Neolithic Cultures of
Western Asia

Sherds of Samarra painted fine ware from Shimshara

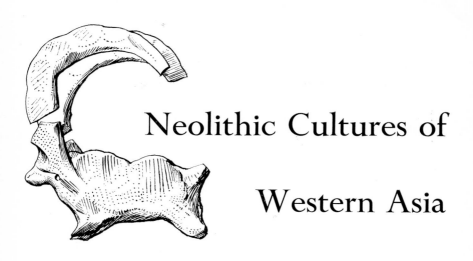

Neolithic Cultures of

Western Asia

PURUSHOTTAM SINGH

Department of Ancient Indian History, Culture and
Archaeology, Banaras Hindu University, Varanasi-5
(U.P.) India

SEMINAR PRESS
LONDON AND NEW YORK
A Subsidiary of Harcourt Brace Jovanovich, Publishers

SEMINAR PRESS LTD.
24/28 Oval Road,
London NW1

United States Edition published by
SEMINAR PRESS INC.
111 Fifth Avenue
New York, New York 10003

913.3903
Si 6 N
95796
2 ar. 1976

Library of Congress Catalog Card Number: 73–7041
ISBN: 0–12–785795–8

PRINTED IN GREAT BRITAIN BY
Willmer Brothers Limited
Birkenhead

Acknowledgements

The present monograph embodies the results of my work at the Institute of Archaeology, University of London during 1970–72. The study was made possible through award of a fellowship by the Commonwealth Scholarship Commission, U.K. My grateful thanks are due to Professor David Oates, Professor of Western Asiatic Archaeology, University of London for supervising this work and providing encouragement at every stage of its preparation. The typescript was read, in parts, by Dr. Joan Oates, Cambridge; Dr. Kathleen M. Kenyon, Oxford; Mrs. Diana Kirkbride, Baghdad and Mr. James Mellaart and Dr. Ian C. Glover, Institute of Archaeology. The author is thankful to them all.

The British School of Archaeology in Iraq gave me a generous grant for travelling to archaeological sites and museums in western Asia. Miss Geraldine C. Talbot helped me in many ways.

The illustrations have been reproduced by the kind permission of the following:
Mrs. Diana Kirkbride, Baghdad (Nos. 3–5; 9–12 and 52–54); Mr. Peder Mortensen and *Acta Archaeologica*, Copenhagen (Nos. 6–8); Dr. Kathleen M. Kenyon (Nos. 13–21); Mr. James Mellaart and the British School of Archaeology at Ankara (Nos. 22–44); Professor Ralph S. Solecki, New York (No. 45); Mr. Peder Mortensen, Aarhus (Nos. 46–51 and 68–70); The Directorate General of Antiquities, Republic of Iraq (Nos. 55–58); Dr. Joan Oates, Cambridge (59–61); Professor Robert J. Braidwood, Chicago (Nos. 62–65); Professor Philip L. Smith, Montreal (Nos. 66–67), Professor Jack R. Harlan, Urbana, Illinois and Professor Daniel Zohary, Jerusalem (Nos. 71–73); and Professor Colin Renfrew, J.E. Dixon and J.R. Cann (No. 74). Map 1 was drawn by Mr. S.G. McDonald and the typescript was prepared by Mrs. M.P. Wyatt. Colour blocks for the frontispiece have been very kindly lent by Det Kongelige Danske, Videnskabernes Selskab, Copenhagen. The author expresses his deep appreciation to the Seminar Press and particularly to the late Mr. John Cruise, Mr. A.R.K. Watkinson and Miss Geraldine H.G. Knox for their advice and help.

Contents

List of Illustrations

1. Introduction

History of Research and Problem of Terminology

The first attempt to classify relics of man's past into some sort of chrono-logical and technological framework was made by Christian Turgensen Thomsen, who, as early as 1812 proposed a "Three Age System" of of Stone, Bronze and Iron (Childe, 1951:17) and since then, these words have been in common archæological usage. Thomsen's theoretical arrangement was stratigraphically proved to be correct by Worsaae's work on the barrows of Jutland (Daniel, 1971). Thomsen's "Stone Age" was further subdivided into two sub-stages in 1865 by Sir John Lubbock (later Lord Avebury), who used the words Palæolithic and Neolithic for these two sub-phases (Daniel, 1962:40; 1968:37; 1971).

Ever since the establishment of prehistory as a scientific discipline, two terminologies have been in use to designate evolutionary cultural stages through which humanity had to pass. Thus while techno-typological labels like Palæolithic and Neolithic were being used by prehistorians like Sir John Lubbock, Worsaae's colleague, Sven Nilsson was developing a subsistence or economic model incorporating economic stages which he named the Savage, Herdsman or Nomad, Agricultural and Civilisation. A similar approach was advocated by evolutionist anthropologists like Sir Edward Tylor (1881) who classified human story into Savagery, Barbarism and Civilisation. According to Tylor, Barbarism represented a stage of culture beginning with agriculture and thus this stage of the anthropologists coincided with the Neolithic of contemporary prehistorians.

This scheme of cultural division was further enlarged by the unilateral evolutionist Lewis H. Morgan (1877) who distinguished seven "ethnic periods" as he called them, i.e. Lower Savagery, Middle Savagery, Upper Savagery, Lower Barbarism, Middle Barbarism, Upper Barbarism and Civilisation (Daniel, 1968:36). The first four decades of this century witnessed the rise and fall of the hyperdiffusion theory of Elliot-Smith and Perry and during the thirties, prehistorians like, Childe forcefully demonstrated that there was no single culture in the most ancient Near

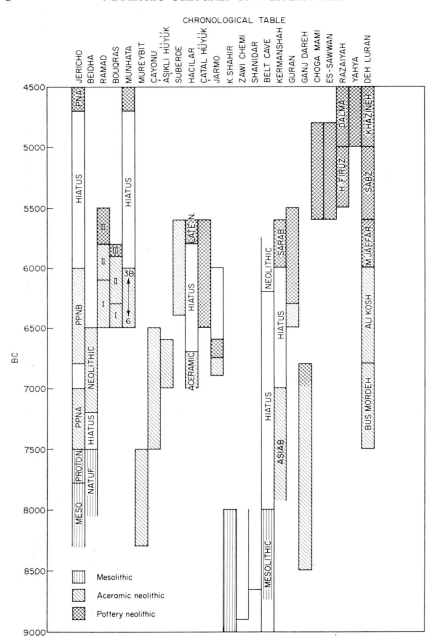

FIG. 1. Chronological table.

East. Childe reinterpreted the old "three Age System" of Thomsen-Worsaae but he believed that all the higher arts came from one particular area, i.e. the Near East. This modified diffusionism of Childe is now being criticised and British prehistorians like Glyn Daniel have begun to talk of seven First Civilisations in different parts of the world, all independent (to a large degree) in origin (Daniel, 1968), and recently an eighth primary and independent civilisation—the Minoan-Mycenean—has been added to this list (Renfrew, 1972).

As noted earlier, the word "Neolithic" was coined by Sir John Lubbock in his *Prehistoric Times* first published in 1865. He used this word to denote the later Stone Age "in which the stone implements are more skilfully made, more varied in form, and often polished" (Avebury, 1900:72). Clearly, the basis of this new label was the shape and the technique of manufacture of the stone tools (especially celts or axes) which was different from that of the Palæolithic age. This criterion formed an important trait of the Neolithic in text-books of prehistory as late as 1956 (Burkitt, 1926, 3rd. Ed., 1956). According to Burkitt (1926:50) the Neolithic comprised the following four characteristic traits:

1. the practice of agriculture,
2. the domestication of animals,
3. the manufacture of pottery and,
4. the grinding and polishing of stone tools.

As will be seen below, recent researches in the prehistory of the Near East have demonstrated that the first two traits are crucial for any prehistoric society to be termed "Neolithic" but the discovery of several pre-ceramic food-producing cultures amply demonstrates that the manufacture of pottery is no longer the hall-mark of the Neolithic. Pottery makes its appearance at least two millennia later than the first domestication of plants and animals and the beginning of the first settled village life. So also, the technique of manufacture of stone celts is not particularly important. The transition from hunting and food-gathering to a food-producing economy had a far-reaching impact on the course of human history and this vital change has been aptly described by the great prehistorian V. Gordon Childe in his phrase "Neolithic Revolution". Childe (1952:23) remarked: "Food production—the deliberate cultivation of food-plants, especially cereals, and the taming, breeding and selection of animals was an economic revolution—the greatest in human history after the mastery of fire". Childe believed that archæologists' "ages" correspond roughly to the economic "stages". However, the word "revolution" used by Childe to denote this change has recently been criticized by several scholars (Daniel, 1968:78; Helbaek, 1969: 402) for "revolution suggests something that happened quickly and purposefully" but the changes from food-gathering to food-producing were "evolutionary rather than revolutionary". As we shall see below, the revolution of Childe was not as sudden as the work suggests today. It was neither rapid nor uniform over the Near East, but was at times an almost imperceptible process. The earliest species of domesticated animals and plants do not appear in one particular area or at one point of time but rather on different sites and at different times. However, considering the extremely slow rate of progress through the scores of millennia during the Palæolithic and the Mesolithic, man's achievements during the early Holocene and especially between the 9th millennium BC and the 6th millennium BC were spectacular indeed. Keeping in view the profound effects this change had on human history, Childe is, by and large, justified in using the term "revolution". Childe himself has clarified his point in the following words: (1950:3):

> The word "revolution" must not of course be taken as denoting a sudden violent catastrophe, it is here used for the culmination of a progressive change in the economic structure and social organisation of communities that caused, or was accompanied by, a dramatic increase in the population affected—an increase that would appear as an obvious bend in the population graph were vital statistics available.

The basic facts realised by Childe have been largely substantiated by recent researches. For example, Childe was quick to realise (1936: 67) that wheat and barley were the two basic cereals domesticated by man in western Asia because they offer enormous advantages over the rest of the cereals.

> These two cereals offer, in fact, exceptional advantages. The food they yield is highly nutritious, the grains can easily be stored, the return is relatively high, and above all, the labour involved is not too absorbing (Childe, 1936: 67).

Similarly, he realised that the food animals kept were not varied: horned cattle, sheep, goats and swine. Both these observations are substantiated by recent work in the prehistory of the Near East. The first domesticated animals in western Asia were sheep, closely followed by goats and pigs. Cattle were domesticated much later. Of course, Childe's remark that pottery is the hallmark of the Neolithic is no longer tenable. Again, his "oasis" theory for the domestication of animals is not being substantiated by the newly-obtained data. Childe believed in the theory of progressive dessication in the climate of the Near East during the early

FIG. 2. The distribution of proto-Neolithic

Holocene, which according to him was the chief factor for the domestication of animals. He remarked (1936:77-78):

> ...The period when the food-producing economy became established was one
> of climatic crises adversely affecting precisely that zone of arid sub-tropical
> countries where the earliest farmers appear, and where the wild ancestors
> of cultivated cereals and domestic animals actually lived. . . . To get food and
> water, the grass-eaters would have to congregate round a diminishing number
> of springs and oases.

Then he further argues:

> Enforced concentration by the banks of streams and shrinking springs would
> entail a more intensive search for means of nourishment. Animals and men
> would be herded together in oases that were becoming isolated by desert
> tracts. Such enforced juxtaposition might promote that sort of symbiosis
> between man and beast implied in the word "domestication".

Childe's "oasis theory" or "propinquity theory" for the domestication
of animals and consequently for the Neolithic revolution has come under
criticism by a number of scholars (Braidwood and Reed, 1957:20; Reed,
1959:1637; 1960:122-23; Butzer, 1964:436-7; also *cf.* Harris, 1971:
44).

Childe based his hypothesis on the assumption that dessication began
in the early post-Würm period and continued throughout the early Recent
period, but this assumption is not borne out by modern researches. Karl
W. Butzer, a leading palæoclimatologist believes (1957, 1958) that there
were a number of climatic fluctuations in the Near East and he classifies
these fluctuations into several phases. The following climatic phases of
Butzer (1958:128) are particularly relevant in the present context:

1. Post-pluvial I—Immediately following the last Pluvial. Wind erosion
   was particularly pronounced; temperatures were apparently a little
   lower and the rainfall of the Near East was somewhat less than that
   of the present.
2. Sub-pluvial I—(probably during the 10th-9th millennia BC). A marked
   but temporary improvement of moisture conditions is evident in the
   Near East.
3. Post-pluvial IIa—(perhaps 8000-6800 BC). Temperatures rose and
   typical post-pluvial conditions of aridity set in with a rainfall a little
   less than that of the present.
4. Post-pluvial IIb—(*c.* 6800-5500 or 5000 BC). An improvement in
   precipitation, characterised by moister conditions closely resembling
   those of the last century of our era.

Butzer concludes (1964:437):

> In conclusion the previous review of paleoclimatic information does not suggest any incisive change in the late glacial and early Holocene record of Western Asia, and the climatic changes that did take place certainly did not follow a simple pattern of progressive desiccation.

Recently, an attempt has been made by van Zeist and Wright (1963; also van Zeist, 1969) to reconstruct the prehistoric environment of Western Asia on the basis of palæobotanical information. They made pollen analyses of sediment cores from Lake Zeribar in the Zagros mountains of western Iran, about 160 km northwest of Kermanshah at an elevation of 1300 m. This study leads them to conclude that between 30,000 and 14,000 years ago the climate of the Near East was not only colder than it is at present, but that it was also considerably drier. During this period the greater part of the Zagros must have been treeless and forests and step-forests were confined to a few areas which at present receive appreciable amounts of rain at lower elevations. From about 14,000 years ago, there was a change in climate from cool to warm and the annual precipitation as well as temperature increased. The trees now started to spread from their refuge areas. Between 10,000 and 6000 BC the precipitation in the autumn, winter and spring was more or less the same as it is at present but the summers were drier. This period witnessed a gradual increase in the tree-pollen percentage and oak-pistachio Savanna forests covered the steppe-forest zone. After about 6000 BC the open oak-pistachio vegetation changed into oak forest which at present constitutes the natural vegetation in this part of the Zagros. This change presumably reflects an increase in precipitation or decrease in temperature to modern levels.

We must now consider how developments in terminology have kept pace with recent research. Following the subsistence model of anthropologists like Morgan, Robert J. Braidwood of the Oriental Institute, Chicago, has been advocating for a subsistence-pattern terminology for the past two decades. Braidwood has been unhappy (and many others, cf. Daniel, 1968:79) with such "Neo-Græcisms" (as he calls them) as "Mesolithic" and "Neolithic" because these terms "lead to more confusion than clarity" (Braidwood and Braidwood, 1953:310; Braidwood and Braidwood, 1960, preface, viii; Braidwood, 1962: 115). So instead of using these typo-technological labels, Braidwood used terms like "Stage", "era" and "Phase", which he defined as follows:

A stage is "one of the steps into which the material development of man...is divided." A stage can be divided into several eras which are "signal stages of history, an epoch." These eras are further sub-divisible into phases where archæological material is sufficient enough to warrant such a classification. In his Condon lectures in the University of Oregon in the spring of 1952, Braidwood (1952) distinguished two major economic stages and designated them "Food-gathering" and "Food producing" respectively. He believed that "gathering" "seems to connote a somewhat more unspecialised and random activity" while "collecting" connotes a more selective and intensified activity (Braidwood, 1960*b*:145, f.n.1). Braidwood believed that the end of the food-gathering stage was marked by a "terminal food-gathering" phase. The succeeding food-producing stage is divisible into many eras and phases like the incipient agriculture and domestication phase and the two successive eras of primary village efficiency and of established village efficiency, followed by the era of incipient urbanisation. This classification was perfected by Braidwood in an important paper in 1960 in which he suggested the following scheme (Braidwood, 1960*b*).

Food-gathering Stage

Food-gathering Era

1. Sub-era of naturally determined mammalian subsistence and free-wandering level, tools *fashioned* but not yet *standardised.*
2. Sub-era within which food-gathering and free-wandering began to be significantly culturally determined; tools of earliest *standardised* traditions.
3. Sub-era of elemental restricted wandering, hunting. Caves commonly occupied, where they existed. Tool standardisation now extends to some variety of standardised tool-forms within one industry. Some regional restriction in the distribution of any one given industry.

Food-collecting Era

1. Sub-era of selective hunting and seasonal collecting patterns for restricted-wandering types of groups. Considerable typological variety and "tools to make tools".
2. Sub-era of intensified hunting and collecting, season-bound activities.
3. Sub-era of highly specialised food-collecting adapted to certain very specialised environments, which allow semi-permanent to permanent sedentary types of groups.

Food-producing Stage

Primary Era, based on individual or family scale efforts,
non-mechanised

1. Sub-era of incipient cultivation (and animal domestication in some regions).
2. Sub-era of the primary village-farming community (or its functional equivalent, settlement-wise), in which a marked proportion of the dietary intake is of produced food.
3. Sub-era of the expanded village-farming community (often also characterised as the sub-era of towns and temples or of "incipient urbanisation").

Braidwood, with his colleagues, has traced the development of the earliest village communities of western Asia (some of which they themselves discovered on a number of sites in the Zagros and Syria) in a number of papers (Braidwood and Braidwood, 1953; Braidwood and Howe, 1962; Braidwood, 1962). In terms of subsistence patterns Braidwood further divided the whole range of development levels of Old World cultural history into eight models (Braidwood and Reed, 1957) which he employed to classify the surface finds from the prehistoric caves and open-air sites in the Kermanshah valley plains and to suggest their chronological position (Braidwood, 1961). However, the terminology and the classification proposed by Braidwood do not find favour among many fellow prehistorians and archæologists. True, the concept of "Neolithic" has been changing through the advancement of research, especially in the prehistory of Western Asia, but Braidwood's own terminology is not free from such ambiguities and it is difficult to delineate his several "stages", "eras" and "sub-eras" from the limited archæological data at our disposal. In fact, Braidwood is fully conscious of the inadequacy of the data and the applicability of his terminology as is demonstrated when he writes:

> "These levels are not yet clearly manifested by archæology, probably because they have not yet been diligently sought after or because evidence for the interpretation of their subsistence patterns has not yet been generally saved or interpreted with sophistication from an eco-systematic point of view." (Braidwood and Reed, 1957: 23).

The neolithic revolution was based on the domestication of six wild plant and animal species, namely, emmer wheat, barley, goats, sheep, pigs, and the ancestors of cattle. What was the *cause* of this revolution? Childe believed in the climatic determinism and the "oasis" theory but as has been shown above, this theory does not withstand the recent studies in the palæoclimate of the Near East. On the other hand, Braidwood believes in the "Natural Habitat Zone" of high piedmonts and intermontane valleys, which, according to him, comprises

> the western and southwestern facing flanks of the Zagros from as far southeast as Shiraz in Iran; thence the zone bore north and westwards about the southern and southwestern flanks of the high Anatolian plateau, while a southern arm fronted upon the Mediterranean along the flanks of the Lebanon and the Judean hills and parts of their trans-Jordanian extensions. The western and northwestern boundary of the natural habitat zone is not yet delimited (Thrace? the Caucasus?) in fact its delimitation is still very imprecise anywhere (Braidwood, 1962:116).

He believes that the classic constellation of the potential plant and animal domesticates were present within the hilly flanks intermontane valley environmental zone, (Braidwood and Howe, 1962:143) and argues that

> the level of incipient cultivation and domestication probably *only* obtained within the natural habitat zone; a zone of general environmental permissiveness but of sub-regional diversity, relatively easy access from intermontane valley to intermontane valley and upper piedmont and within which minor climatic fluctuations (if they really existed) were readily compensated for.

Braidwood further believes that the first phase or phases of his second cultural-historical level, i.e. the primary village-farming level also took place in this natural habitat zone. But as many newly-discovered sites like Ali Kosh, Ganj Dareh, Beidha and Ramad etc. showing the earliest traces of domestication, clearly lie outside this zone, it is obvious that Braidwood's definition of the natural habitat zone needs revision (also *cf*. Gary A. Wright, 1971:457).

As regards the probable causes of the first domestication of food plants and animals, several hypotheses have been put forward, though none of them quite convincing. Changing climate during the early Holocene; technological advancement of early Neolithic communities to a level where they could exploit their environment, and the supposedly rapid increase in the population—all have been taken to be the causes of the first domestication of plants and animals. Although each of these factors may have contributed towards this process, in varying degrees, none of them is capable alone of providing an adequate explanation. Thus Herbert E. Wright and Charles A. Reed, two natural scientists who worked with Braidwood, propose different hypotheses. Earlier in 1960, Wright argued that the economic revolution was not necessarily tied down with climatic change during the early Holocene. He believed that technological advancement and consequently culture complexity in this age was largely responsible for this. He remarked (1960:97):

> Favourable habitats for animals and plants had long been available, but man had not reached the technological level to exploit them. It seems to the writer that the gradual evolution of culture, with increasing complexity and perfection of tool technology may have been a more potent factor in bringing about this economic revolution than was the climatic change at the end of the glacial period.

However, after his work with van Zeist on the sediment analysis and the study of pollen deposits from lake Zeribar he has modified his stand. These studies show that climatic change from cool steppe to a warm oak-pistachio savanna took place approximately at the same time (about 11,000 years ago) as the first manifestations of domestication of plants and animals. Therefore Wright argues (1968:338):

> Although I have always felt that cultural evolution—general refinement of tools and techniques for controlling the environment—is a stronger force than climatic determinism in the development of early cultures, the chronological coincidence of important environmental and cultural change in this area during initial phases of domestication is now well enough documented that it cannot be ignored. A much greater problem, of course, will be to prove that the environmental change was the cause of the cultural revolution.

On the contrary, Charles A. Reed believes that the increasing complexity of human culture coupled with incipient cultivation was a conducive situation where domestication followed automatically. He remarks (1960:124):

> It is seemingly the age-old habit of pet-keeping of the young of the wild animals by women and children that led to taming and eventually to the keeping and breeding of the adult animals. In a primitive hunting and food-gathering society such pet-keeping may have continued for a long time with nothing more happening. The basic factor leading to the higher degree of intergroup co-operation that we know as domestication was, it seems to be, the development of incipient cultivation, which was associated with increased human population and a more sedentary life.

More recently Lewis R. Binford has proposed an equilibrium model to explain post-Pleistocene changes in the archæological record. He believes that equilibrium systems regulate population density below the carrying capacity of an environment. A change in demographic structure upsets an established equilibrium system. This increase in the population density of a region beyond the carrying capacity of the natural environment offers selective advantage to increases in the efficacy of subsistence technology. Binford remarks that

> It is in the context of such situations of strain in environment with plant and animal forms amenable to manipulation that we would expect to find conditions favouring the development of plant and animal domestication.

He also argues that the locus for the origin of agriculture should not be sought in the heart of the "Natural habitat zone" but in those places "where a population frontier or adaptive tension zone intersects a 'natural habitat zone' ". These observations find support from earlier studies of Harlan and Zohary (1966) who argue that

> domestication may not have taken place where the wild cereals were most abundant and farming may have originated in an area adjacent to, rather than in, the regions of greatest abundance of wild cereals.

In an ecological approach to the study of the origins of food-production, Flannery applies the equilibrium model to the Near East and argues that

> the changes leading to intensive food-production are here viewed as a series of responses to disturbances of density equilibrium in human populations around the margins of favoured areas caused by the fact that these areas were the zones of population growth and emigration (Flannery, 1969:95).

However, this model does not explain the cause of this disequilibrium in the first place.

We see from the above that different scholars have tried to explain, the process of and the circumstances leading to, the first domestication of plants and animals in different ways but no one explanation is complete. What is important is the realization that this was a process which took considerable time and the domestication of each type of potentially domesticable animal and plant species might have taken place in different ecological niches at different times. Here it may be pertinent to point out that even the natural habitat zone of the hilly flanks of the Fertile Crescent was 2000 km in extent and the domestication of the six species noted above covered a time-span of more than two millennia. But as is clear from the pattern of obsidian trade and the occurrence of other antiquities on the sites, not native to the areas in which the sites are situated, these Neolithic communities were in contact with each other. It is logical to believe that ideas travelled faster than material objects and any knowledge of discoveries made in any one region would be transmitted to other parts in a short while. The mechanics of the process of domestication are not clear in the archæological record at the moment but more extensive and more detailed archæological and palæecologic studies of the crucial period between 10,000 BC and 7000 BC closely controlled by radiocarbon dating will help us to understand this process in more detail.

Here a word may be said about the radiocarbon dates and the comparative chronology of early village cultures. The chronology adopted here (Fig. 1) is based on the radiocarbon dates calculated on the Libby half-life of 5568 years and thus represents radiocarbon years rather than the true calendar years. However, two new phenomena have been observed during recent years. Earlier, radiocarbon dates were calculated on the assumption that the radiocarbon content of the atmospheric carbon dioxide has remained constant during the Pleistocene and recent times. But this assumption is no longer valid and most of the nuclear physicists now agree that the radiocarbon content has been fluctuating. Secondly, the development of a 7100-year tree-ring chronology for bristlecone pine in the White Mountains of eastern central California (Suess, 1970) has considerably helped in determining the variations of the carbon-14 content of the atmospheric carbon dioxide throughout this period of time. However, the correction chart prepared on the basis of this study is not yet applicable for radiocarbon dates falling between the ninth and the sixth millennium BC—the period with which we are primarily concerned here.

A word of caution must be given regarding the use of the radiocarbon dates. Some prehistorians, in the absence of any other method of dating precisely, have been putting heavy reliance on a handful of dates available for these cultures. But as Neustupný (1970; also cf. Waterbolk, 1971) has pointed out, radiocarbon dates not only contain the inherent deviations of a century or more, but also may be fraught with errors of measurement in the laboratory; errors resulting from the age of the material (the tissues of a sample dating some event might have been biologically dead for several decades or even centuries when it was used by ancient man) and variations in the concentration of the radiocarbon itself. Most of these errors can be checked and reduced if we have a series of radiocarbon dates from successive levels at a particular site. But unfortunately most of the Neolithic sites of the Near East do not have many dated samples and sometimes, perhaps due to the factors noted above, there are widely divergent dates from a single site. A typical example of this vast time span is Jarmo where the dates of the radiocarbon samples range between 3310 BC and 9300 BC giving a time-span of 6000 years for a cultural deposit of only seven metres.

It is heartening to note that research in the Prehistory of the Near East has reached a new phase during the last few years by adoption of interdisciplinary approach for problem-oriented work. New methods of data-recovery like water sieving to retrieve macroscopic material has been successfully applied by David French at Can Hasan (French, 1971; also *cf.* Weaver, 1971) and it is hoped that this new technique will be increasingly applied at future digs in Western Asia. Similarly, Hans Helbaek (1969:385; also Helbaek, 1972:48) has developed and used buoyancy technique for segregating plant remains from mineral samples. The process is

> carried out by drying the soil or ash sample and then pouring it into a basin with water. Under cautious stirring, the water is slowly poured through a fine mesh sieve, the plant matter floating on the surface and being retained in the sieve. When the mineral matter approaches the lip of the basin, the process is stopped and the sediment, as circumstances indicate, either thrown away, or dried again and subjected to other kinds of examination. After drying in shade, the plant material is ready for the microscope.

Among the scientific examination of the excavated antiquities, the analysis of obsidian from different sites has brought forth interesting data. Several techniques like trace-element analysis by optical spectroscopy, fission-track analysis, neutron-activation analysis etc. have been successfully applied by Gordus and Renfrew *et al.* and valuable results obtained. A similar advancement is being made regarding the interpretation of the archæological data. It is now no longer enough to dig and publish the remains of structures and house-plans, pottery-drawings and tool-types alone (important though these are even today) scholars have begun asking such questions as the role of changes in population pressure on other factors like land-use, subsistence exploitation, settlement patterns, technology, social and political organisation, economic exchanges etc. (Smith, 1972). It is hoped that this new awareness among the prehistorians and the increasing co-operation of natural scientists will open new vistas for research in Near Eastern prehistory.

Scope of the Present Work

The present monograph deals with the early village cultures of Western Asia. The word "Neolithic" has been used in a broad sense. As we have pointed out, scholars like Braidwood are averse to using this term but their own terminology is not adequate enough to be adopted, without creating more confusion. For the present, the data at our disposal are not sufficient and we shall have to wait for more research to be carried out in Near Eastern prehistory before any better terminology can be devised and adopted. This is clear from the recent writings of Professor Braidwood himself. Even after two decades of research, writing in 1969 Braidwood has candidly admitted that at the same time we cannot yet define the ancient boundaries of a "natural habitat zone for the potential domesticates", nor can we yet identify a level of incipience by any specific artifactual type fossil (Braidwood, 1970:83).

So the word "Neolithic" is here retained, although food-production is the only one of the classic criteria by which it may now be defined. The existence of pre-ceramic cultures is already an established phenomenon in the Near Eastern prehistory. Now the discoveries made at Mureybit seem to demonstrate that a village with solid architecture could flourish on the basis of hunting and collecting alone.

The area covered comprises the region from the eastern coast of the Mediterranean to the eastern boundaries of Iran. Neolithic cultures of Afghanistan and Turkmenia have not been included because they are chronologically later than those in the area covered, and they are not, in our opinion, relevant to the crucial region where domestication of food plants and animals took place. The division of chapters on the basis of modern political boundaries is made purely for convenience of description and no culture groupings, let alone cultural centres, are implied. Most of these sites have been discovered only recently, during the last two decades, and definitive reports of most of these excavations, are not forthcoming. Preliminary communications of these results are scattered in various journals, and an attempt has been made here to analyse and collate the latest data and to see whether a general pattern emerges out of this analysis. In the last chapter, we examine the antiquity of such important cultural traits of the Neolithic as the origin of the domestication of each important species of plant and animal and also ancient trade-patterns as known from the study of obsidian artefacts. This is, in fact, a synopsis without pretension to original research, but as such it may well prove useful to students and specialists alike.

References

AVEBURY, LORD. (1900). *Prehistoric Times* (6th Ed.) London: Williams and Norgate.

BINFORD, L. R. (1968). Post-Pleistocene Adaptations in *New Perspectives in Archœology* (L. R. Binford and S. R. Binford, eds). Chicago: Aldine Press, pp. 313-341.

BRAIDWOOD, ROBERT J. (1951). *Prehistoric Men* (3rd Ed.). Chicago: Chicago Natural History Museum.

BRAIDWOOD, ROBERT J. (1952). *The Near East and the Foundation of Civilization*, Oregon.

BRAIDWOOD, ROBERT J. (1960a) Prelude to Civilization in *City Invincible* (Carl H. Kraeling and Robert M. Adams, eds). Chicago: University of Chicago Press.

BRAIDWOOD, ROBERT J. (1960b). Levels in Prehistory: A Model for the Reconsideration of the Evidence, *The Evolution of Man* (Sol Tax, ed.). Chicago: University of Chicago Press.

BRAIDWOOD, ROBERT J. (1961). The Iranian Prehistoric Project. *Iranica Antiqua*, **1**, 3-7.

BRAIDWOOD, ROBERT J. (1962). The Earliest Village Communities of Southwestern Asia Reconsidered. *Int. Congr. Prehist. Protohist. Sci.*, 6th Session Rome, **1**, 115-126.

BRAIDWOOD, ROBERT J. (1970). Prehistory into History in the Near East. *Nobel Symposium on Radiocarbon Variations and Absolute Chronology* (I. U. Olsson, ed.) Stockholm: Almqvist and Wiksell Förlag AB, pp. 81-91.

BRAIDWOOD, ROBERT J. AND BRAIDWOOD, LINDA (1953). The Earliest Village Communities of Southwestern Asia. *J. Wld. Hist.*, **1**, 278-310.

BRAIDWOOD, ROBERT J. AND BRAIDWOOD, LINDA (1960). *Excavations in the Plains of Antioch*. Chicago: Chicago University Press.

BRAIDWOOD, ROBERT J. AND HOWE, BRUCE. (1962). Southwestern Asia Beyond the Lands of the Mediterranean Littoral. *Courses Toward Urban Life* (Robert J. Braidwood and Gordon Willey, eds). Edinburgh University Press.

BRAIDWOOD ROBERT J. AND REED, C. A. (1957). The Achievement and Early Consequences of Food Production: A Consideration of the Archæological and Natural-Historical Evidence. *Cold Spring Harb. Symp. quant. Biol.* **22**, 19-31.

BURKITT, M. C. (1926). *Our Early Ancestors*, Cambridge: Cambridge University Press.

BUTZER, KARL W. (1957). Late Glacial and Postglacial Climatic Variations in the Near East. *Erdk. Arch. Wiss. Geogr.*, Band XI, Lfg. **1**, 21-35.

BUTZER, KARL W. (1958). *Quarternary Stratigraphy and Climate in the Near East*, Bonn: Ferd, Dummlers Verlag.

BUTZER, KARL W. (1964). *Environment and Archæology*, Chicago: Aldine Publishing Co.

CHILDE, V. GORDON. (1936). *Man Makes Himself* (4th Ed.). C. A. Watts and Co., The Fontana Library, 1970.

CHILDE, V. GORDON (1950). The Urban Revolution. *Tn Plann. Rev.*, **21**, 3-17.

CHILDE, V. GORDON (1951). *Social Evolution*, London: Watts & Co.

CHILDE, V. GORDON (1952). *New Light on the Most Ancient East* (2nd. Ed.). London: Routledge & Kegan Paul.

DANIEL, GLYN (1962). *The Idea of Prehistory*, London: C. A. Watts & Co.

DANIEL, GLYN (1968). *The First Civilizations*, London: Thames & Hudson: Published in Pelican Books, 1971.

DANIEL, GLYN (1971). From Worsaae to Childe: The Models of Prehistory. *Proc. Prehist. Soc.* **37**, (2), 140-153.

FLANNERY, KENT V. (1969). Origins and Ecological Effects of Early Domestication in Iran and the Near East. *The Domestication and Exploitation of Plants and Animals* (Peter J. Ucko & G. W. Dimbleby, eds). London: Duckworth, pp. 73-100.

FRENCH, DAVID (1971). An Experiment in Water-Sieving. *Anatolian Stud.*, **21**, 59-64.

HARLAN, J. R. AND ZOHARY D. (1966). Distribution of Wild Wheats and Barley, *Science, N.Y.*, **153**, 1075-80.

HARRIS, C. J. (1971). Explanation in Prehistory. *Proc. Prehist. Soc.*, **37**, 38-55.

HELBAEK, HANS (1969). Plant Collecting, Dry Farming, and Irrigation Agriculture in Prehistoric Deh Lurhan. *Prehistory and Human Ecology of the Deh Luran Plain* (Frank Hole, Kent V. Flannery and James A. Neely, eds). Ann Arbor, pp. 383-426.

HELBAEK, HANS (1972). Samarran Irrigation Agriculture at Choga Mami in Iraq, *Iraq*, **34**, 35-48.

NEUSTUPNÝ, E. (1970). The Accuracy of Radiocarbon Dating *Nobel Symposium on Radiocarbon Variations and Absolute Chronology* (I. U. Olsson, ed.). Stockholm: Almqvist and Wiksell Föslag AB, pp. 23-34.

REED, CHARLES A. (1959). Animal Domestication in the Prehistoric Near East *Science, N.Y.* **130**, 1629-39.

REED, CHARLES A. (1960). Review of Archæological Evidence on Animal Domestication in the Prehistoric Near East. *Prehistoric Investigations in Iraqi Kurdistan*, SAOC-31 (Robert J. Braidwood and Bruce Howe, eds). Chicago: University of Chicago Press, pp. 119-145.

RENFREW, COLIN (1972). *The Emergence of Civilization*, London: Methuen & Co.

SMITH, PHILIP L. (1972). Changes in Population Pressure in Archæological Explanation. *Wld Archæol.*, **4** (1), 5-18.

SUESS, H. E. (1970). Bristlecone-pine calibration of the Radiocarbon time-scale 5200 B.C. to the Present. *Nobel symposium on Radiocarbon Variations and Absolute Chronology* (I. U. Olsson, ed.). Stockholm; Almqvist and Wiksell Föslag AB, pp. 303-311.

WATERBOLK, H. T. (1971). Working with Radiocarbon Dates. *Proc. Prehist. Soc.*, **37**, 15-33.

WEAVER, M. E. (1971). A New Water Separation Process for Soil from Archæological Excavations. *Anatolian Stud.*, **21**, 65-68.

WRIGHT, GARY A. (1971). Origins of Food Production in Southwestern Asia: A survey of Ideas. *Curr. Anthrop.* **12** (4-5), 447-478.

WRIGHT, HERBERT E. (1960). Climate and Prehistoric Man in the Eastern Mediterranean. *Prehistoric Investigations in Iraqi Kurdistan*, SAOC-31 (Robert J. Braidwood and Bruce Howe, eds). Chicago: Chicago University Press, pp. 71-97.

WRIGHT, HERBERT E. (1968). Natural Environment of Early Food Production North of Mesopotamia. *Science, N.Y.*, **161**, 334-339.

VAN ZEIST W. AND WRIGHT, H. E. (1963). Preliminary Pollen Studies at Lake Zeribar, Zagros Mountains, Southwestern Iran. *Science, N.Y.*, **140**, 65-69.

VAN ZEIST, W. (1969). Reflections on Prehistoric Environments in the Near East. *The Domestication and Exploitation of Plants and Animals*, (Peter J. Ucko and G. W. Dimbleby, eds). London: Duckworth, pp. 35-46.

2. The Levant

The Levant was one of the first regions in the Near East where traces of the earliest food-producing cultures were identified. The first of these with evidence of an incipient food production, the Natufian, has been known since 1928 through the pioneering researches of Dorothy Garrod in the valley of Wadi en Natuf on Mt. Carmel. Similarly, a late stage of the Neolithic, comprising distinctive dark burnished pottery and stone tools together with remains of permanent villages, was known from such coastal sites as Byblos and by the discovery of the Yarmukian culture in the Beth-Shan valley. Now the recent excavations at El Khiam, Einan and Nahal Oren in Israel and Beidha and Jericho in Jordan have not only bridged the gap between the two cultures noted above, but have also helped in identifying some new intermediary stages previously unknown. Similarly, recent work at Ramad, Bouqras, Mureybit, Munhata and Al Kowm has demonstrated that inland Syria also witnessed the transition from the food-gathering to the food-producing stage. Again, survey and excavation of other pottery-bearing Neolithic sites like Hazorea, Mukhtara and Ghrubba demonstrate the regional variations among the late Neolithic cultures as well as their transmutation to the succeeding chalcolithic cultures like the Ghassulian in the south and the Yarmukian, Amuq A-B and Ras Shamra VA and IVC in the north. These cultures tie up the sequence with Mersin, Tarsus and other sites in the Cilician plains. However, it may be pointed out that the chronological chart is far from complete and as Henri de Contenson has pointed out in a recent paper (de Contenson, 1966a), there remains a cultural hiatus of nearly 1500 years (between 6000 BC and 4500 BC) very prominently witnessed at Jericho, Farah, Munhata and Sheikh Ali. This gap is partially filled by the recent work at Ramad, Ras Shamra and in the Amuq valley but it remains to be bridged in Palestine. In the present context, accepting the Jericho sequence as the representative one, the following cultural stages can be identified:

1. An incipient food-producing stage—The Natufian culture identified at the type-site, Al Khiam, Einan, Abu Gosh and the earliest levels at Jericho and Beidha.

2. Proto-Neolithic—the least known phase of all, identified at Jericho and Nahal Oren.
3. Pre-Pottery Neolithic (divisible into sub-phases A and B) Jericho, Beidha, Ramad, Bouqras, Munhata and Mureybit.

Cultural Hiatus

4. Pottery Neolithic (divisible into sub-phases A and B). Upper levels at Jericho, Ramad, Munhata, Ghrubba, Byblos, Ras Shamra etc.

Excellent summaries of these works have been presented from time to time by several scholars like Garrod (1957), Anati (1963), Kenyon (1970), Albright (1965), Watson (1965), de Vaux (1966) and de Contenson (1966a) but detailed study has not been possible mainly because most of the early sites have been excavated during the last decade and their definitive reports are not yet available. However, an attempt will be made in the following pages to examine the cultural assemblages of the principal sites as obtained from the preliminary communications.

The excavations at Jericho and Beidha have not only placed the well-known Natufian culture in its stratigraphic context vis-a-vis the Neolithic cultures of that area but have also demonstrated that the latter have their roots in the former. So before proceeding to examine the results of these two sites, it is as well to give a basic idea of the Natufian culture itself. This culture was first found in stratigraphic context in the cave of Shukba on the western slope of the Judæan hills by Dorothy Garrod in 1928. The name itself derives from Wadi en Natuf in which the Shukba cave is situated. It is now known that the Natufian settlements are found not only in caves and rock-shelters but also on open-air sites like Jericho, Beidha and Ain Mallaha. The culture is characterised by a microlithic flint industry although rough picks and massive scrapers were used for heavy work. Lunates are the principal type and sickle blades are found together with bone hafts in which these blades were mounted. Hunting of gazelle, wild goat, horse and half-ass together with fishing was the main source of livelihood and the presence of sickle-blades, bone-hafts, querns and grinding stones etc. has been taken to show that agriculture was practised. Vessels of limestone and basalt are present and dentalia shells were used for beads. Natufian art included the carving of animal figures on bone and stone. The dead were buried inside the habitation area, on their sides with limbs extended or tightly flexed. In communal graves, the dead bodies were placed one on the top of the other. The personal ornaments included head-dresses of dentalia and necklaces. The contribution of this culture towards a settled way of life has been summed up by Emmanuel Anati (1963:142):

The Natufian people developed fishing and began the domestication of animals; they made the earliest attempts at agriculture and trade and sped up greatly the rhythm of evolution in their region. The Natufians developed a new and sophisticated religion, a highly realistic art and a refined material culture and they founded the earliest known permanent settlements in the world.

The excavations by Jean Perrot (1960) at Eynan (Ain Mallaha), a Natufian site on the shores of Lake Huleh have supported the remarks of Anati. These excavations have brought to light the remains of large curvilinear houses. One of these with a diameter of 7 m was exposed and near the centre of the room was found a stone-lined square fireplace bounded on the north and east sides by a rough pavement of large stones. A mortar stone and some broken pestles were found scattered on this floor together with a beaker-shaped basalt vessel 12 cm in height. A house was built at least twice on the same spot with minor variations in the furnishings, clearly showing the permanence of settlement before the stage of food-production was reached. However, the presence of grindstones, pestles, mortars and sickles shows that "the Natufians had already gone very far along the path from gathering wild grains towards planned agriculture" (Anati, 1963:146). This process of sedentarisation was greatly accelerated in the succeeding proto-Neolithic and Neolithic cultures.

The progress from the Natufian to "Neolithic proper" is marked by a transitional stage best identified at Nahal Oren (Wadi Fallah) and Jericho. Nahal Oren encompasses an area of 500 sq. m on the western cliff of Mt. Carmel and six seasons of work by Stekelis and Yizraely (1963) has brought forth the remains of Atlithian, Kebaran, Natufian and proto-Neolithic (called "pre-pottery Neolithic" by the excavators) phases. Two strata of the last named phase have been identified. Stratum I yielded the remains of a large building, with walls built of large boulders taken from the stream bed and floors made of flat, thin stones. The flint tools found comprise axes, burins, scrapers, knives (arrowheads) sickle-blades and retouched tools. The heavy tools include axes of basalt, flint and limestone with finely polished cutting edges; adzes of flint and querns of limestone and basalt, oval in shape. Stratum II at Nahal Oren has yielded remains of no less than 14 houses, elliptical in plan and each covering an area of 9 to 15 sq. m. The walls are made of large undressed stones and floors are of *terre pisée*. The stone tools belong to the well-known Tahunian* industry.

*The use of the term "Tahunian" given to the industry immediately succeeding the final phase of the Natufian at Al Khiam, is now under criticism and is being discarded in recent writings (*cf.* Jean Perrot (1962) in *Courses Toward Urban Life* (R. J. Braidwood and G. Willey, eds), p. 152, f.n.2).

More details of architectural and artefactual remains of the pre-pottery Neolithic phase at Nahal Oren have been obtained in the recent work of Noy and Higgs (1971) at this site. This has provided a sequence of cultures from the Mousterian, Kebaran and Natufian to the pre-Pottery Neolithic. Traces of a building and a complete human burial of the Natufian culture have been found. The pre-pottery Neolithic phase yielded remains of buildings and floors and an almost intact house was excavated in the third season. The house was erected on stone foundations and the walls were built of small and middle sized stones and preserved to a height of 50 cm. In the north east corner of this building, a human skull was discovered and below the floor, skeletons of three adults and one youth. In the corner, a child's skeleton was found without a skull. This level yielded many animal bones, the majority of them goat. Gazelle bones were dominant in the Natufian and the Neolithic levels. An enormous amount of seed (such as beans and cereals) was collected by flotation. Their study will provide valuable data regarding the prehistoric economy of the Mount Carmel area.

Beidha (Seyl Aqlat)

Seyl Aqlat is a seasonal torrent bed situated in Wadi el-Beidha about one hour's walk to the north of Petra. The pre-pottery settlement is located on a 6 km wide terrace, 1000 m above sea-level. This settlement was discovered by Diana Kirkbride (now Mrs. Hans Helbaek) in 1956 who excavated it for 7 field-seasons between 1958 and 1967. The site is presently about 70 m long and 60 m wide, though an unknown area has been eroded away down the Seyl bank. The earliest culture of Beidha is Natufian, characterised by such tool-types as lunates, micro-burins, trapezes, triangles and obliquely truncated bladelets. Also, great numbers of end-scrapers, notched blades and a number of dentalia shells have been recorded. The Natufian assemblage was discovered in two soundings made in the eroded talus of the Seyl bank and during this first season a large circular hearth area partially outlined by slabs of sandstone with animal bones and horn cores was exposed. Diana Kirkbride observes that the Natufian of Seyl Aqlat parallels that of Mugharet el-Wad level B2 and it can, therefore, be assigned to the lower Natufian (Kirkbride, 1960a:141). In another sounding made in 1965, she recorded brick shapes in the Natufian levels and surmises that the Natufians came from an alluvial environment and brought with them a tradition of building in clay or *pisé* (Kirkbride, 1960b:172; 1967:12). However, there is no continuity from the Mesolithic (Natufian) to the Neolithic at Beidha and the two cultures are separated by 2 or 3 m of windborne sterile sand.

B

Fig. 3. Beidha: General view of structures in Level II. Copyright: Diana Kirkbride.
Beidha Excavations.

The Neolithic newcomers to Beidha belonged to the aceramic group
who came and settled on the site towards the close of the 8th millennium
BC. Their cultural relics are stratigraphically divisible into six* building
levels, numbered from the top downward. The inhabitants of Beidha
lived in semi-subterranean houses which were entered by three descend-
ing stone steps. The rooms were very small and the walls made of dry

*In the 1965 season in a sounding on the north of the excavated area (squares E 4-6) on
the site, the possible existence of two more levels (Levels VII and VIII) was discovered.
Traces of post-holes indicating the remains of huts and large expanses of plaster-floor
together with a small hearth have been noticed there (Kirkbride, 1967:5-6).

FIG. 4. Beidha: Remains of earliest buildings (Level VI) with wall slots for posts. Copyright: Diana Kirkbride. Beidha Excavations.

stone with small stones set in interstices. The rooms divided from each other by immensely thick, solidly built stone baulks. The houses of the first definitely identifiable level (Level VI) are small circular buildings arranged in separate clusters like cells in a honeycomb. Four of the five segmented houses of this level have five plastered floors and walls and two contained central post-holes, presumably to support the roof. Each cluster of houses had an encircling wall behind which lay the courtyards with hearths while floors and walls were usually plastered. Three separate clusters of houses have been located and excavated to varying extents.

(a)   (b→)

FIG. 5 a, b, Beidha: The "Butcher's Shop" unit Level III. Copyright: Diana Kirkbride. Beidha Excavations.

The contents of the rooms have been carefully noted by Kirkbride who believes that specialisation of crafts had already taken place at this early stage (Kirkbride, 1966b). An architectural evolution is noticeable in the succeeding level (Level V) where one finds single-roomed free standing buildings. But it is in Level IV that one encounters the finest building techniques where the houses comprise one-roomed rectangular structures or circular ones which have continued from the preceding level. The architecture and general layout of houses in Levels III and II are similar. They are now very large, single roomed and free standing with walls and floors plastered with a strong lime plaster which had been relaid and recoated many times. Red bands noticed on the floors in these levels are comparable to those of aceramic Hacilar and Çatal Hüyük. It is suggested that grinding was done on the flat roof and from the contents of the rooms, a beadmaker's workshop and a butcher's shop have been identified (Kirkbride, 1966c). Enclosures or pens, presumably for the safe-keeping of the herds of animals by night, have been exposed. A single house comprising a rectangular room 4 by 4 m with slightly curved walls made of flattish stone slabs and with a floor of white plaster has been recorded from Level I.

Fig. 5.   (b)

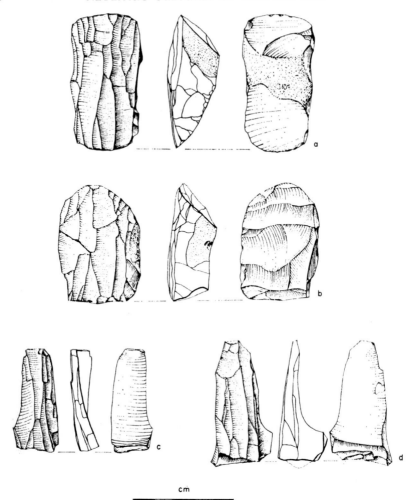

cm

FIG. 6. Beidha: Chipped stone industry of the PPNB phase; *a–b* double-ended blade-cores, *c–d* plunging flakes. With kind permission from *Acta Archaeologica*.

The chipped stone industry of Beidha Neolithic is principally made of local flint, and obsidian accounts for only 3 pieces (one borer and two blades), one coming from each of the Levels II, III and V. A trace element analysis by Renfrew *et al.* suggests that the pieces from Levels II and III came from the Çiftlik source in central Anatolia and the single blade from Level V came from one of the obsidian sources in the Lake Van district, almost 900 km northeast of Beidha (Mortensen, 1970:15). The chipped

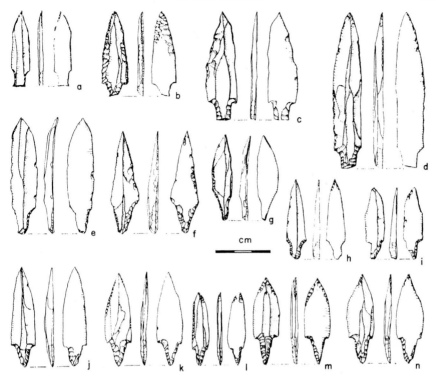

FIG. 7. Beidha: Chipped stone industry, arrowheads. With kind permission from *Acta Archaeologica*.

stone artifacts of Beidha have been studied by Mortensen (1970) who has identified several types of arrowheads made on blades with converging edges; borers made on longitudinal flakes, burins, scrapers, knives, sickle-blades, flakes, notched blades, beaked blades, firestones and re-touchers. The core tools include chisels, celts, picks, and spherical hammerstones. As regards the occurrence of individual types Mortensen observes (1970:45):

> The development seems to be gradual, with a few types appearing and re-appearing in the course of time.

He concludes that:

> the type stability at Beidha is so high (93.3%) that we must conclude that the chipped stone industry from level VI to level I represents a development from generation to generation within the same group of people. There are no reflections in the material of new population elements (1970:47).

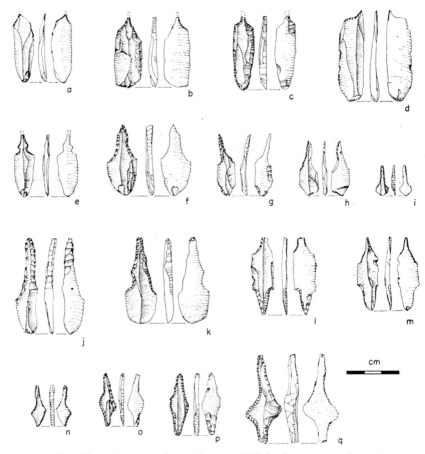

Fɪɢ. 8. Beidha: Chipped stone industry, borers. With kind permission from *Acta Archaeologica*.

He further adds:

Also we must conclude, that it is most unlikely that the change from round to rectangular houses in Palestine reflects a migration of people from the North or even a new population element (Mortensen, 1971).

It is not clear whether the change from round to rectangular houses represents a change in roofing technique.

Two animal figurines of baked clay (one a rough representation of a possible female goat and another a well modelled ram's head) were found in Level VI (Kirkbride, 1967). A tiny mother goddess, only 2·8 cm high, armless and with head missing, was found in a work-shop of Level II. An ibex figure and ibex horn cores found in the shafts of graves indicate that the ibex, in preference to the bull, was the chief sacred animal of Neolithic Beidha (Kirkbride, 1966c:26). The personal ornaments include a large number of beads of pierced and unpierced cowrie, and slender

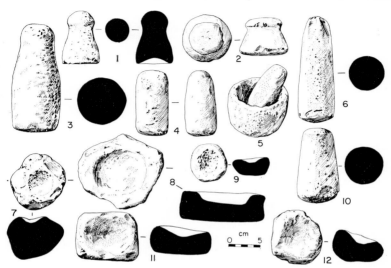

FIG. 9. Beidha: Pestles and stone bowls. Copyright: Diana Kirkbride. Beidha Excavations.

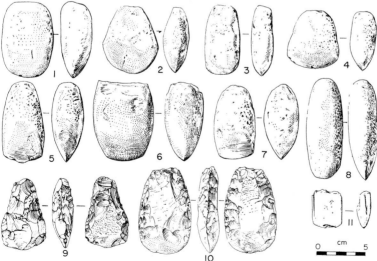

FIG. 10. Beidha: Basalt axe heads. Copyright: Diana Kirkbride. Beidha Excavations.

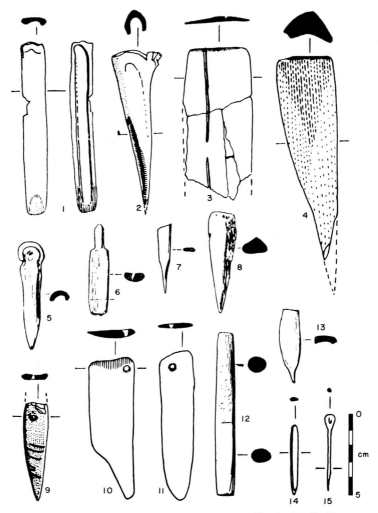

FIG. 11. Beidha: Bone implements. Copyright: Diana Kirkbride. Beidha Excavations.

long bones of gazelle, and long barrel-shaped beads of stone and carved stone amulets. A wooden palette, 40 cm in diameter, and a bitumen-coated basket with a diameter of 45 cm were also recorded. An oval wooden box, represented only by shadows in the soil, contained 114 flint arrowheads and points (Kirkbride, 1968b:267).

The burial customs of Beidha are of somewhat macabre type. Forty-three burials (10 of adults and 33 of children and infants) have been un-

covered so far. Two distinct methods of the disposal of the dead were
practised at Beidha. The infants and children were buried intact under
house-floors. One child had been buried with its personal ornament of a
little bracelet of cowrie shells. The other method of burial was also
under the house-floor, but after decapitation, and practised in the case
of adults. However, an intact adult burial was found in 1965 so it is
assumed that decapitation was practised in the cases of death only after

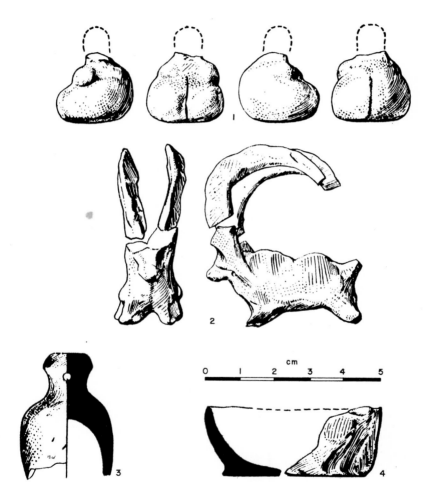

FIG. 12. Beidha: 1 Clay mother goddess from Level II; 2 baked clay ibex figurine,
Level VI; 3 bell shaped stone amulet, Level II; and 4 baked clay bowl, Level VI.
Copyright: Diana Kirkbride. Beidha Excavations.

a certain age. This custom was also prevalent at Jericho in the pre-Pottery Neolithic B (PPNB) phase. However, considering the occurrence of plastered skulls at places like Jericho—hypothetically associated with an ancestral cult—it may be argued that the deceased was decapitated only if he or she had descendants. The occurrence of a large number of child burials suggests a high mortality rate and the comparative paucity of adult burials suggests the existence of a cemetery as yet unidentified (Kirkbride, 1968b:272). It is interesting to note that a group of carefully built edifices with huge flat stone slabs and basins was discovered in the 1967 season by Kirkbride (1968a) and she believes it to be a "sanctuary" for some kind of religious observance.

Our knowledge regarding the economy of protoneolithic Beidha is based on thousands of grain imprints found in the burnt plaster of a house destroyed in a violent fire. The economy was based on the cultivation, as the chief crop, of hulled 2-row barley (Helbaek, 1966) but emmer wheat was also grown on a limited scale. The Beidha emmer is believed to be wheat in a transitional form on the way to full domestication (Kirkbride, 1968b:267). Food was supplemented by collection of pistachio nuts, acorns, and seeds of various leguminous plants. Three weed grasses, characteristic of the earliest corn-fields, viz. goat-faced grass, rye grass and wild oats, have been recognised. Animal domestication seems to be limited to the goat but evidence is not yet conclusive (Perkins, 1966, Kirkbride, 1968b:267). Aurochs, bezoar (considered to be the ancestor of the domesticated goat), ibex, gazelle, wild boar, hare, jackal, and members of the horse family (horse or half-ass, Equus sp.) lived in the vicinity and were hunted for their meat, skin and bones (Kirkbride, 1966a; Perkins, 1966). The Neolithic occupants of Beidha had trade contacts with their contemporaries elsewhere in the Levant. Thus obsidian came from Anatolia and pumice and shell may have been carried from the Mediterranean and the Red Sea. The locality around Beidha is rich in such minerals as hæmatite, malachite and ochre and it is probable that Beidha traded with these (Kirkbride, 1966a). In fact, it has been claimed that Beidha was the bazaar of the district (Mellaart, 1965:44).

The absolute chronology of this settlement is based on a series of 14 radiocarbon dates which, though not very consistent internally, fall within a time-bracket of 7200 BC to 6600 BC on the Libby half-life. Allowing a century for the latest deposits at the settlement, it seems reasonable to believe that Beidha Neolithic flourished between 7200 and 6500 BC. There are close parallels between the Beidha Neolithic and the PPNB culture at Jericho. Kirkbride observes that there is similarity of ground stone and bone implements and of querns obtained from both sites and in their burial practices (Kirkbride, 1962:11-12).

Jericho

The settlement of old Jericho, an oval mound now called Tell Es Sultan, on the outskirts of the modern oasis, has been known to antiquaries for more than a century. The site was discovered by Warren on behalf of the Palestine Exploration Fund as early as 1868 and systematic excavations were undertaken by Sellin and Watzinger in 1907-9 (Garstang, 1932). Archæological investigations were resumed after nearly three decades in 1930-36 and the neolithic origin of the site was discovered by Garstang (1935) who found a 6·5 m deposit of this period divisible into two main phases on the basis of the presence of pottery above the 5 m level (i.e. in a stratum about 1·5 or 2 m thick), but not below. The antiquity of this site was further emphasised by a third expedition led by Kathleen M. Kenyon who worked for seven field seasons from 1952 to 1958. These campaigns showed that the site was occupied from Mesolithic times through various phases of the Neolithic, Chalcolithic, Bronze Age down to the Iron Age with occasional breaks in the sequence. What has attracted people to occupy and reoccupy the same place time and again? The reason for this long and almost continuous occupation has been summed up by Kenyon (1953b:603) in the following words:

> As one flies over the modern oasis of Jericho, one realises why it was an important site for many thousands of years. The oasis stands out as a patch of brilliant green in the dazzling whiteness of the rest of the Jordan valley. Its luxuriant vegetation is nourished by a perennial spring which wells out at the foot of the mound which marks the site of the ancient city, and which was the reason why man first settled there.

The culture-sequence of Jericho is as follows:
1. Bronze Age (divisible into Early, Middle and Late).
2. Chalcolithic and Early Bronze/Middle Bronze.
3. Pottery Neolithic (divisible into A & B).
4. Pre-Pottery Neolithic (divisible into A & B).
5. Proto-Neolithic.
6. Mesolithic (Natufian Culture).

The first settlers of Jericho were Mesolithic hunters and food-gatherers whose cultural relics have been identified in the lowest 45 cm deposit in square E towards the north-eastern end of the tell (Kenyon 1960:100). Their artefacts include numerous blades, lunates, borers and sickle-blades. Scrapers and burins are scarce and no microburins or obsidian were reported (Kirkbride, 1960b). Among the bone objects one must mention a harpoon head. A structure associated with this assemblage is a clay

Fig. 13. Jericho: A Mesolithic structure in Square E1, possibly a sanctuary.

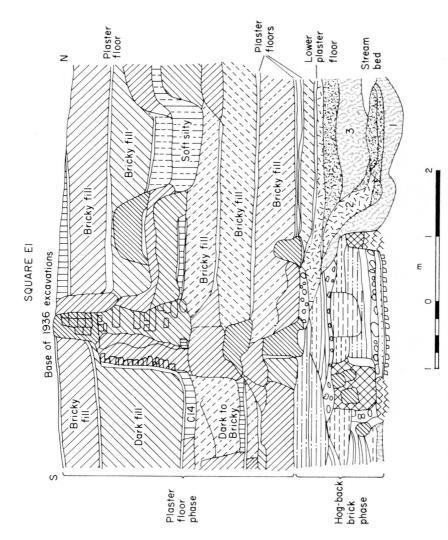

SQUARE EI

Base of 1936 excavations

N

Plaster floor

Bricky fill

Bricky fill

Soft silty

Plaster floors

Bricky fill

Bricky fill

Lower plaster floor

Bricky fill

Stream bed

3

2

S

Bricky fill

Dark fill

C14

Dark to Bricky

Plaster floor phase

Hog-back brick phase

1

8

m

0   1   2

Fig. 14. Jericho: Section showing two phases of the Pre-Pottery Neolithic.

Fig. 15. Jericho: A typical round house of the PPNA phase.

platform measuring 6·50 m by 3 m, bounded by a substantial stone wall. It is rectangular in plan and has two stones with sockets presumably to hold "totem poles" set in the wall. Kenyon believes it to be a sanctuary or a shrine (Kenyon, 1959a:40; 1959b:8). Two radiocarbon samples (F.69, F.72) give dates of 7900±240 and 7850±240 BC respectively, but

FIG. 16. Jericho: Neolithic town wall with earlier one beneath it.

FIG. 17. Jericho: Pre-Pottery Neolithic tower; at base, entrance to passage. The man at the top is at the head of the stairs.

a sample from this phase dated by Philadelphia laboratory (P. 376) gives
9216±107 BC on the Libby half-life and this has led Kenyon to assign a
date of *c.* 9000 BC for the appearance of the first Mesolithic hunters and
food-gatherers at Jericho (Kenyon, 1969:151).

The Mesolithic hunters were succeeded by people of a Proto-Neolithic
stage which characterises a transition from the nomadic to the settled
way of life. Four metres of cultural deposit of this phase was encountered
in Square M on the west side of the tell, beneath a long succession of the
typical rounded houses of the PPNA stage. No well-defined walls were
found but slight humps, supposed to be the bases of hut-like shelters
and an innumerable succession of floors have been identified (Kenyon,
1959*a*:40). The flint industry of the Proto-Neolithic phase comprises
arrow-heads, sickle-blades, burins, core-scrapers, chisels and adzes;
small axes and numerous fine points or blades and flakes (Kirkbride,
1960*b*:116). The implements are better made and show more retouching
than in the succeeding PPNA period. Another noteworthy feature is the
occurrence of obsidian during this period suggesting that Jericho was in
trade contact with obsidian sources in Anatolia. It is believed that an
economy based on agriculture must have developed during this stage
(Kenyon, 1960:99) although there is no positive proof of this.

The succeeding stage at Jericho, termed Pre-pottery Neolithic A
(PPNA) or "hog-back brick phase" marked a sudden increase in the
development of the Neolithic culture. The people now lived in mud-
brick houses, round or rectilinear in plan. The walls were made of plano-
convex bricks usually with a hog-backed profile and were thick and well-
built, indicating permanence of architecture. The houses certainly had
two rooms and altogether 22 structural phases of this period have been
identified in site D (Kenyon, 1957*a*:102). Floors were made of beaten
mud but not of burnished plaster as in the succeeding period (Kenyon,
1956*a*:72). The flint industry comprising arrowheads, sickle-blades,
numerous burins and borers, small chisels, adzes and picks which is
"distressingly monotonous with few characteristic implements" (Kirkbride, 1960*b*) was supposed to be derived from the preceding Natufian
industry (Kenyon, 1959*a*:39). Obsidian was frequently used and there
was an extensive bone industry while polished stone tools included
querns, grinders and bowls.

A noteworthy feature of the PPNA stage is the discovery of a defensive
system suggesting that by about 8000 BC the settlement had reached the
status of a town which covered an area of 10 acres. The evidence for this
defensive system comprises a town-wall, a massive tower and a rock-cut
ditch. The ditch, measuring 8·25 m wide and 2·75 m deep, was traced
on the west side of the mound in front of the town-wall which stands to a

Fig. 18. Jericho: A rectilinear house of Pre-Pottery Neolithic B phase.

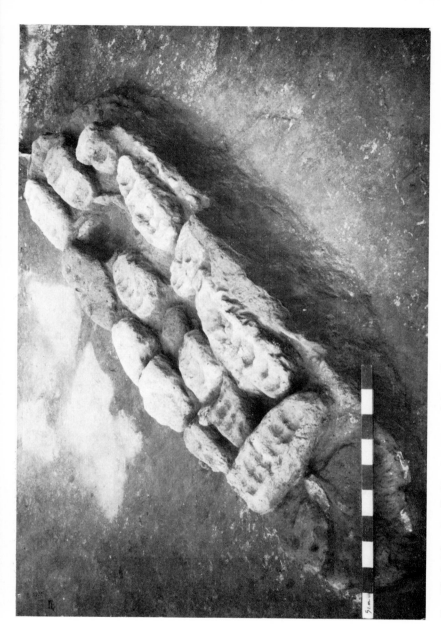

Fig. 19. Jericho: A wall of Pre-Pottery Neolithic B phase.

height of 6 m at this point. The town-wall has also been traced at the north and south ends of the settlement and it has three structural phases. In the area cleared on the west side, the wall is backed by a massive tower measuring 12·20 m in diameter at the base, 9·15 m at the summit and surviving to a height of 9·15 m. The tower is provided, in its centre with a staircase of 22 steps for an unknown purpose. The discovery of such a defensive system at such an early date and its interpretation has been a matter for much discussion among scholars (Wheeler, 1956; Kenyon 1956c; Braidwood, 1957; Kenyon, 1957b; 1959a.) Here, without going into the merits of the arguments it will suffice to say that the construction of such an elaborate defensive system requires a central leadership coupled with either considerable degree of communal organisation or surplus wealth to pay the workers. This also presupposes the possibility that increased wealth had come to the town-dwellers which made it imperative to protect themselves from nomads and marauders. This wealth could only have come by the discovery of agriculture and as will be seen below, emmer was grown during this period. In fact, even the existence of an irrigation system has been suspected (Kenyon, 1959a:40) but this remains to be proved by archæological or botanical evidence. However, the discovery of other neolithic townships such as Çatal Hüyük in Anatolia, although without a town-wall and belonging to a somewhat later date, does suggest a hitherto unsuspected degree of social organisation and technological advancement in this early stage of the Neolithic.

The PPNA folk buried their dead in regular graves, about a metre deep. The dead bodies lay in contracted position at the base of the grave-pits (Kenyon 1957a:106). Ten radiocarbon dates are available for this period and with the exception of one date, (B.M. 250) 8350±500 BC, all the other dates fall between a time-bracket of 7825 BC to 6770 BC.

There is a stratigraphic gap between the end of the PPNA stage and the beginning of the succeeding stage termed Pre-Pottery Neolithic B (PPNB) or the Plaster Floor Stage. This new phase is marked by a change in architecture, artefacts and burial practices from the preceding phase. However, like the preceding phase, PPNB also spans a long duration of time and up to 26 structural phases have been excavated in different areas (Kenyon 1956c). The basic unit was a succession of large, well-proportioned rooms communicating through entrances flanked by walls. Adjoining the principal rooms were smaller ones some of which may have served as storage rooms. Walls were now made of flattened cigar-shaped bricks with a herring-bone pattern made on their surface by brick-worker's thumbs. Elaborate care was taken for the preparation of floors which were covered with gypsum plaster and rush mats have been

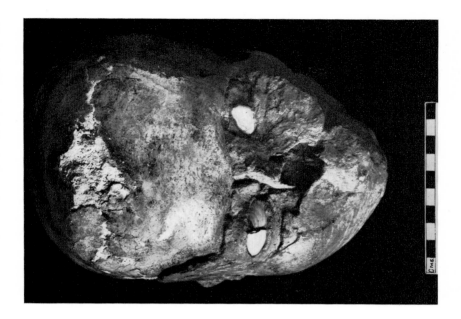

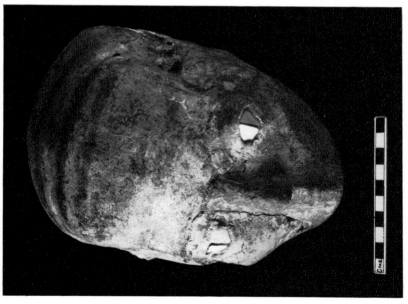

Fig. 20. Jericho: Portrait heads.

FIG. 21. Jericho: Portrait head.

traces of architecture and some hearths (Kenyon, 1954a). Structures built of bun-shaped bricks are typical of the latter sub-phase. The ceramics is hand-made and mostly soft and friable. The forms are simple, flat-based saucers and jugs with a globular body. In addition, a decorated ware, with a cream slip and a pattern of chevrons and triangles in dark red colour, is also present in the Pottery Neolithic A (Kenyon, 1954b: 109). The ceramic ware of Pottery Neolithic B is comparable with that from Byblos. It seems that the Pottery Neolithic occupation was short-lived, as compared with the preceding two phases, and the site was then deserted. Soil analysis carried out by Zeuner (1954), indicated that there is a stratigraphic gap of at least 300 ± 100 years between the end of the Pottery Neolithic and the arrival of the Early Bronze Age I people at the site.

El-Khiam

Mention may be made in this context of the prehistoric site of El-Khiam situated near the cliffs of Wadi Khareitun in the desert southeast of Bethlehem. It was excavated by Neuville in 1933 and the results were published by Perrot in 1951. This work was resumed by Echegary (1964) who made small soundings in 1962. The 7 m thick cultural deposit of El-Khiam is divisible into 12 layers, the first layer from the top repre-senting the Tahunian I industry characterised by abundant flints, typical arrowheads and remains of a large wall, 1 m wide and recalling the walls of Jericho PPNB. The next 60 cm deposit attests the transition from the Mesolithic to the Neolithic cultures. The former are represented by a series of industries termed Khiamian I and II, Kebaran and Atlitian from the top downward. The earliest culture is Middle Arvignacian which lies over a sterile layer. The sequence at El-Khiam, although it does not give much information about the Neolithic culture, furnishes an uninter-rupted sequence from the Upper Palæolithic down to the beginning of the Neolithic.

Ghrubba

A number of neolithic-chalcolithic sites were located in 1953 during the survey of the Yarmuk and the Jordan valleys by Mellaart (1962). One of these sites, Ghrubba, is situated on the southern side of Wadi Nimrin about 2 km west of the police post of Shunah on the main Jerusalem-Amman road. It is a flat mound, only one metre in height. Here, below the Ghassulian (Chalcolithic) deposits were found remains of a Neolithic culture (Mellaart, 1956). It is characterised by a homogeneous pottery, all hand-made both painted and plain, two clay spoons, a fragmentary figurine, a clay spindle-whorl, two flint axes and two sickle-blades of brown flint together with a bun-shaped brick. Mellaart observes that Ghrubba presents a neolithic culture distinct from that of Jericho IX and the so-called Yarmukian of Sha'ar ha-Golan (Mellaart, 1956:32-33). The Neolithic pottery has been compared with that of Mersin and Amuq B culture (Tell Judeidah XIV) and Mellaart believes it to be a western variant of the Hassuna-Sammara complex in northern Mesopotamia.

Besides the two excavated and two partially tested sites described above, some neolithic material has been picked up in surface explorations in different parts of Jordan. Thus Neolithic artefacts like arrowheads, sickle-blades, backed blades, burins, drills, cores and fragmentary basalt querns, pestles, and mortars, digging sticks and hammerstones have been found at Abu Suwan near Jerash (Kirkbride, 1958). Some flint artefacts of neolithic character and animal bones, along with three hearths, were found at Abu Sewan in a test-pit of 2 sq. m. Again, a few fragments of hand-made bowls with flat bases and flint artefacts assignable to the pottery Neolithic period have been picked up from Salihi, a site between Amman and Jerash (Kirkbride, 1959). Further, ground stone artefacts of coarse-grained basalt and flint implements like sickle-blades assignable to an early Neolithic date have been collected at Wadi el Yabis in the Jordan valley, between Deir Alla and Khirbet esh Shuneh, on the east side of the Jordan (Kirkbride, 1956).

Hazorea

Recent excavations of pottery-Neolithic cultures of Palestine (December, 1970 to April, 1971) were made at Abu Zureiq, near Hazorea, 20 km southeast of Nahal Oren (Anati, 1971). Here the Neolithic settlers lived in semi-subterranean pits excavated in the earth or a soft limestone down to about a metre and a half below the ground. The floors had fireplaces and various stone structures presumably used for storage and cooking. These houses were roofed with straw mixed with mud. The stone tools comprised axes, saw-blades and sickle blades, well made arrow- and javelin-heads, borers and scrapers. The ground tools comprised grinding stones, pestles and mortars mostly made of basalt. The pottery was thick and heavy but relatively well-fired and the shapes included deep and large bowls with flat, rounded bases; jars with very broad hole-mouths and almost vertical sides; shouldered and handled jars as well as platters. This assemblage has been compared with those from Jericho, Byblos and other sites in northern Syria and Cilicia. Anati believes that the culture persisted for a relatively longer period at Hazorea as five successive occupation levels have been distinguished in one of the excavated areas.

Ramad

Ramad is located 15 km southwest of Damascus at the foot of the Hermon range on a fertile plateau about 900 m above sea-level in the dry-farming rainfall zone. The settlement measures 150 m north-south and 175 m east-west and the thickness of deposit is about 5 m. The site was tested for 7 field seasons (from 1963 to 1970) by de Contenson and van Liere (van Liere, 1963; de Contenson and van Liere, 1964a, 1966a, 1966c, de Contenson, 1970, 1971), and levels of three main occupations were encountered.

Level I

Level I (the earliest) with its remains of habitation concentrated mostly in the eastern part of the site, is represented by a two-metre thick deposit. This level, divisible into two sub-phases A and B, shows a succession of half-buried huts made of *pisé* with thick layers of white plaster and furnished with ovens and shallow basins hollowed in the base of the rock. The chipped stone industry found had two types of flint sickle, with characteristic sheen, together with a few blades and flakes of obsidian. The study of the latter material reveals that 90% of it came from Cappadocia, the remaining 10% being an import from the Lake Van region through the Euphrates valley. Among the implements of flint, arrowheads with short tangs and notches on the base, burins, awls, blades and retouched bladelets are characteristic tool-types of phase IA and leaf-shaped arrowheads are present in IB. The ground stone industry comprised pestles, mortars and hammerstones of basalt and the bone tools included spatulæ and points. Carved limestone spindle-whorls have been reported from phase IA and stone bowls and numerous unbaked clay figurines of both animals and humans, occur in IB. de Contenson believes that phase IA represents a population based on agriculture and hunting. This interpretation is supported by the study of the flora by van Zeist and Bottema (1966) who believe that agriculture was practised from the very beginning of the settlement. The inhabitants cultivated grains including barley in its more primitive stage (*Hordeum distichum*), emmer wheat (*Triticum dicoccum*), einkorn (*Triticum monococcum*) and club wheat (*Triticum compactum*). Of these, emmer was the most important species while einkorn and club-wheat occurred in small quantities. They also grew lentils and collected wild grasses such as bromus and wild vegetables including vetch. Their diet was supplemented by a number of wild fruits such as almond and pistachio. The study of the faunal remains suggests that hunting was the only source of meat supply, and the bulk of the material consists of gazelle and deer. Two radiocarbon samples (Gr. N. 4428, 4821), of which the first comes from the upper phase of Level I just below the base of Level II (de Contenson and van Liere, 1966c), give dates of 6250 ± 80 BC and 6140 ± 50 BC on the Libby half-life (Vogel and Water-bolk, 1967). As one sample comes from the upper stratum of Level I, the beginnings of Ramad probably goes back to around 6500 BC.

Level II

Level II is the most prosperous period in the history of tell Ramad as it marks a definite advancement in architectural styles. Straight walls on stone foundations have been exposed. The foundation of these walls are made of two rows of unbonded blocks, bedded in gravel, 40 to 70 cm thick; their extant height does not exceed half a metre. The super-structure is made of bun-shaped or rectangular mud-bricks measuring 40 by 30 by 8 cm. The best excavated house had been rebuilt at least four times on the same spot with slight changes and shifts in orientation. Parts of rectilinear walls were also exposed in the northwestern corner of the northern square. These houses appear to have been built around large courtyards and are provided with numerous hearths.

Level II at Ramad is not preceramic but marks a stage of transition to the use of proper ceramics. White vessels in moulded plaster (*vaisselle blanche*) are present in this level. These vessels are made of lime and silica, with ochrous, friable cores containing large grits. The outer layer on some vessels is more white and fine; sometimes the whole body is homogeneous. The surface is smooth and a change in curvature is sometimes marked by bright red bands. The large receptacles like large bowls with rounded rims and short, flat bases were doubtless made in moulds but they are always found in very fragmentary condition. This ware is widespread, it occurs on the coast at Byblos etc., inland at Al Kowm and as far as Bouqras on the Euphrates.

The chipped stone industry discovered at this level comprises two types of sickle blades, one with small and more or less regular teeth and the other with large, well-spaced teeth. The blunted back is rare in the latter type. Many types of knives made of tabular flint, and leaf-shaped and tanged javelin points with flat retouch continue from Level IB. We also recognise a revival of the short or elongated arrowheads. Sometimes flat retouch produces fine serration along the edges. Other types include circular scrapers often made on thick flakes and bifacial elements similar to those of Level IB. Obsidian is well represented and includes long blades with retouch. The basalt industry continues the same tradition but one polished axe is added to the repertoire. The bone industry discoveries comprise a fine needle 11 cm long, stubby awls and spatulæ, polishers and hafts decorated with grooves on the exterior. Personal ornaments found include a cylindrical bead and a ring, both of bone, one cylindrical bead of hæmatite and one of green stone, and 6 perforated shells. Figurines of unbaked clay are now abundant although they are preserved only when accidentally fired and among these, horned quadrupeds are frequent and animals with short tails and twisted horns are reminiscent of capra-ovids (sheep/goat) rather than bovids. The schematic human figures have discoid heads, appliqué eyes and club-shaped limbs. Small, pawn-shaped figurines with pinched nose are also present. Several child burials were found, as well as two adult skeletons. One of the adults lay in a crouched position, with head to the west, outside the houses, and a second contracted burial was found in the seventh season (1970), the only ornament was a jadeite bead, found under the right arm. The discovery of 12 plastered human skulls modelled and partly painted in red ochre, reminded one of similar finds from PPNB levels at Jericho. These had been placed in an oval cavity surrounded by mud-bricks in House 10, not far from the child burials. They were divided in small groups separated by lumps of clay, plastered and painted. They were originally thought to belong to Level II but have now been ascribed to Level I (de Contenson, 1971:281). The flora and fauna does not differ from that in Level I and the inhabitants of Ramad still depended on hunting and agriculture. Two radiocarbon samples (Gr. N. 4427, 4822) from this level have been dated to 5970 ± 50 BC and 5950 ± 50 BC respectively on the Libby half-life. But another sample (Gr. N. 4426) said to have come from Square H. 10, together with the plastered skulls has been dated to 6260 BC and these may now be ascribed to Level I where it is in conformity with the other two dates from Level I mentioned earlier. Thus Level II flourished during the first half of the sixth millennium BC.

Level III

Level III at Ramad has been identified only in the western square of the mound and it has been argued that the village had shifted towards the west. No complete building has been excavated and the architecture includes fragments of walls and platforms of stone. Two structural phases have been observed in the western square. This level witnesses the arrival of true ceramic of the style known as Dark Faced Burnished ware. The pottery is hand-made and always presents a smooth surface with forms which include hemispherical bowls, cups with ring base and jars with flaring neck. A new shape which was discovered is a plate with flat base and flaring rim which faintly recalls Halaf forms. The decoration is found on the exterior and burnishing is confined to a band on the neck. de Contenson points out that this pattern fits into the group of burnished ware which is the earliest in Anatolia and Palestine, but is far from homogeneous. The pottery of Ramad does not have the richness of forms and decoration of the Syro-Cilician province and it does not attain the technical perfection of the fine vessels of Amuq B or Ras Shamra VA.

Among the flint tools found, sickle elements with large teeth are the principal type and blunted backs are less rare. Knives with large teeth have become important and only the cutting edge is retouched on the lower face. Obsidian is rare but basalt is found used for the manufacture of pounders and querns, while limestone was more commonly used for bowls and plates. However, the bone industry remains the same as in Level II. The fauna shows an important change and goats, sheep, pig, ox and dog have all become domesticated. This is attested by the discovery of abundant juvenile remains of *Capra*, *Ovis*, and *Sus*. However, gazelle and red deer were still hunted (Hooijer, 1966). A single radio-carbon sample (Gr.N. 4823) has been dated to 5930±55 BC.

Bouqras

The pre-pottery settlement of Bouqras is situated on the west bank of the Euphrates, on its confluence with the Habur, about 40 km south of Deir-ez-Zor. Two five-metre squares dug by de Contenson and van Liere, (de Contenson 1966b; de Contenson and van Liere, 1966b; van Liere and de Contenson, 1963) in 1965 yielded a 5 m thick cultural deposit divisible into three layers numbered from the bottom to the top.

Level I

Level I had two superimposed villages with houses made of *pisé* and roughly rectangular in plan. The floors were made of beaten earth and covered with a coating of plaster and sometimes with matting of simple crossweave. A hut measuring 5 m by 6 m with rounded corners has been uncovered. The extant walls rise to a height of 60 cm and the houses were provided with horseshoe shaped ovens made of burnt clay. The flint industry was made of blade tools. End-scrapers are found to be the commonest tools but two types of arrowheads and sickle elements are associated with obsidian bladelets and angle burins while burins and knives are not common and awls are rare. Ground tools found include pestles in basalt and grinders in diorite, basalt and sandstone. A cylindrical bead of green stone and one human figurine in unbaked clay complete the inventory of Level I. The fauna studied by Hooijer (1966) suggests that intensive hunting of bezoar (*Capra aegagrus*), Asiatic mouflon and a large wild ox was practised. In the total absence of grains, van Zeist suggests that the presence of sickles does not indicate a grain economy but only food-supply of vegetables. de Contenson believes that the architecture and the stone industry suggest a connection with Jarmo on the one hand and with Jericho PPNA and Ain Mallaha on the other. Two radiocarbon dates (Gr. N. 4818, 4852) from the bottom and the top of this level read 6190 ± 60 BC and 6290 ± 100 BC on the Libby half-life (Vogel and Waterbolk, 1967:128-9). These dates compare well with those of Ramad I.

Level II

Level II marks an overall development in the architecture and four successive villages with mud-brick constructions and plastered floors have been identified. Outlines of a network of rectangular structures with a system of pillars and pilasters coupled with extensive use of wood in the architecture of the successive villages have been found. Plastered hearths, a rectangular bin and a drain are other interesting features. The flint industry derives from the preceding levels and the discovery of scrapers, arrowheads and burins becomes more frequent. Obsidian is rarely found but the bone industry includes spatulæ, highly polished burnishers and vertebræ of ovids polished by use. An interesting fact is that sickles, pestles and grindstones have disappeared but this is probably due to the limited scope of the excavation which exposed only a small area because they reappear in the succeeding level. There are, however, bowls with carefully polished sides, made of locally available alabaster and gypsum, and beads of blue or green stone and of alabaster have been reported. As at Ramad, *vaisselle blanche* is present but is coarser in character. A jadeite seal, translucent in colour, in the form of a truncated cone and with impression of a series of chevrons has been recorded from village IV. A single radiocarbon sample (Gr. N. 4819) gives a date of 6010 ± 55 BC. The remains of wild species of animals are very abundant and de Contenson believes that this is a sedentary hunting settlement.

Level III

Level III, represented by the 7th village on the site is marked by the occurrence of 14 sherds of dark burnished pottery devoid of any surface

C

decoration. The pottery was hand-made with red or brown surface colour and micaceous core, with forms including cylindrical goblets with flat base. There was no change in architectural style and the mud-brick walls followed the same orientation as in the preceding level. The flint industry found does not differ from that of Level II and the typical tool-types of burins, knives, scrapers and arrowheads are present. Obsidian is now discovered in plenty and among the retouched tools are crescents. Alabaster vessels have also become more common and globular bowls, goblets or cups are found. The red veins of alabaster have been used for decorative effect, a feature common in the alabaster vessels of Tell Es-Sawwan. Mortars and grindstones of sandstone and basalt now reappear. The bone industry discovered includes spatulæ, handles, polishers and beads. Discoid beads of alabaster and carnelian, one dentalium shell, and a small trapezoidal plaque in mother-of-pearl were also recovered. The faunal remains have not been studied but it is believed that there may have been domesticated goat and cattle side by side with wild species. A single radiocarbon sample (Gr. N. 4820) from this level is dated to 5990 ± 60 BC. It is noteworthy that Bouqras is situated 100 km south of the rainfall zone* and cultivation is not possible without irrigation, so it is likely that the neolithic folk of Bouqras may have had an economy like that of the present day Bedouin in that area.

Besides the excavated sites of Ramad and Bouqras, de Contenson and van Liere have located three more early neolithic settlements in surface explorations (van Liere and de Contenson, 1963) in the Damascus basin. Of these, Sahl el Sahra, a wide level plain in between the foot-hill ridges of the Anti-Lebanon mountains, yielded hut floors and a predominantly flake industry with crude retouching together with large instruments of chert such as axes, adzes, chisels and picks. de Contenson remarks that unless the stratigraphical position shows the industry to be Neolithic, it is so crude that it can not easily be recognised as such. A similar collection of beaked burins, thick assymetrical arrowheads, scrapers and an axe with polished working edge have been picked up on the springs of the Barada in the Damascus basin. This collection again gives the impression of a Mesolithic industry but the presence of a polished stone axe has been taken to be indicative of a neolithic industry. The third settlement was located at Saidnaya in the same basin. Here, the collection is one of fine-grained flint and chert showing important microlithic elements, backed bladelets, a large variety of burins, a few borers and scrapers and notched arrowheads. Again the industry shows a strong Mesolithic tradition but in this case with a possible Tahunian influence.

*Modern limit of reliable rainfall for cultivation (200 mm per annum).

Our knowledge, in recent years, of the Neolithic cultures of inland Syria has been appreciably augmented by excavations at Mureybit and Al Kowm but before discussing this we will examine the data furnished by Munhata in the Jordan valley.

Munhata

A sequence generally comparable to that of Ramad and Bouqras but without the white vessels in moulded plaster (*vaisselle blanche*) has been discovered at Munhata, located 15 km south of the Lake Tiberias in the Jordan valley, 215 m below sea level. The site has been explored by Jean Perrot for six field seasons from 1962 and a total area of 1250 sq. m has been investigated. The maximum depth of 3 m has been divided into six levels numbered from the top downward, with stratigraphical and cultural breaks between the upper three levels. The lowermost layers are aceramic, while pottery appears in Level II with a cultural break after the end of the preceding level of nearly 1500 years (de Contenson, 1966a).

The earliest traces of human occupation are found on virgin soil (Level VI) and comprise stone-paved areas that were probably hut foundations, together with fragmentary bones, flint flakes and a number of unbaked animal and human figurines. It is not until Level V that a substantial mud-brick wall is found 8 m long, and 1 m thick, built on stone foundations and standing to a height of 50 cm. The shape of the bricks has not been recognised. Level IV has rectangular houses with plaster floors exposed in an area of 200 sq. m. The walls are made of loaf-shaped bricks 30 cm long and 6 or 7 cm in diameter. A room of this level measures 4·20 m by 4 m and the fine floor had been plastered five times in one case. These rooms have been provided with hearths and small compartments built of flat stones. The equipment consists of flat blocks of basalt, grinders and pestles, limestone bowls, large thin flint flakes and tools among which the most common are sickle-blades, arrowheads and javelin heads. Level III yielded a large circular construction 20 m in diameter consisting a central area paved with pebbles and several rooms measuring 2·50-3 m by 5-6 m arranged around the circumference. The floors of the rooms are paved with flat stones. A novelty of Level III is the appearance of a number of small fragments of reddish baked clay with imprints coming from walls and roofs destroyed by fire. Jean Perrot observes that some of the fragments (Perrot, 1964) have been intentionally modelled. The floor of this circular building is covered with animal bones and faunal remains of gazelle (*Gazella*), sheep and goat (*Ovis* and *Capra*), two species of cattle (*Bos taurus*), dog species (*Canis* sp.), pigs (*Sus scrofa*), and a few bones of ass (*Equus asinus*) have been identified. Of these, sheep and goat are abundant, cows and pigs are common, but equids and dogs are rare.

The chipped stone industry of the preceramic levels at Munhata is made of two types of flint, and obsidian is rare. The débitage is reminiscent of the Levallois technique. The industry comprises very fine blades and points, various types of javelin heads and arrowheads. Arrowheads with a central mid-rib and points with barbed tangs are a characteristic feature of Munhata. The ground stone industry comprises saddle querns, or flat querns of basalt, pestles, grinders, polishers, bowls of limestone and a few small beads of grey stone. A large number of human and animal figures of sun-dried clay, mostly fragmentary, have been recorded from preceramic levels. These figures are very small and remain very crude but some (Perrot, 1966 Pl.6.3), show care in the modelling. Perrot observes that the houses, stone industries, basins, grinding stones etc. of the aceramic levels at Munhata show a relationship with the PPNB at Jericho.

As noted above, there is a major break between Level III (aceramic) and Level II (ceramic bearing level). Hut floors with hearths and stone benches have been noted in Level II. Several trenches also yielded small bun-shaped bricks, measuring 15 cm across and 8 cm thick. The pottery found is characterised by the use of fine clay, with vegetable and mineral tempering. The firing is not very hard and the pots have a yellowish brown surface colour. Some of the pots have light burnish and the bottoms of some have mat impressions. The shapes include bowls, basins, hollow footed cups, pots with small, low neck; small jars with no neck or curved neck. Tongue-shaped lugs and small ring lug are the usual methods of handling. Decoration is common and almost half of the pots are incised or painted or both. The painted decoration includes chevrons and oblique parallel lines and the incised decoration comprises herringbone incision and single and double bands on the body. The pottery found includes the Dark Faced Burnished ware, characteristic of this region. Figures discovered of baked and unbaked clay include animal and human figurines. Terracotta human figurines have long heads and typical "coffee bean" eyes and are decorated with red paint. These figures remind us of similar female figures from Choga Mami in Iraq. The stone industry is found in less abundance and differs from that in the preceding levels. The chipped stone industry uncovered includes a small number of arrowheads with small barbs; sickle-blades with large, regularly spaced teeth; awls, scrapers and burins. Also present are picks, grinders, pounders and perforated stones of hard limestone or basalt. Perrot compares this level with Jericho Pottery Neolithic A and B; Byblos, (Middle Neolithic); and Ras Shamra IV.

The site was abandoned at the end of Level II and it was re-occupied after a long time gap. Level I has stone constructions and a few walls have been traced. The pottery of this phase differs from that in Level II. The clay is now better levigated and the shapes include vases with carinated profile decorated with appliqué bands, usually beneath the lip. Sherds of grey lustrous ware or burnished ware are another characteristic feature. This level has been compared with Levels XVII-XVI at Beth Shan. Moving east from the coastal sites one encounters two early sites, Mureybit and Al Kowm excavated in recent years.

Mureybit

The prehistoric settlement of Mureybit, siutated on the left bank of the Euphrates, near Meskene, about 86 km east of Aleppo was discovered by Maurits van Loon under the auspices of the Oriental Institute, University of Chicago, in the survey of the area to be flooded by a proposed dam on the Euphrates. It is one of the 56 settlements of different periods explored in that region. This five-acre village mound was tested in 1964 and an area of 240 sq m on the western slope of the mound was exposed in 1965 (van Loon, 1966a, b, c, 1968). The excavations have revealed that early man lived in permanent settlements long before he had learned to practise either agriculture or animal husbandry. The 6 m high conical mound measures 75 m in diameter and has a cultural deposit of 10 m divisible into 17 strata numbered from bottom to top, all neolithic and about two-thirds of which is without any pottery. The only other period represented is the Islamic, with glazed pottery and glass bracelets.

The first settlers at the site lived in permanent houses which show a gradual evolution in the art of building techniques. Thus Strata I to VIII are marked by round or curved buildings made of red clay walls with roofs built of wood or reeds and the pavements of large limestone blocks (van Loon, 1966a). The middle levels (Strata VII to XIII) were honeycombed by 16 perfectly round, vertical pits 80 cm in diameter and 70 cm in depth. The pits were lined with red clay and filled with ash and rounded river-pebbles. It is suggested that these pits may have been used as bread ovens of the type used even today in that area (van Loon, 1966a) or they may have served for the parching of the wild grains (van Loon, 1968). The upper levels (Strata X-XVII) are characterised by typical rectilinear structures built of loaf-shaped limestone slabs measuring 25 by 13 by 9 cm and laid like bricks with red clay covering them from all sides. The best-preserved rectilinear structure measured only 3·50 by 3·50 m and it was divided into four diminutive rooms of 1·50 by 1·50 m. These rooms had no doors but between two pairs of rooms there were tiny peep-holes. It is presumed that the entrance was through the roof— a practice commonly encountered at the later Neolithic settlement of Çatal Hüyük. Near the hearth-like depression in the corner of one room was found the jaw-bone of a large carnivore and cattle-horns had actually been built into other walls of the same levels. These features are also met with at Çatal Hüyük and these may be the precursors of similar manifestations at the latter site. The top two building levels were completely burned by fire but one could recognise the emplacement of vertical wooden posts and of round wooden beams placed horizontally over the stone wall foundations and covered on all sides with clay.

The inventory of artefacts for Mureybit is very large and no less than 70,000 pieces of chert, flint and obsidian were collected. The chipped stone industry was made up of two components, a heavy industry comprising scrapers, adzes, picks and hammers made of chert and a light tool industry essentially made of flint and consisting of such tool-types as burins, perforators, notched blades, borers and tanged points. Sickle blades make their appearance in the fourth level from the bottom along with querns and grinding stones. van Loon remarks that the tool-making industry is one continuous tradition and the changes demonstrate shifts of emphasis rather than revolutionary changes. A sample of about 15,000 chipped artefacts was studied by James H. Skinner (in van Loon, 1968) who also confirms van Loon's observation that it essentially represents a single industry reflecting a continuous technological tradition from the lowest to the highest level. Obsidian is extremely rare and only 5 pieces have been collected from the top seven layers at the site. The bone implements comprised only awls, occurring throughout the sequence in small numbers, and a cache of needles found in stratum VII. The ground stone tools consisted mostly of querns and mortars. Cylindrical pebbles with traces of use at both ends were apparently used as pestles. The rim of a bowl was found in one of the upper levels and it was carved out of a soft dark brown stone and carried a wavy band in relief, very much like a stone bowl fragment found at Çayönü. Some limestone plates with diameters ranging from 23-35 cm were also recorded. There is also some rudimentary evidence for the disposal of the dead. In the two burned layers at the top of the pre-pottery debris were found three instances in which human skulls had been buried in the angle between floor and wall of a structure and covered with debris and red clay. Nearby, but in no way connected with the skulls, other groups of human bones were also buried (van Loon, 1966a; 1968:275).

As noted above, the economy of neolithic Mureybit was based on

hunting and collection of wild species of cereals and no trace of domestication of animals or plants has been found. Preliminary study of animal
bones by Dexter Perkins Jr. shows that wild cattle, gazelle and onager
account for 30% each of the animal bones. Among the remaining 10%
are fallow deer, boar/pig, wolf and hare. It is rather curious that the neolithic folk did not eat fish although the site is situated on the banks of a
major river. However, it must be remembered that fish bones rarely
survive. Many thousands of bones of the Equid family have been found at
Mureybit and in a study of these remains Ducos (1970) observes that the
Mureybit *Equus* differs from *Equus hemionus hemippus* and it fits into the
Equus (Asinus) palestinae series. In a study of the vegetal remains from the
site van Zeist (1970) identified wild barley and two varieties of wild
einkorn wheat. The Neolithic inhabitants also collected wild lentil, vetch
and pistachio nuts. van Loon estimates that the number of families living
in the village at any one time may have totalled about 200 (van Loon,
1966c). There are six radiocarbon dates from this settlement spanning
from the earliest stratum to the latest which give a time-bracket of 8265
BC to 7542 BC on the Libby half-life.

Al Kowm

In 1967, a brief five-day sounding was made by Rudolph H. Dornemann of the Oriental Institute, Chicago, at Al Kowm, situated about 120
km northeast of Palmyra in the pass between Jebel Abu Rujmein and
the Jebel Bishri (Dornemann, 1969). This 25 m high conical mound is
one of the several early sites explored by Giorgio Buccellati. The trial
excavations revealed a cultural deposit of about 15·20 m of neolithic
strata of which the lowest 10 m belongs to the pre-pottery phase making
Al Kowm one of the richest and most promising aceramic settlements in
that area. Virgin soil could not be reached and the limited area under
excavation did not give a complete idea of the architectural patterns but
cream or white mud plaster floors have been reported from the aceramic
levels. The inventory of artefacts comprises a large number of flint tools,
several bone tools like awls and the top of a spatula, stone bowl fragments, a polished stone celt and fragments of thick, hard, red
burnished plaster. Obsidian blades were present throughout the neolithic strata but were most frequent in the lowest three metres. This
collection has been compared with Jericho PPNB, Ramad I, Ras Shamra
Vc and the highest levels of Beidha.

Architectural remains become more conspicuous in the overlying
4·90 m of deposit which has yielded well preserved remains of two superimposed buildings. Portions of 11 rooms of different sizes have been

exposed. The walls are 40 cm thick and have been covered with thin white lime plaster. True pottery is still absent but "plaster vessels" similar to the *vaisselle blanche* of Ramad II and Ras Shamra Vb have been reported. However, it seems that true pottery comprising a coarse yellow ware and the Dark Faced Burnished ware of Amuq A and B type occurs in the debris of the structures noted above. Other objects found include stone bowl fragments, bone tools, loom weight, a stone bead and a stamp seal. Pattern-burnished sherds comparable to those of Amuq B have been recorded from the upper 75 cm deposit of this phase.

The upper 4·80 m deposit yielded what seems to be part of a 1·80 m thick defence wall. The economy of the lower levels was based on hunting and agriculture. A similar situation is found in the aceramic levels at Ramad. Wheat and barley are said to be present and bones of gazelle, onager, cattle, sheep and goat (all wild) have been collected from the lower levels.

References

ALBRIGHT, WILLIAM F. (1965). Some Remarks on the Archæological Chronology of Palestine before about 1500 B.C. *Chronologies in Old World Archæology* (Robert W. Ehrich, ed.), Chicago: University of Chicago Press, pp. 47-60.

ANATI, EMMANUEL (1962). Prehistoric Trade and the Puzzle of Jericho. *Bull. Am. Sch. Orient. Res.*, **167**, 25-31.

ANATI, EMMANUEL (1963). *Palestine Before the Hebrews*. London: Jonathan Cape.

ANATI, EMMANUEL (1971). Hazorea. *Israel Explor. J.*, **22** (2-3), 172-73.

BARKER, H. AND MAKAY, JOHN (1968). British Museum Natural Radiocarbon Measurements V. *Radiocarbon*, **10** (1), 4-5.

BARKER, H., BURLEIGH, R. AND MEEKS, N. (1969). British Museum Natural Radiocarbon Measurements VI. *Radiocarbon*, **11** (2), 290-91.

BRAIDWOOD, R. J. (1957). Jericho and Its Setting in Near Eastern History. *Antiquity*, **31** (122), 73-81.

CECILIA WESTERN, A. (1971). The Ecological Interpretation of Ancient Charcoals from Jericho. *Levant*, **3**, 31-40.

CLUTTON-BROCK, J. (1969). Carnivore Remains from the Excavations of Jericho Tell. *The Domestication and Exploitation of Plants and Animals* (Peter J. Ucko and G. W. Dimbleby, eds). London: Duckworth. pp. 337-45.

CLUTTON-BROCK, J. (1971). The Primary Food Animals of Jericho Tell from the Protoneolithic to the Byzantine Period. *Levant*, **3**, 41-55.

DE CONTENSON, H. (1963). New Correlation Between Ras Shamra and al Amuq. *Bull. Am. Sch. Orient. Res.*, **172**, 35-40.

DE CONTENSON, H. (1966a). Notes on the Chronology of the Near Eastern Neolithic. *Bull. Am. Sch. Orient. Res.*, **184**, 2-6.

DE CONTENSON, H. (1966b). Decouvertes recentes dans le domaine du Néolithique en Syrie. *Syria*, **43,** 152-54.

DE CONTENSON, H. (1970). Septieme campagne De Fouilles A Tell Ramad En 1970: Rapport Préliminaire. *Ann. Archeol. Arabes Syriennes*, **20,** 77-79.

DE CONTENSON, H. (1971). Tell Ramad, A Village of Syria of the 7th and 6th Millennia B.C. *Archæology*, **24** (3), 278-85.

DE CONTENSON H. AND VAN LIERE, W. J. (1964a). Sondages a Tell Ramad en 1963: Rapport Préliminaire. *Anns Archeol. Syrie*, **14,** 109-24.

DE CONTENSON, H. AND VAN LIERE, W. J. (1964b). Holocene Environment and Early Settlement in the Levant. *Annls Archeol. Syrie*, **14,** 125-28.

DE CONTENSON, H. AND VAN LIERE, W. J. (1966a). Second Campagne a Tell Ramad, 1965: Rapport Preliminaire. *Ann. Archeol Arabes Syriennes*, **16** (2), 167-74.

DE CONTENSON, H. AND VAN LIERE, W. J. (1966b). Premier Sondage a Bouqras en 1965: Rapport Preliminaire. *Ann. Archeol. Arabes Syriennes*, **16** (2), 181-92.

DE CONTENSON, H. AND VAN LIERE, W. J. (1966c). Premiers Pas vers Une Chronologie Asolu A Tell Ramad. *Ann. Archeol. Arabes Syriennes*, **16** (2), 175-76.

CORNWALL, I. W. (1956). The Prepottery Neolithic Burials, Jericho. *Palestine Explor. Q.* . **1956,** 110-24.

DE VAUX, O.P., R. (1966). Palestine During the Neolithic and Chalcolithic Periods. *Camb. Ancient Hist.* **1,** (1), 499-538.

DORNEMANN, R. H. (1969). An Early Village: Al Kowm. *Archæology*, **22** (1), 68-70.

DUCOS, PIERRE (1970). The Oriental Institute Excavations at Mureybit, Syria: Preliminary Report on the 1965 Campaign. *J. Nr. East. Stud.*, **29** (4), 273-89.

ECHEGARY, J. G. (1964). Excavations in El Khiam. *A. Dep. Antiqu., Jordan*, **8-9,** 93-94.

GARROD, DOROTHY A. (1957). The Natufian Culture, The Life and Economy of a Mesolithic People in the Near East. *Proc. Br. Acad.*, **43,** 211-27.

GARSTANG, JOHN (1932). Jericho: City and Necropolis. *Ann. Archæol. Anthrop., Liverpool*, **19,** 3.

GARSTANG, JOHN (1935). Jericho: City and Necropolis. *Ann. Archæol. Anthrop, Liverpool*, **22,** 166.

HELBAEK, HANS (1966). Pre-Pottery Neolithic Farming at Beidha: A Preliminary Report. *Palestine Explor. Q.* . **1966,** 61-66.

HOOIJER, D. A. (1966). Preliminary Notes on the Animal Remains Found at Bouqras and Ramad in 1965. *Annls Archeol. Arabes Syriennes*, **16** (2), 193-6.

HOPF, MARIA (1969). Plant Remains and Early Farming at Jericho. *The Domestication and Exploitation of Plants and Animals* (Peter J. Ucko and G. W. Dimbleby, eds). London: Duckworth. pp. 355-59.

KENYON, KATHLEEN M. (1952). Excavations at Jericho, 1952. *Palestine Explor. Q.* . **1952,** 62-82.

KENYON, KATHLEEN M. (1953a). Excavations at Jericho, 1953. *Palestine Explor.* Q., **1953,** 81-95.

KENYON, KATHLEEN M. (1953b). *Ill. Lond. News,* **1953,** 603.

KENYON, KATHLEEN M. (1954a). Excavations at Jericho, 1954. *Palestine Explor.* Q., **1954,** 45-63.

KENYON, KATHLEEN M. (1954b). Excavations at Jericho. *J.R. Anthrop. Inst.,* **84,** 103-10.

KENYON, KATHLEEN M. (1954c). Jericho, Oldest Walled Town. *Archæology,* **7** (1), 2-8.

KENYON, KATHLEEN M. (1955). Excavations at Jericho, 1955. *Palestine Explor.* Q., **1955,** 108-117.

KENYON, KATHLEEN M. (1956a). Excavations at Jericho, 1956. *Palestine Explor.* Q., **1956,** 67-82.

KENYON KATHLEEN M. (1956b). The World's Oldest Known Township: Excavating the Jericho of 7000 years and Earlier. *Ill. Lond. News,* **1956,** 504-6.

KENYON, KATHLEEN M. (1956c). Jericho and Its Setting in Near Eastern History. *Antiquity,* **30,** 184-95.

KENYON, KATHLEEN M. (1957a). Excavations at Jericho 1957. *Palestine Explor.* Q., **1957,** 101-107.

KENYON, KATHLEEN M. (1957b). Reply to Professor Braidwood. *Antiquity,* **31,** 82-84.

KENYON, KATHLEEN M. (1959a). Some Observations on the Beginnings of Settlement in The Near East. *J. R. Anthrop. Inst.,* **89** (1), 35-43.

KENYON, KATHLEEN M. (1959b). Earliest Jericho, *Antiquity,* **33,** 5-9.

KENYON, KATHLEEN M. (1960). Excavations at Jericho, 1957-58. *Palestine Explor.* Q., **1960,** 88-108.

KENYON, KATHLEEN M. (1969) The Origins of the Neolithic. *Advm. Sci.,* **26** (128), 144-160.

KENYON, KATHLEEN M. (1970). *Archæology in the Holy Land* (3rd Ed.). London: Benn.

KIRKBRIDE, DIANA (1956). A Neolithic Site at Wadi El Yabis. *A. Dep. Antiqu., Jordan,* **3,** 56-60.

KIRKBRIDE, DIANA (1958). Notes on a Survey of Pre-Roman Archæological Sites Near Jerash. *Bull. Inst. Archæol., Lond.,* **1,** 9-20.

KIRKBRIDE, DIANA (1959). Short Notes on Some Hitherto Unrecorded Prehistoric Sites in Transjordan. *Palestine Explor. Q.,* **1959,** 52-54.

KIRKBRIDE, DIANA (1960a). The Excavations of a Neolithic Village of Seyl Aqlat, Beidha, Near Petra Interim Report. *Palestine Explor. Q.,* **1960,** 136-45.

KIRKBRIDE, DIANA (1960b). A Brief Report on the Pre-Pottery Flint Cultures of Jericho. *Palestine Explor. Q.,* **1960,** 114-9.

KIRKBRIDE, DIANA (1962). Excavation of the Pre-Pottery Neolithic Village at Seyl Aqlat, Beidha. *A. Dep. Antiqu. Jordan,* **6-7,** 7-12.

KIRKBRIDE, DIANA (1966a). Beidha, An Early Neolithic Village in Jordan. *Archæology*, **19** (3), 199-207.

KIRKBRIDE, DIANA (1966b). Beidha: 1965 Campaign. *Archæology*, **19**, 168-72.

KIRKBRIDE, DIANA (1966c). Five Seasons at the Pre-Pottery B Neolithic Village of Beidha. *Palestine Explor. Q.*, **1966**, 8-72.

KIRKBRIDE, DIANA (1967). Beidha 1965: An Interim Report. *Palestine Explor. Q.*, **1967**, 5-13.

KIRKBRIDE, DIANA (1968a). Beidha 1967: An Interim Report. *Palestine Explor. Q.*, **1968**, 90-96.

KIRKBRIDE, DIANA (1968b). Beidha: Early Neolithic Village Life South of the Dead Sea. *Antiquity*, **42**, 263-74.

VAN LIERE, W. J. AND DE CONTENSON, H. (1963). A Note on Five Early Neolithic Sites in Inland Syria. *Annls Archeol. Syrie*, **13**, 173-210.

MELLAART, JAMES (1962). Preliminary Report on the Archæological Survey in the Yarmuk and Jordan Valley. *A. Dep. Antiqu., Jordan*, **6-7**, 126-57.

MELLAART, JAMES (1965a). The Neolithic Site of Ghrubba. *A. Dep. Antiqu. Jordan*, **3**, 24-40.

MELLAART, JAMES (1965b). *Earliest Civilizations of the Near East*. London: Thames and Hudson.

MORTENSEN, P. (1970). A Preliminary Study of the Chipped Stone Industry from Beidha. *Acta Archæol.* **41**, 1-54.

MORTENSEN, P. (1971). On the Reflection of Cultural Changes in Artefact Materials—with Special Regard to the Study of Innovation Contrasted Against Type Stability. *Research Seminar on the Explanation of Culture Change: Models in Prehistory*, Sheffield, December, 1971.

NOY TAMAR, AND HIGGS, E. (1971). Nahal Oren. *Israel Explor. J.*, **21** (2-3), 171-72.

PERKINS JR. D. (1966). The Fauna from Madamagh and Beidha. *Palestine Explor. Q.*, **1966**, 66-67.

PERROT, JEAN (1960). Excavations at Eynan ('Ein Mallaha): Preliminary Report on the 1959 Season. *Israel Explor. J.*, **10** (1), 14-22.

PERROT, JEAN (1962). Palestine-Syria-Cilicia. *Courses Toward Urban Life* (Robert J. Braidwood and Gordon Willey, eds). New York: Wenner-Gren Foundation.

PERROT, JEAN (1964). Les deux premieres Campagnes de fouilles a Munhatta (1962-63). *Syria*, **41**, 323-45.

PERROT, JEAN (1966). La Troisieme Campagne de Fouilles a Munhatta, (1964). *Syria*, **43**, 49-63.

PRAUSNITZ, M. W. (1970). *From Hunter to Farmer and Trader*. Jerusalem: Rudolf Hebelt.

RAIKES, R. L. (1966). Beidha: Prehistoric Climate and Water Supply. *Palestine Explor. Q.*, **1966**, 68-72.

STEKELIS, M. (1957). Oren Valley (Wadi Fallah). *Israel Explor. J.*, **7**, 125.

STEKELIS, M. (1960a). Oren Valley (Wadi Fallah). *Israel Explor. J.*, **10**, 118-9.

STEKELIS, M. (1960b). Oren Valley (Wadi Fallah). *Israel Explor. J.*, **10**, 258-9.

STEKELIS, M. AND YIZRAELY, T. (1963). Excavations at Nahal Oren, Preliminary Report. *Israel Explor. J.*, **13** (1), 1-12.

STUCKENRATH, JR. R. (1963). University of Pennsylvania Radiocarbon Dates VI. *Radiocarbon*, **5**, 82-103.

TZORI, N. (1958). Neolithic and Chalcolithic Sites in the Valley of Beth-Shan. *Palestine Explor. Q.*, **1958**, 44-51.

TAUBER, H. (1968). Copenhagen Radiocarbon Dates IX. *Radiocarbon*, **10** (2), 323-4.

VAN LOON, M. N. (1966a). First Results of the 1965 Excavations at Tell Mureybat Near Meskene. *Annls Archeol. Arabes Syriennes*, **16** (2), 211-17.

VAN LOON, M. N. (1966b). Mureybat: An Early Village in Inland Syria. *Archæology*, **19**, 215-6.

VAN LOON, M. N. (1966c). Pre-Neolithic Village. *Scient. Am.* **214** (5), 53-54.

VAN LOON, M. N. (1968). The Oriental Institute Excavation at Mureybit, Syria: Preliminary Report on the 1965 Campaign, Parts I, II. *J. Nr. East. Stud.*, **27**, 265-90.

VAN ZEIST, W. AND BOTTEMA S. (1966). Palæobotanical Investigations at Ramad. *Annls Archeol. Arabes Syriennes*, **16** (2), 179-80.

VAN ZEIST, W. (1970). The Oriental Institute Excavations at Muryebit, Syria: Preliminary Report on the 1965 Campaign, Part III: Palæobotany. *J. Nr. East. Stud.*, **29** (3), 167-76.

VOGEL, J. C. AND WATERBOLK, H. T. (1967). Groningen Radiocarbon Dates VII. *Radiocarbon* **9**, 128-9.

WATSON, P. J. (1965) The Chronology of North Syria and North Mesopotamia from 10,000 B.C. to 2,000 B.C. *Chronologies in Old World Archæology*. (Robert W. Ehrich, ed.). Chicago: University of Chicago Press, pp. 61-100.

WHEELER, SIR MORTIMER (1956). The First Town? *Antiquity*, **30**, 132-6.

ZEUNER, F. E. (1954). The Neolithic-Bronze Age Gap on the Tell of Jericho. *Palestine Explor. Q.*, **1954**, 64-68.

ZEUNER, F. E. (1955). The Goats of Early Jericho. *Palestine Explor. Q.*, **1955**, 70-86.

ZEUNER, F. E. (1958). Dog and Cat in the Neolithic of Jericho. *Palestine Explor. Q.*, **1958**, 52-55.

3. Turkey

Anatolia, the name given to Asiatic Turkey has been put on the Neolithic map of the Near East only recently and as late as 1955 it was written by an eminent archæologist that "... The region more correctly described as Anatolia shows no sign whatever of habitation during the Neolithic period" (Seton Lloyd; 1956:53). The only Neolithic site known was Mersin in Cilicia and some tools of protoneolithic facies were recorded from Beldibi caves C and B. However, the discovery of the Neolithic mound of Hacilar in December, 1956 and its excavation in the subsequent four seasons opened a new vista and Anatolia became one of the foremost centres of the Neolithic revolution in the Near East. The excavations at Hacilar brought to light two cultures, the first called "Aceramic Neo-lithic" and the second known as "Late Neolithic" with a gap of one thousand years between the two. This hiatus was filled by the discoveries at Çatal Hüyük some 320 km east of Hacilar in the Konya plain. Sub-sequent discoveries made at Suberde, Çayönü, Erbaba and Can Hasan have added more colour in the diffused picture of the Neolithic culture. The investigations at Çatal Hüyük west, Can Hasan and the upper levels at Hacilar continue the story of human evolution from the Neolithic to the chalcolithic phase.

There are two distinct phases of the Neolithic cultures in Anatolia (Mellaart: 1972) and their comparative stratigraphy is as follows:

1. Aceramic Phase (before 6500 BC)—Aşilki Hüyük, Aceramic Can Hasan, Suberde, Aceramic Hacilar and Çayönü.

2. Neolithic with monochrome pottery (c. 6500-5500 BC)—Çatal Hüyük east, Can Hasan 4-7; Reis Tumegi, Ilicapinar, Mersin, Tarsus etc.

The second phase is followed by a chalcolithic phase often with red-on cream painted pottery and is identified at Çatal Hüyük west, Can Hasan 3-2b and Mersin (Levels XXIV-XX). This phase is tentatively datable to 5500-5000 BC.

Hacilar

The inconspicuous mound of Hacilar is located 26 km to the southwest of the town of Burdur in southwest Anatolia. The settlement measuring 135 m in diameter, rises to a height of 5 m. It is situated in an intra-montane valley of the Taurus range at an elevation of 940 m above sea-level. Archæological investigations were carried out by James Mellaart for four seasons from 1957 to 1960 and remains of Neolithic and chalco-lithic phases were brought to light. The stratigraphic sequence at Hacilar is as follows (Mellaart, 1970:92):

Hacilar	ID	Squatter Levels
	IC	
	Ib	Repairs followed by destruction
	Ia	Fortress
	IIb	Last phase of the fortified enclosure
	IIa	First phase of the fortified enclosure
	III	
	IV	
	V	
	VI	Final Late Neolithic settlement
	VII	
	VIII	
	IX	First Late Neolithic occupation

Lacuna in occupation

Aceramic Hacilar
I-VII

Aceramic Levels

As evident from the Table above, the earliest culture is Aceramic Neolithic with seven building levels. This culture was discovered in the fourth and last field season and the work was restricted to a small sounding in area Q on the southwestern portion of the mound. As only an area of 150 sq. m could be investigated in a five-day exploration, it was not possible to determine the extent of this early settlement. However, it is believed that Aceramic Hacilar was a small village comparable to the Aceramic village of Jarmo. The cultural deposit of 1·5 m is divisible into seven building levels numbered from the top downward. The first settlers lived in permanent houses, practising agriculture and possibly animal husbandry supplemented by hunting. The houses comprised small rooms rectangular in plan. The walls were made of large mud-bricks measuring 72 by 28 by 8 cm on average. Most walls were one brick thick but the

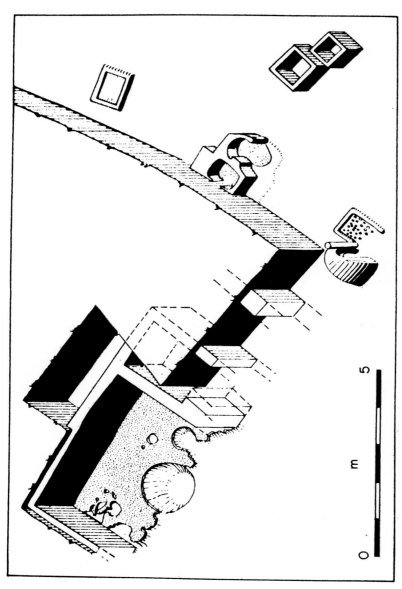

Fig. 22. Hacilar: Aceramic village; Isometric drawing of Level V.

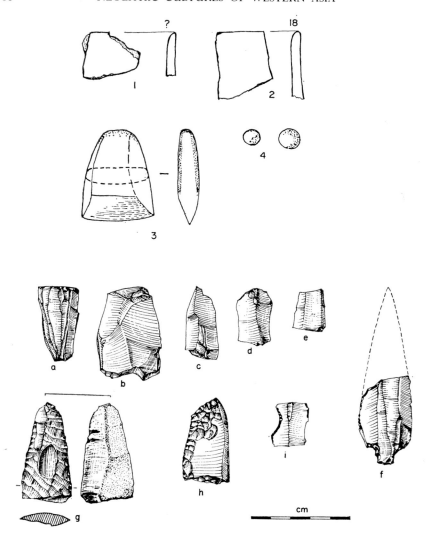

FIG. 23. Hacilar: Aceramic levels; Polished stone industry and stone tools.

courtyard walls were over a metre in thickness. The bricks were laid in
headers and stretchers in alternate courses with black mortar in between.
Walls and floors were covered with mud plaster. Heavy walls were
provided with stone foundations and floors of important rooms were laid
on a bed of small stones or pebbles covered over with lime plaster. The
floors were occasionally decorated with red ochre. No house-plans could

be traced and no doorways recognised due to the limited area under ex-cavation. It is suggested that the inhabitants had access from the roof as at Çatal Hüyük (Mellaart; 1970:4). Rooms were provided with hearths and ovens. In Aceramic V were found two bins, both empty, but a big patch of white ash, found just to the west of them, revealed the silica skeletons of numerous food-plants and weeds.

Apart from the structural remains, finds were disappointingly few. A fully polished green stone axe-head, a few stone beads, some stone awls, two fragments of marble bowls and some flints complete the inventory. The chipped stone industry finds comprised only 11 pieces primarily made of blades and blade-cores of which four are made of obsidian which after analysis revealed that the material was brought to Hacilar from a source 8 km east of Acigöl-Topada and 11 km southwest of Nevşehir on the Akşaray road. There are no burials but several human crania found set-up on house-floors may suggest ancestor-worship.

The economy of Aceramic Hacilar was based on agriculture and hunt-ing. Dog was the only domesticated animal but bones of sheep, goat, cattle, fallow deer and hare have been identified (Mellaart, 1970:246). However, the number found is too small to prove whether some of these species were domesticated. A similar situation prevails at Suberde, the nearest aceramic site to Hacilar. In an analysis of ash deposit found in Aceramic V level at Hacilar, Helbaek has identified grains and seeds of emmer, wild einkorn, naked barley, hulled two-row barley, lentil and five species of weed which definitely show that agriculture was practised in the aceramic levels. Helbaek observes:

> Both Wild Einkorn and Wild barley (*Hordeum spontaneum*) were presumably members of the flora of the virgin Hacilar environment, but even so, the Aceramic plant list suggests that agriculture was introduced from the East (Helbaek in Mellaart, 1970:239).

The chronology of Aceramic Hacilar is based on a single radiocarbon determination (BM 127) from Level V which gives a date of 6740 ± 180 BC on the Libby half-life. Calculated on the higher half-life of 5730 years, this date comes to nearly 7000 BC. Mellaart observes:

> The seven building levels then may cover any period from a few centuries to half a millennium. In any case, the aceramic settlement falls mainly within the early half of the seventh millennium and may just extend into the late eighth millennium B.C. (1970:6).

Late Neolithic Period

For reasons unknown to us the Aceramic settlement was abandoned by its inhabitants to be occupied by new settlers of the Late Neolithic period after a gap of a thousand years in around 5750 BC. The site then witnessed an unbroken sequence of habitation from the Late Neolithic to the chalcolithic period and remained under occupation for some eight hundred years. The new folk of Hacilar built their houses partly on the mound and partly on the virgin soil. The architectural remains of the earliest phases of the Late Neolithic settlement (Level IX-VII) are poorly represented but solid stone walls, ash and rubbish containing pottery sherds and some figurines are found. This culture saw a sudden improvement in phase VI where the houses were constructed around a large central courtyard with a length of 35 m and a width more than 16 m. No streets have been found but blocks of rooms, separated by courtyards show signs of planning. The houses were now large and two-storied, rectangular in plan measuring 6·5 m to 10·5 m in length with an average width of 5·5 m. The walls were approximately 1 m thick and had stone foundations. The walls were built of square, oblong and flat bricks of different dimensions and covered with several layers of plaster. The floors were made of beautifully smoothed clay plaster and houses were kept very clean. The construction of the houses was very accurate and perfect right angles are a noteworthy feature. Unlike the houses at Çatal Hüyük and probably Aceramic Hacilar, the houses of Level VI were entered through a wide doorway in the middle of the long side. There were ovens and hearths inside the rooms and plaster screens in some large rooms for greater privacy.

The pottery of Late Neolithic Hacilar is believed to have been developed from that of Çatal Hüyük or its western equivalent, the Kizilkaya ware. The evidence from Çatal Hüyük shows that pottery was made in Anatolia at least a millennium before the Late Neolithic settlement was founded. The pottery found at Hacilar is largely monochrome and almost invariably burnished. Light grey and cream wares were found predominantly in Levels IX and VIII and red brown and buff wares in Levels VII and VI. The principal shapes are cups, bowls, and jars. In Level VI, the vessels found are somewhat larger in size and the shapes include bowls, jars and theriomorphic vessels. Another new trait of this phase is the occurrence of white marble vessels, totally absent in the first three phases at the site. These vessels are well carved and polished and sometimes have three or four feet with shapes that include bowls ranging in diameter from 11·5 cm to 40 cm. These stone vessels are a characteristic feature of this phase. The number found gradually diminishes in the chalcolithic levels and they disappear altogether in phase I.

The chipped stone industry discovered is made of flint and obsidian, the latter accounting for 42 % of the tools. In all, 533 tools were col-

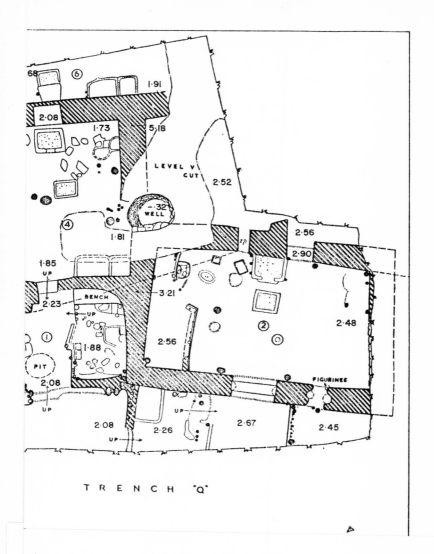

68　⑥　　　　1·91

2·08　　1·73　　5·18

LEVEL V
CUT
2·52

·32
WELL

④　　　　　　　2·56

1·81　　　　　　2·90

1·85
UP

2·23　BENCH　　3·21

①　　　　　　　　　2·48

PIT　　1·88

2·08

UP　　　　2·56

②

FIGURINES

2·08　　　2·26　　2·67　　2·45
UP

T R E N C H "Q"

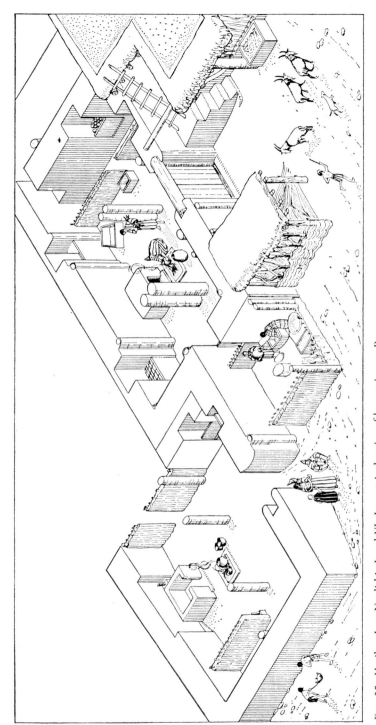

Fig. 25. Hacilar: Late Neolithic Level VI; Isometric drawing of houses in area P.

lected from the late Neolithic levels. The types include blade-cores, cores with irregular scars, flakes, blades, scrapers, angular blade knives, sickle blades, serrated blades and micro-points. Other antiquities comprise polished stone axes of green stone, baked clay missiles, probably used as sling balls, pounders of green stone, beads of white marble, limestone and obsidian and six complete and several fragmentary sickles of antler.

Another important trait of this culture is the presence of sizable numbers of terracotta female statuettes found mainly in two buildings of Levels IX and VI respectively. These statuettes vary in height from 7 cm to 24 cm with the head, body and legs made separately and pressed together. The head was pegged in the body before baking. Mellaart believes that these statuettes have been modelled by artists who had intimate knowledge of female anatomy and the ability to reproduce it in clay. They are represented by seated, standing, resting or enthroned form. Some of these figures wear "briefs" and others hold a leopard to their breasts or under the left arm. Mellaart (1961c:231) believes that these statuettes are domestic cult statues representing the Anatolian Fertility Goddess in a variety of aspects.

He observes,

> In fact all the statuettes from Hacilar VI represent certain aspects of the life of the goddess; the maiden, the mature matron, the pregnant mother, a full-breasted nursing mother, the mother with her child and the Mistress of Animals, the goddess of nature and wild life (Mellaart, 1970:170).

This observation is supported by the fact that these statuettes have been found in private houses and most of them in Level VI were found clustered near the hearth.

The economy of the Neolithic folk was primarily based on farming supplemented by stock-raising and hunting. The people grew wheat, barley, lentils, peas and bitter vetch. Grains of einkorn, emmer, bread wheat, 2-row hulled barley, 6-row hulled barley and 6-row naked barley have been identified together with lentil, purple pea and bitter vetch from samples from Level VI (Helbaek in Mellaart, 1970:200). The crop was harvested with antler sickles and grains stored in plastered square bins, standing a metre or more in height arranged along the walls. The presence of spindle whorls in Hacilar VI attests spinning and weaving. With the exception of dog, the domestication of other animals could not be positively established from the small number of bones but the possibility of cattle, sheep and goat being domesticated may not be unreasonable. Hunted animals include red and roe deer, aurochs, wild sheep and goat and probably leopard. Bones of domesticated dog, pig, red deer,

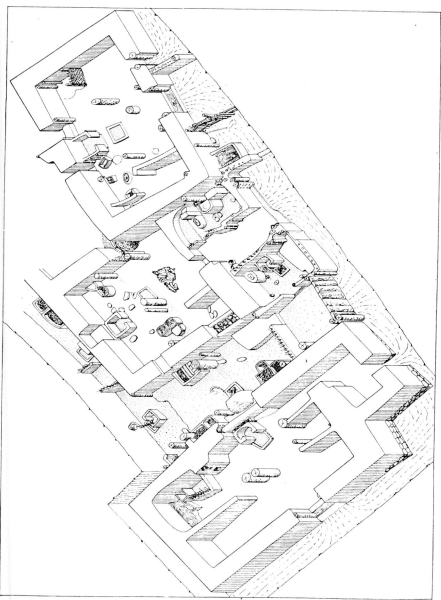

Fɪɢ. 26. Hacilar: Late Neolithic Level VI; Isometric drawing of houses in area Q.

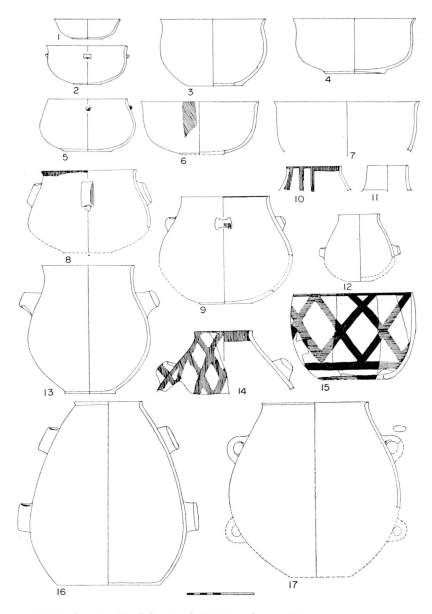

FIG. 27. Hacilar: Late Neolithic Level VII; Monochrome Ware.

Fig. 28. Hacilar: Late Neolithic Levels VI and VII; Painted vessels and miniatures.

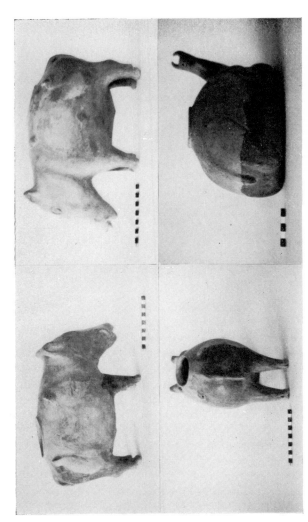

Fig. 29. Hacilar: Late Neolithic; Theriomorphic vessels.

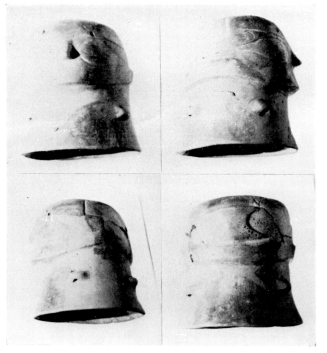

FIG. 30. Hacilar: Late Neolithic; Cup in the form of a woman's head.

mouflon (with no evidence of domestication), wild cattle, wild goat and roe-deer have been identified (Westley in Mellaart, 1970:245). There is no evidence of fishing during this period or any other at Hacilar.

The chronology of Late Neolithic Hacilar is fairly established by three consistent radiocarbon dates from various levels except one sample (P.314-A) from Hacilar IX which gives a somewhat later date. Thus the radiocarbon date for Level VIII is 5820 ± 180 BC (BM 125) and for two samples from Level VI is 5590 ± 180 BC and 5399 ± 79 BC (BM 48, P.313-A) respectively on the Libby half-life. Keeping in view the standard deviation as also the fact that the dates were more often obtained from thick beams which may have been robbed from earlier buildings and re-used, Mellaart (1970:94) proposes c. 5750 BC for the beginning of the settlement (Level IX) and c. 5600 BC for the destruction of the last Neolithic settlement (Level VI). Mellaart (1970:22) believes that Hacilar VII-VI may have comprised about 50 houses with a minimum of about 240 souls. Hacilar VI was destroyed by fire but the survivors continued to live on the site in light buildings of impermanent nature, presumably

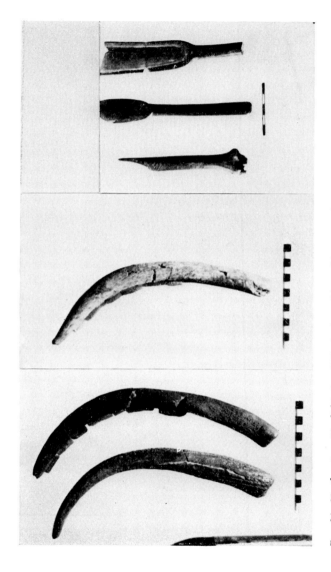

Fig. 31. Hacilar: Late Neolithic Level VI; Antler sickles and bone spatulae.

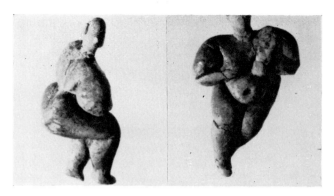

FIG. 32. Hacilar: Late Neolithic Level VI; Two views of an unbaked figure of a pregnant woman resting on her left side.

built of wood, lath and plaster. This culture gave rise to the succeeding chalcolithic culture with the first painted pottery tradition in southwest Anatolia.

Aşikli Hüyük

Before proceeding to examine other neolithic sites of Anatolia with pottery, mention will be made of other Aceramic Neolithic sites explored and excavated in recent years. The protoneolithic site of Aşilki Hüyük was visited by Todd in the summer of 1964 (Todd, 1966*b*, 1968; also *cf.* Mellink, 1967:157). This site lies in the vilayet of Niğde *c.* 25 km southeast of Akşaray on the right bank of the Melendiz Çay. The site originally comprised a very large hüyük but a considerable portion of this mound has been eroded by the river leaving bare 6 m high sections in places. The site has not been tested as yet but chipped stone tools and other artefacts have been collected and published. Traces of mud-brick walls are seen on the exposed sections and obsidian seems to occur in large quantities in all levels. Although our knowledge is based on intensive surface collection alone, it seems that obsidian is almost the only material used for the manufacture of tools. In a total collection of 6200 pieces, only one implement was made of chert. An analysis of obsidian from this site (Renfrew, Dixon and Cann, 1968) reveals that the material was brought from Çiftlik source about 50 km south southeast of this site.

The chipped stone industry of Aşikli was a homogeneous industry and there is no apparent difference between the tool-types found from the top of the mound and the base of the eroded section and the industry discovered is characterised by very large quantities of blades and scrapers. Borers, burins, sickle-blades and cores also occur in varying quantities while projectile points are comparatively few and unifacial retouch is scarce and complete bifacial retouch is totally absent. The discovery of the presence of sickle blades would give some idea about the economy of the people and a small number of blades with considerable evidence of use chipping are believed by Todd (1966b:154-55) to probably have been used as sickle blades. However, no querns have been reported and the only vegetable matter collected from the site has been identified by Helbaek as Hackberry (*Celtis Australis*). The ground stone industry collected comprises two diabase polished stone axes, one quartzite celt, one diabase rubber, a small gabbro pounder and a fragment of a heavy pestle made of an igneous rock. Bone tools include a complete and two fragmentary awls and a belt hook. Five samples taken from the eroded sections of the mound give dates which range from 7008 BC to 6661 BC on the Libby half-life (Todd, 1968:157-58). However, on the higher half-life of 5730 years the earliest date (P. 1240) comes to 7277 ± 134 BC. Todd argues that allowing a certain depth of occupation below the level from which the sample was taken, it would confirm a date of *c.* 7600 BC for the beginning of the settlement. If the tolerance is not taken into account, a date nearer to 7500 BC would probably be more in accordance with the facts.

A surface collection was made of nearly 400 implements and waste flakes of obsidian from the terraces of the Avla Dağ mountains, 8 km south southeast of Ürgüp on the east side of the Damra Çay valley in the vilayet of Nevşehir (Todd and Giorgio, 1965). The industry uncovered comprises parallel-sided blades, projectile points, scrapers and flakes. However, it remains to be ascertained whether the industry is ascribable to the protoneolithic phase noticed at Aşikli Hüyük. Similarly, a number of neolithic sites have been discovered in surface explorations from other sites in central Anatolia (Todd, 1965) but their nature remains far from clear.

Obsidian tools and weapons, some bifacially retouched, have been picked up from the south and east flanks of the hüyük at Ilicapinar, *c.* 12 km south of Cihanbeyli at the north end of the Acituz Gölü. The tools collected by Todd (1966a) comprise 33 complete and fragmentary blades. This settlement was earlier known to be a factory-site but the absence of raw-material (obsidian) and cores makes it difficult to believe that it was an establishment of an obsidian working community. A small quantity of reddish-brown and burnished pottery sherds have also been picked up from the site but their association with obsidian tools has in no way been proved. Some polished stone axes, worked flint and obsidian and pottery sherds have been found at Morali Akhisar, a mound *c*. 3 km west of Kennez in western Anatolia (French, 1965). Other polished stone axes but without pottery or obsidian tools have been found from Muğla vilayet and Antalya vilayet (Biernoff, 1964).

Suberde

The geographical gap of 200 km between Hacilar and Çatal Hüyük—the two best known Neolithic settlements of southwestern Anatolia—has been closed by the recent work in the Taurus mountains, around Lake Suğla. This region was explored by Ralph Solecki of Columbia University in 1963 (Solecki, 1964; also *cf*. Mellink, 1964:154) who located nine neolithic settlements. The most promising of these, Suberde, an Aceramic Neolithic site was investigated by Jacques Bordaz for two seasons in 1964 and 1965 (Bordaz, 1965, 1966, 1968, also *cf*. Mellink, 1966:142-43). Suberde is situated on the northwestern shores of the Suğla lake, 11 km southeast of Seydişehir, at an elevation of approximately 1100 m in the Taurus mountains. The settlement covers an area of 70 by 70 m or 1·25 acres and the cultural deposit ranges from 3·5 m to 4 m. This deposit represents three distinct layers, termed Surface layer, Middle layer and Lower layer from the top. The earlier two layers represent neolithic occupation and the latest belongs to the Byzantine and Islamic periods.

The first settlers of Suberde probably lived in structures of perishable nature as no trace of permanent structures has been reported from the base of the Lower layer. The only traces of human occupation comprise a number of undisturbed hearths with lenses of ash and charcoal. However, a few remains of structures with unplastered wall, floors and benches are reported from the uppermost part of this layer. A number of clay-lined circular bins or basins measuring 80 cm in diameter and 40 cm in depth have been found in this level. These basins, once thought to be fired *in situ* are now believed (perhaps correctly) to have been fired in accidental burning of the dwellings in which they had been built. More remnants of architectural activity are seen in the Middle Layer where a structure 5·25 m in length with another structure 2·80 m in length, at right angles to it, have been discovered. The structures are made of alternate courses of mud of two different colours (and not of unfired bricks as reported earlier in the first preliminary reports) with the walls built on foundations of flat stones. Remains of superimposed plastered floors have been found in poor condition, made of white plaster laid over a 2-3 cm thick foundation of small stones. The settlement seems to have been deserted after the Neolithic period as no Chalcolithic or Bronze Age material occurs on the mound but it was occupied again in historical times as the 1·25 m thick surface layer has yielded Byzantine building remains, pottery-sherds of Byzantine and Islamic periods and large numbers of late burials.

The discoveries at Suberde of neolithic culture include a chipped stone industry, ground stone tools, bone tools, some stone and bone beads and a few terracotta figurines. The existence of pottery and copper, suspected earlier, has now been discounted. The chipped stone industry found is characterised by the small size of tools which rarely exceed 4 cm in length. Obsidian was the principal material for the manufacture of tools and it accounts for no less than 90 % of them. The rest were made of flint. The types uncovered include projectile points, piercing tools (blades retouched into drills or perforators), backed blades, microliths (including three triangles and seven lunates), end-scrapers, side-scrapers, flakes and blades. Besides all these, no less than 320 sickle-blades of flint with characteristic sickle sheen on their edges were found from both prehistoric strata (Bordaz, 1968:54). Bordaz observes:

> ...Stratigraphic group II has the highest percentage of sickle blades of all groups. This might indicate a greater reliance on a vegetable diet but stratigraphic group II is at the same time proportionately the richest in projectile points.

This would suggest that hunting activity was also intensified in stratigraphic group II along with the new modes of acquiring food.

Polished and pecked stone artefacts from Suberde include 52 celts and celt fragments—all of green diabase, most of them being comparatively small, measuring 4 to 7 cm in width and 1 to 2 cm in thickness. Small polished stone chisels and rectangular shaft-straighteners and a large number of river pebbles, both plain and incised, have been found. The worked bone industry collection comprises 200 awls and a large flat needle and the personal ornaments a barrel-shaped bead, small cylindrical, circular and winged beads and perforated ground pendants—all of stone. Four roughly cylindrical beads and two small bead spacers have been reported from the lower levels. Clay objects are present in sizable number. They include 13 sherd-whorls, 17 spindle whorls, 33 small cones of low-fired clay, and 21 low-fired figurines. Among the figurines is one of a fragmentary female and also four almost complete figures of boars.

As noted earlier, there have been conflicting reports about the occurrence of metal (copper) in the Neolithic strata at Suberde. In the preliminary reports (Bordaz, 1966) it was noted that a 4 cm long awl and 3 heavily corroded pieces of copper wire as well as what might be copper ore were found in the prehistoric layers. These are now being studied by

Dr. Ufuk Esin of the University of Istanbul. An analysis by Dr. S. Tung-hams (Bordaz, 1968:50-51) showed the objects to be clearly of bronze with a tin content of 8·4%. Regarding their stratigraphic position Bordaz observes:

> The artefacts were believed to be in context but the possibility of a fraud can not be excluded at the time of the find and a prehistoric date for this object should and must evidently be rejected. (Bordaz, 1968: 50-51.)

A similar situation prevails regarding the presence of pottery. In the first season's work about 40 sherds of crude, undecorated pottery were found concentrated in a small area of one pit in the lower layer (Bordaz, 1965, 1968:51). But in the resumed work in 1965 it was confirmed that the "sherds" noted above were the fragments of the linings of the basins referred to above. However, other ceramic items in the form of animal figurines and a few anthropomorphic figurines did occur.

Suberde has been exceptionally rich in zoological remains and has yielded the largest collection of animal bones obtained from any neolithic site of southwestern Asia. In the removal of 230 cubic yards of earth no less than 300,000 pieces of bone weighing a ton and a half, have been collected. This collection has been studied by Dr. Dexter Perkins Jr. and Patricia Daly (1968). It consisted mostly of sheep (the Anatolian mouflon *Ovis orientalis anatolica*) and goats (the Asian bezoar, *Capra hircus aegagrus*) both of which were wild at Suberde. The proportion was 85% sheep to 15% goats. Other bones include those of pigs (*Sus scrofa*) and oxen—both being of wild variety. The Neolithic man also hunted badger, hedgehog, hare, red deer, roe deer and fallow deer. Bones of jackal, fox, bear, wild cat and marten have also been identified. The very small number of fish bones suggests that they played no significant role in the economy of the Neolithic man. Freshwater clam shells and bird bones (which seem to belong to a species of pelican) have been reported. Better represented than any of these aquatic animals was the land tortoise. The only domestic animal present at Suberde was dog. Perkins suggests that the "Schlepp effect" (after the German word meaning "to drag") was practised by the hunters of Suberde. When a wild ox was killed, it was butchered on the spot and the meat carried home in the animal's own hide. The feet were left attached to the hide presumably because they made convenient handles for dragging the meat-filled hide.

No recognisable carbonised seeds could be obtained from the dig. Hence no information is available regarding plant domestication. Dr. Aytug, Director, Polynological Laboratory, of the University of Istanbul suggests that cedars, pines, juniper trees as well as chestnut trees, birches and poplars were present in relatively large numbers in the area during the lower prehistoric period. He also suggests that the variety of trees was much greater than today.

The dating of Suberde is based on seven radiocarbon dates—all coming from Layer III or the lower prehistoric layer. These range in date from about 6600 to 6200 ± 100 BC on the half-life of 5730 years and from 6400 to 6000 ± 100 BC on the Libby half-life. Bordaz believes that Layer II at Suberde is earlier than Level VI at Çatal Hüyük, that is, earlier than 5800 to 5900 BC (on the higher half-life of 5730 years). Consequently, he dates the upper prehistoric occupation at Suberde to a period between 6200 and 5800 BC on the higher half-life or 6000 and 5600 BC on the Libby half-life.

Çayönü Tepesi

Until 1963 southwestern Turkey was the only area known for neolithic settlements but the explorations of Professor Braidwood and Halet Çambel in that year in the Diyarbakir and Siirt provinces of southeastern Turkey brought to light no less than 134 archæological sites ranging in date from early Palæolithic (Acheulian) through Neolithic and Chalcolithic sites. Of these, Çayönü Tepesi, an early neolithic settlement near Ergani has been under excavation for three field seasons in 1964, 1968 and 1970 (Braidwood, Çambel and Watson, 1969; Çambel and Braidwood, 1970; Braidwood, Çambel, Redman and Watson, 1971; also *cf*. Mellink, 1965: 138,1969:204-5). The low, oval mound of Çayönü measures 250 m by 150 m and is situated 5 km southwest of the town of Ergani, adjacent to a tributary of the upper Tigris. This aceramic settlement has yielded evidence of a high degree of architectural sophistication. The people had not yet learned the potter's craft but made simple metal tools by cold hammering native copper—a feature unknown hitherto on the Aceramic Neolithic levels in western Asia. Preliminary observations on the flora and fauna represented at the site, demonstrate for the first time, the transition from an almost totally wild inventory of plant and animal food resources to one including those of the domesticated species.

Two trenches, a 10 by 15 m area on the crest of the mound and a 5 by 8 m area cut into the mound on the river side, were excavated in the first two seasons. An area of 600 sq. m was excavated during the third season and over 800 m^3 of earth removed. The cultural deposit varies from 4-5 m and it is divisible into five successive phases of occupation— all belonging to the preceramic stage.

Bearing in mind the early age of this settlement, Çayönü has given some impressive architectural remains. The earliest prehistoric layer (Phase I) is known from a 6 by 6 m sounding in the centre of the mound. Small fragmentary walls and pit-ovens varying from 1·2-2 m in diameter and 30-50 cm in depth, have been found. Phase II, termed "grill building level" is known from two soundings made during the first two seasons when two grill-like structures were found, one of which consisted of a succession of at least three superimposed buildings. The middle structure of this series measures 5 by 10 m and contains interior foundations. Phase III is poorly represented in terms of domestic architecture but has yielded a terrazzo floor, which is a characteristic feature of Çayönü. Braidwood *et al* (1971:1239) observe:

> This floor is constructed basically of white limestone cobbles and pebbles set in concrete and varies from 5 to 20 cm in thickness. The limestone was evidently crushed for this purpose. A surface layer of primarily salmon pink pebbles, 1-3 cm in diameter, was set into the concrete while still wet, as were at least two sets of parallel strips of white pebbles, to make white bands 5 cm wide and over 4 m long. After the concrete had bonded, the entire surface of the floor was ground smooth and polished. Not only was the bond strong enough to support this grinding, but the concrete has remained extremely hard for over 8500 years.

Phase IV witnessed the use of mud-bricks for structures which were still provided with stone foundations. A 5 x 8 m building made of 6 or 7 small rooms has been exposed. Phase V, the final preceramic occupation, is represented by a number of complete and some fragmentary structures. A single-room structure, 5 by 9 m in size, was found during the third season.

The Neolithic folk of Çayönü made and used chipped tools of flint and obsidian with a heavy emphasis on flint blades, most of which were untouched. Less than 10% of the blades found showed sickle-sheen. Retouched tools uncovered constituted about 5-10% of the pieces of flint, with cutting, scraping, and piercing tools predominating. Also recorded are ground stone implements such as celts, querns, handstones and hammerstones. Ground stone beads, pendants and bracelets were common finds in Phases I and II as were bone tools. A crude clay figure, representing perhaps a pregnant woman, has also been found. An outstanding contribution of Çayönü is the discovery of use of metal ornaments in a preceramic neolithic economy. The collection comprises drilled beads of malachite found below the fourth occupation level; part of a tool (one end of a reamer with square cross-section); two tiny pin fragments and a complete pin—all of copper. It may be useful to add that copper ores and related minerals such as malachite are available in areas less than 20 km from this settlement.

Another noteworthy contribution of Çayönü is the position of faunal and botanical remains. On preliminary observation of faunal resources, Charles A. Reed suggests these were predominantly wild in the early history of the site (Phases I and II). They include bones of *Bos primigenius*, *Sus*, *Cervus*, *Dama ovis*, and *Capra* sp. Dog is the only domesticated animal in these levels. However, domesticated sheep, goat and pig were found in Phases IV and V. Nevertheless, food was supplemented by hunting wild cattle and deer. The macrobotanical remains also give evidence of this. Wild forms of emmer and einkorn have been reported from the earliest levels. The collection of pistachio, almond and wild vetch is also suggested in these levels. But the top levels show the presence of cultivated emmer, peas, lentils and vetch. If these preliminary observations are substantiated by detailed examination of these samples then Çayönü will be the first settlement showing the transition from wild to domesticated form of both plants and animals—a fact which had profound effect on the course of human history for the following millennia.

Two radiocarbon samples from Levels IV and V (M. 1609, M. 1610) give dates of 6840 ± 250 BC and 6620 ± 250 BC on the Libby half-life (Crane and Griffin, 1968:108-9). These are the dates from the upper levels, so the dates for Levels I and II should be earlier still, probably somewhere in the latter half of the eighth millennium BC. Two more samples (Gr. N. 4458, 4459) have been dated to 7570 ± 100 BC and 7250 ± 60 BC, respectively (Nandris, 1969:56). Redman (1971) observes that:

> available radiocarbon dates (Libby half-life, uncorrected) indicate that prehistoric occupations at Çayönü fall within the range of 6500 to 7500 B.C.

Çatal Hüyük

One now finds that on returning to southwestern Anatolia, the cultural gap of approximately one millennium between the Aceramic and the Late Neolithic cultures at Hacilar has been successfully filled by the excavations at Çatal Hüyük, a neolithic township situated some 325 km east of the former site in the Konya plain. Çatal Hüyük is located 52 km southeast of Konya city and 11 km north of Çumra, on the banks of the Çarsamba Çay—a river which flows from the lake of Beyşehir into the Konya plain. The settlement consists of two mounds, the eastern one being Neolithic and the western, Chalcolithic. The Neolithic mound alone measures 500 m by 300 m, rising to a height of 17·5 m and covering an area of 32 acres, making it the largest Neolithic settlement discovered so far in the Near East. This area is three or four times larger than prepottery Jericho and the sheer size of the settlement qualifies it to be a town and not an ordinary Neolithic village. This settlement was dis-

D

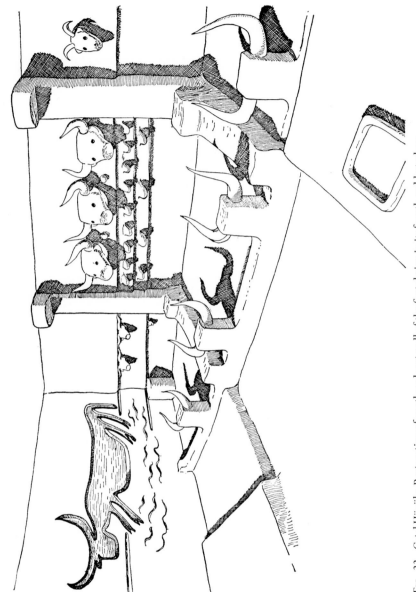

Fig. 33. Çatal Hüyük: Restoration of north and east wall of the first shrine in its fourth and last phase.

Fig. 34. Çatal Hüyük: Great bull (transcript), main section of north wall, Shrine F V, 1.

covered by James Mellaart in his survey of the Konya plain in November, 1958 and was excavated by him from 1961 through 1965 (Mellaart, 1962a, b, c, 1963a, b, c, d, 1964, 1965, 1966, 1967). About an acre of the western slope of the Neolithic mound has been excavated and the miraculous preservation of perishable materials has given a wealth of new information making Çatal Hüyük a unique site in many ways. This settlement has been securely dated by a series of 18 consistent radio-carbon dates from successive levels. However, in spite of four season's work, virgin soil has not been reached and no information is available about the first settlers at this site. In the deepest excavated trench, 12 building levels have been identified with traces of a 13th visible before the work was interrupted. Even this depth is 1·82 m above the level of the plain and it is believed that "there is still at least 7 m of deposit to come and possibly considerably more" (Mellaart, 1966:167). In the third field season a narrow test-trench sunk below the floor of Room X 8, yielded four metres of occupation deposit without touching the virgin soil (Mellaart, 1964:73).

The neolithic folk of Çatal Hüyük lived in well-planned and carefully plastered mud-brick houses. The walls did not have stone foundations as stone was not available in the alluvial plain in which the site is situated. Most houses were rectilinear in plan consisting of living rooms approximately 4 by 5 m in size and one or more subsidiary rooms—all provided with standard furnishings which included platforms for sitting and sleeping with a bench at the southern end placed along the eastern side of the room. The main rooms usually contained a large bin placed in the north-western corner and one or more raised rectangular hearth with rounded kerb and a vaulted bread-oven built into the southern wall. The flat roof was made of compressed mud laid on beds of reeds and supported by two stout main beams and numerous small beams. A characteristic feature of Çatal houses is the fact that they were entered through a shaft from the roof. These shafts, carefully plastered, could not have been open to the sky and in the absence of mud-brick staircases, they must have had wooden ladders. Mellaart observes that entry from the roof is still found in numerous villages in the most remote parts of Turkey (1962a:46). The secondary rooms were entered from the main room through low, open doorways; square, rectangular or oval in shape and up to 77 cm in height. As such, one could only move through them in a squatting or crawling position. The houses were closely packed together and as many as 40 houses have been excavated in an area of two-thirds of an acre. The settlement does not have any street or lane but open court-yards have been found in between the main blocks of houses.

There is another class of buildings at Çatal Hüyük which has been uncovered and these buildings are decorated with wall paintings, reliefs in plaster and animal heads and contain cult statues. These have been designated "shrines" or "cult rooms". Some of these have horns of cattle set into benches, rows of bucrania and *ex-voto* figurines stuck into the walls and human skulls set upon platforms. In plan and construction they are no different from the ordinary dwellings and contained all built-in furniture such as platforms, benches, hearths and ovens but the curious decorations on the walls and the contents of the rooms suggest them to be sanctuaries. Small deposits of grain, tools, pots, bone utensils and animal bones—supposed to be offerings—have been found in all shrines which are interspersed among ordinary dwellings and vary in ratio from two houses to each shrine in Level VII to five or six houses to one shrine in Level IV. This gives the impression that there are more shrines in the lower building levels but it must be borne in mind that the lower levels remain inadequately explored. In a total of 156 houses excavated in the first three seasons, as many as 48 were shrines. These shrines were found to contain human burials. "Ochre burials" are supposed to be special features of the shrines as no such burial has been found in a building which can definitely be described as an ordinary residential house. Frontal bone and horn-cores of wild bulls are found set in benches in a number of shrines of Level VI and ram's heads are frequently discovered at the base of the posts against the north walls. A collection of four skulls perhaps used in funeral rituals was found on the floor of Shrine VII, 21. As mentioned above the walls of these shrines were decorated with paintings or plaster reliefs or both. Wall paintings have been noticed as early as Level X and they continue to occur as late as Level II. Some of the plaster reliefs were also painted. Cut out figures in sunk reliefs were first found in Level IX and animals and goddesses in low reliefs are found depicted in Level VIB. The plaster reliefs un-covered include goddesses in anthropomorphic form and many animal heads were set in superimposed rows on posts or they were used to attach the animal head to the wall. Benches decorated with horns are found only in Levels VIB and VIA but the bucranium continued to be used till the end of Level II. The decoration of shrines follows certain rules. Mellaart (1967:104) observes:

Scenes dealing with death are always placed on the east and north walls below which the dead were buried. Scenes dealing with birth occupy the opposite west wall and bulls are found only on the north wall facing the Taurus Mountains perhaps not a coincidence. Animal heads associated with red painted niches are always on the east wall but goddesses and bull and ram heads have no special place and may occur on any wall. It is however, rare

Fig. 35. Çatal Hüyük: *Kilim* pattern (transcript) from Shrine VI, A. 50.

Fig. 36. Çatal Hüyük: Red deer stag surrounded by bearded men (transcript).

for the south wall (the kitchen end of the shrine) to be decorated although there are a few cases where this happened.

A small shrine of Level VII had both its long walls covered with animal heads fixed on wooden posts. Another shrine of the same level shows a still more complex symbolism. Here, one large bull's head spans the main panel of the north wall; two small ones are found beside it on the same wall and a large ram's head appears below a red painted niche on the east wall. Next to the niche a pair of human breasts appears above the animal's right horn and a second pair, placed vertically, appear above the ram's head. From the open nipples protruded the teeth of a fox and a weasel's skull respectively which were incorporated in this pair of breasts. The traditional use of plaster relief in shrines, already fully developed in Level VII, reaches its climax in Levels VIB and VIA. Many more elaborate presentations of complex symbolism are present in the temple decorations at Çatal Hüyük. One of the shrines bore the familiar representation of a goddess originally about 1·2 m in height, with raised arms and upturned feet, a position indicative of the act of child-birth. Immediately below her, a large bull's head with spreading horns, modelled in clay and plaster is shown. Mellaart thinks that the scene shows the goddess having given birth to a bull. In another shrine of Level VI, a goddess is shown giving birth to a ram.

Yet another characteristic feature of Çatal Hüyük are the paintings used for decorating houses and temples alike. They are found from the earliest excavated level and continue to occur till the end of the settlement. The decoration was confined to the interior of the buildings. The paintings were executed by brush in a flat wash in dark or light red paint in monochrome series or in red-pink, while geometric designs of great intricacy are found in polychrome. The background was of fine smoothed cream or pinkish white plaster, which itself was superimposed on a sandier and coarser mud plaster which covered the mud-brick walls. The colours were waterproof and they did not run after rain. However, a fine pink turned light grey within 20 min of exposure. These frescoes were subsequently covered with numerous coats of white plaster of varying thickness. The position of the frescoes on the walls varied; often they went nearly to the floor, whereas in other cases the horizontal ribs served as base-lines. The subject matter used includes scenes comprising isolated groups of animals and deer hunt; the figures normally being 15 to 20 cm in height. Some of the animals used in a deer-hunt scene are just over 30 cm in length while the great auroch bull measures nearly 2 m. Both naturalistic and geometric motifs continue to occur in the same levels. Among the human representations found the males are shown in red whereas women

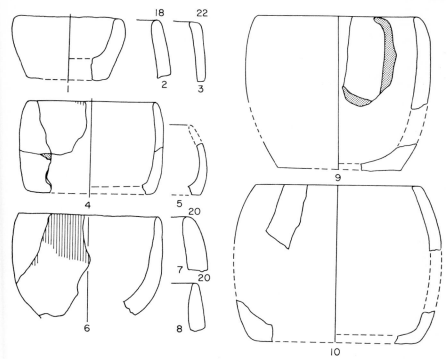

FIG. 37. Çatal Hüyük: Pottery from Levels XII and XI.

are painted white. Some of the geometric patterns uncovered represent textiles and their resemblance to modern Anatolian *kilims* (i.e. thin woven rugs) is striking. Wall paintings of vultures attacking human bodies are found only in three shrines of Levels VII and VIII and Mellaart believes that they illustrate the preliminaries of the burial practices at Çatal Hüyük which consisted of secondary burial of skeletons cleansed by vultures. On the basis of their themes, the wall paintings are divided into 6 groups (Mellaart, 1967:132-33):

1. Plain panels of paint without any motif.
2. Panels of geometric patterns with repetitive motifs; rectilinear or curvilinear, in monochrome or polychrome.
3. Panels with symbols; solid circles, quatrefoils, crenellations, stylised flowers or stars, etc.
4. Human hands, either isolated or grouped into panels.
5. Naturalistic paintings; goddesses, human figures, bulls, birds, vultures, leopards, deer, found either by themselves or grouped into elaborate scenes like deer hunts, bulls with human figurines, funeral rites etc.

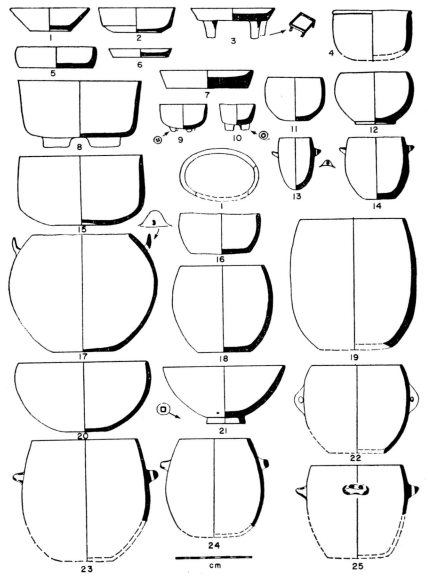

FIG. 38. Çatal Hüyük: Early Neolithic pottery.

6. Representations of landscape and architecture; volcano and town and mortuary structures.

Of these, the deer-hunt scenes are very realistically portrayed and one such scene found in a large shrine (A. III. I) shows 5 or 6 men of different sizes, some naked and others dressed in animal skins and armed with bows, slings or maces attacking a herd of red deer. The herd consists of 3 stags, 2 does and 2 young fawns fleeing to the right of the picture. Many of the animals turn their heads towards their pursuer and in the bottom of the register a fine stag has been brought down by two men.

The Neolithic folk of Çatal knew the art of pottery-making but it was not so common or so developed as that of Late Neolithic Hacilar. Pottery is present in all levels from VIB to XII but only a total of 300 sherds have been found. This is partly because wooden vessels and baskets were in use. As pottery has been reported from the earliest excavated levels, it is suspected that aceramic levels still lie buried in the unexcavated strata (Mellaart, 1966:170). The earliest pottery was heavily built in cream or light grey ware with grits and straw and burnished. This has been termed Cream Burnished ware. The shapes found were few and simple; deep bowls with heavy flat bases being most common. However, simple bowls, shallow basins and one or two oval vessels were also present. Firing was very poor and heavy black cores predominated. This pottery gives way to Dark Burnished ware which occurs from Level VIII onwards. As its name implies, it belongs to the dark burnished category known from Mersin and other sites in Cilicia. The pots were built-up in the coil technique on a flat base but were frequently finished with paddle and anvil. The types found include cooking pots and storage vessels while ornaments were rarely discovered. Half a dozen sherds from Level II bear incised designs near the mouth of the vessel. As pottery is present in Level XII, the earliest level excavated so far, Mellaart (1966:170) argues that pottery at Çatal is considerably earlier than any pottery elsewhere in the Near East. However, this statement needs revision as a small quantity of pottery has been found from Level D at Ganj Dareh in Iran which has been dated to 7018 BC on the Libby half-life. Numerous wooden vessels were also discovered in burnt Level VI. Most of these were found as burial gifts but some came from the store-room of a shrine. The shapes collected include large dishes, 50 cm in diameter, with carved handles, oval bowls with ledge handles, deep and shallow round bowls and dishes; boat-shaped vessels and small boxes of many varieties, square, oval and oblong, each with a well-fitting lid and frequently having small lugs. Besides these, the round baskets presumably made of wheat straw, are very common in all layers. However, less than a dozen stone vessels were found from the shrines and burials but they comprise a thin-walled

Fig. 39. Çatal Hüyük: A well-preserved wooden dish from Level VI.

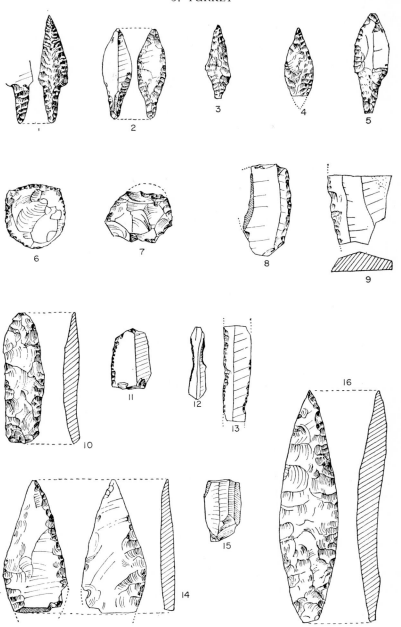

FIG. 40. Çatal Hüyük: Chipped stone tools from Level VIII.

marble bowl on crescent feet from Level IV, four spouted dishes in fine red limestone from various shrines of Level VIA and a similar white marble dish from a male grave of Level VIA (Mellaart, 1964:84). In comparison with other sites in the Near East, it seems that stone vessels were a luxury for the people of Çatal and their use was confined to ritual purposes only.

The chipped stone industry of Çatal is an improved version of that of Mersin. The material used was almost exclusively obsidian, usually jet black, only slightly translucent on the edges of the tools and was brought from the Acigöl region, some 200 km northeast of Çatal Hüyük (Renfrew, Dixon and Cann, 1966). Chert and flint was used mainly for scrapers and inferior tools. Projectile points (lance and arrow-heads), often beautifully pressure-flaked on both sides, were the principal tool-type. Scrapers are common finds but drills and awls are not very prominent. Microlithic tools are conspicuous by their absence. The tool-types uncovered indicate that hunting played an important part in the economy of Çatal. The chipped stone tools recorded during the first season have been studied by Bailor (1962) who has identified numerous tanged arrowheads and lance-heads, some awls and drills, scrapers of various kinds, laurel-leaf daggers, typical parallel-sided blades, a couple of heavily retouched fabricators and some heavy pointed blades. He believes that the industry was homogeneous from the bottom to the top.

However, the earlier tools are definitely larger than those found in the later levels (V-II). By Level II, the industry declines and blades predominate. Sickle blades can be identified and they are now found frequently. An antler sickle haft was found in Level VI.

Among the polished stone tools found, mace-heads are very common in all strata. Axes remain rare but adzes and chisels abound. Small flat greenstone celts are often uncovered and polishers and pallettes are also present. Obsidian mirrors collected show excellent craftsmanship and the carving of minute beads is unsurpassed. Stone bowls are found less frequently than in the Late Neolithic Hacilar but, as noted above, a few trays and spouts were found in Level VI.

Çatal Hüyük has yielded a large number of figurines modelled in clay and carved in stones like alabaster, limestone and marble. These are mostly found in shrines. Crude clay figures of wild animals like boar, wild cattle, pig and deer (?) have been identified. Human figures collected commonly include female figures, either standing or seated with hands supporting the breast or placed on the stomach. These have been taken to be the representation of a Fertility Goddess. The context in which these figures are found strongly suggests that these are cult-statues. A group of 18 such statues were found in the excavations of 1962. Among

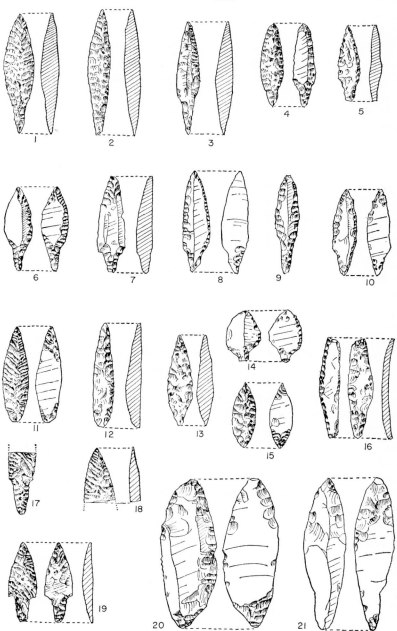

FIG. 41. Çatal Hüyük: Chipped stone tools from Level III.

them was a twin-goddess in white marble. It has 2 heads with schematic rendering of nose and eye-brows, 4 breasts and 2 arms shown over a clearly indicated belt. Also, one impressive figure of a goddess in the act of giving birth to a child was found from the grain-bin of a shrine of Level II. She sits on a throne supported on either side by lions, her feet resting on human skulls depicting perhaps the Neolithic man's belief that the goddess is Mistress of Life and Death (Mellaart, 1963d). Comparatively few male figurines have been found but the figure of a boy-god riding a leopard has been recorded.

The people buried their dead below the platforms of both residential houses and shrines. Some 400 individuals were found in the first three season's dig (Mellaart, 1965:202) and about 80 burials were recorded in the fourth season. Of these, 21 had been treated with red ochre. The ochre burials were usually found in shrines and predominantly in the lower levels. Thus while children were buried anywhere below the house-floors, the adults were buried in contracted position on the left side with legs towards the east and the head to the west, below the platforms on the eastern side of the house. The burial was made at an average depth of about 60 cm but in no specific grave. The burials found outside the platform areas were made in oval graves. Mellaart (1962a: 52, 1964:92) believes that secondary interment was practised at Çatal after complete or partial decomposition of the flesh. It has been argued that excarnation took place in special morgues or charnel houses as shown in the wall paintings and vultures carried out this task. Individual graves are rare and most houses were used as family burial sites. Some of the burials were accompanied by obsidian mirrors and personal ornaments like necklaces and armlets of various stones, bone and dentalium shell. Female burials were provided with articles of personal ornaments while weapons were the prerogatives of males. In a room in Level VI was found a burial consisting of 7 or 8 bodies and some of the bones were wrapped in textiles (Helbaek, 1963). In another case, a little girl had been buried in a basket. The body of a prematurely born child was found to be carefully wrapped in very fine cloth, and the bones had stains of red ochre. The funeral gift, in this case, comprised a tiny bit of bright shell and a small chip of obsidian (Mellaart, 1967:83). Demographic studies of the human skeletal remains from Çatal reveal that the average adult length of life is 34·3 years for males and 29·8 for females. It is interesting to note that there is an excess of females as out of 222 adult dead, 136 are females (Angel, 1971).

The economy of Çatal was based on agriculture and animal domestication supplemented by hunting, fishing, collection of edible fruits and roots. As compared to the recently excavated site of Suberde, the faunal

Fig. 42. Çatal Hüyük: Two flint daggers, pressure-flaked on one side, smooth on the other.

remains are surprisingly scarce, presumably because the excavations seem to have been carried out in the priestly quarters. The bulk of the excavated material comes from Level VI and Levels X to XII. Preliminary examination of these bones by Charles Reed points to the preponderance of cattle over other animals. These observations have been confirmed by the subsequent studies of Çatal animal bones by Perkins Jr. (1969) who observes that cattle provided more than 90% of the meat diet during both the occupation levels (Levels X-XII and VI). He believes that domestic cattle were certainly present in Level VI and were probably domesticated during Levels X-XII, 500 years earlier. The only other domestic animal was the dog (Canis familiaris) identified by Miss B. Lawrence of the Harvard University. In addition to the cattle, bones of the following species were identified: Anatolian mouflon (Ovis orientalis anatolica), Asian wild goat (Capra hircus aegagrus), red deer (Cervus elephus), wild boar (Sus scrofa,) and onager (Equus hemionus). There is no evidence for domestic sheep or goat at any level. An interesting feature is the complete absence of leopard bones, an animal commonly depicted in the frescoes and the plastic relief figures. Bones of red deer, wild boar and onager—the other animals depicted in the paintings and in figurines—are also relatively uncommon in the faunal remains from Çatal Hüyük. Among the large collection of food grains, the main crops are wheat and barley. Field pea, lentil as well as apple, pistachio, hackberry, almond and acorns were also collected. Helbaek, (1964) observes that the principal agricultural products were einkorn, emmer, bread wheat, naked barley and pea, and seeds of all these occur in great quantities. The occurrence of stamp seals demonstrates the existence of private property. These seals are made of baked clay and decorated with fine geometric ornament in pseudo-meander style. None of the designs is repeated and not more than one seal has been found in one house-complex. Mellaart (1962a:56) suspects that the seals may have been used to stamp clothes as well as produce stored in sacks.

The presence of weaving needles, loom weights and spindle-whorls suggests that weaving was an established industry. This has been proved by the discovery of actual remains of carbonised textiles in the excavations of 1962 and 1963. As noted above, the specimens were found from burials under the low clay platforms in the shrines and houses of Level VI. Human skeletal remains had been wrapped in textile pieces. The fibre of these fabrics has not been identified conclusively. All the yarns are evenly spun and most of them were clearly two-ply. Helbaek (1963) and Burnham (1965) think that they are wool but Ryder (1965) identifies them as flax. However, he does not rule out the possibility that wool might also have been used (Ryder, 1965:176). Here it may be well to

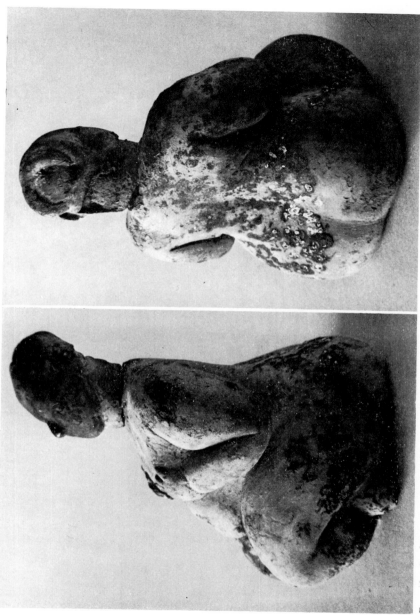

B

A

FIG. 43. Çatal Hüyük: A and B: Two views of a complete seated clay figure, Shrine II, A.1. Height 8 cm.

Fig. 44. Çatal Hüyük: Level VI. Human mandible in its cloth wrapping.

point out that there is no indication of the domestication of sheep at this site.

The chronology of Çatal Hüyük has been established by a series of 18 radiocarbon dates coming from Levels X to II. Calculated on the Libby half-life they fall between 6300-5600 BC while on the higher half-life of 5730 years, they give a time-bracket of 6500-5700 BC giving a time-span of 700 to 800 years for Levels X to II. A later series of Philadelphia dates (P-1361 etc) gives a range of c.6000-5500 for Levels X-V and thus suggests a slightly later date for the end of this site and more of an overlap with Hacilar. As regards the upper levels, a century may safely be given for Levels I and O, and it seems, the Neolithic mound was abandoned around the middle of the sixth millennium BC and for reasons unknown to us, the people settled on another site, Çatal Hüyük West, across the river. As to the origins of the settlement, no plausible guess can be hazarded unless lower levels are explored further. As regards the population of Çatal Hüyük, Mellaart estimates that the Neolithic city's population was 8000 to 10,000 (Mellaart, 1965:202).

Can Hasan

Further southeast of Çatal Hüyük is the prehistoric settlement of Can Hasan. It has been under excavation for several years and, until recently, was known for its Chalcolithic deposits. But recently a Neolithic phase has been identified in Layers 4 and 5 at this site (French, 1968; Mellink, 1968, 1970). House complexes with remains of fragmentary buildings have been identified in both layers. The walls of mud-brick and *pisé* are considerably thinner than those of the later periods. Some floors were coated with red ochre. Bins, containing grains and seeds in considerable quantities, have been found in an area in Layer 5. Pottery found consists of plain burnished ware with a rich black or chocolate surface colour and black core with the main shapes bowls and jars, some of them with elaborate lips. Tools of obsidian and rarely of flint; beads, pendants, stamps, polished axes of stone and points, awls, spatulæ, chisels, gauges, beads and pendants of bone complete the inventory. Grains of hulled six-row barley (*Hordeum hexastichum*) have been identified by Renfrew (1968) from this level. Animal bones show extensive hunting. No radiocarbon dates are available for this period but these collections have been ascribed to the seventh millennium BC although this date remains to be corroborated by other evidence.

Erbaba

Another Neolithic settlement with thin, black micaceous pottery has been recently excavated by Bordaz at Erbaba, 10 km north northwest of Beyşehir (Mellink, 1970:159). This settlement covers an area of 1·2 acres with a 3 m thick occupational deposit. Architectural remains comprise thick north-south walls joined by thinner east-west walls forming a series of parallel rooms. Such remains became more dense in the upper layers. The thin, micaceous pottery gives way to red and brown mono-chrome ware which contains large amounts of fragments of gastropods in the upper levels. The chipped stone industry uncovered consists of obsidian blades, flakes and some bi-facial projectile points. The polished stone objects recovered comprise grinding stones, pestles, beads, awls, spatulæ, and buckles of bone. Human figures of clay have also been re-ported. Extensive botanical remains of cereal plant food and faunal material mainly of domestic sheep and cattle suggest an assured supply of food for a sedentary society less dependent on hunting and collecting.

Cilicia

As mentioned in the beginning of the Chapter, Cilicia was the only known region in Anatolia where Neolithic remains had been identified as early as 1936. These relics were exposed on the northwestern slope of the prehistoric mound of Yümük Tepe, 3 km to the northwest of Mersin. The mound, situated in the river valley of the Soğuk Su, covers an area of 12 acres and rises to a height of 25 m. The culture-sequence at this site runs from Neolithic through Chalcolithic, Bronze Age, Hittite, Greek, and early Islamic periods. This site was under excavation from 1936 to 1939 and again in 1946-47 (Garstang, 1953). Virgin soil could not be reached due to high water table but two phases of Neolithic; the earliest or Lower (Levels XXVII-XXXIII) and the Upper (Levels XXV-XXVI), have been distinguished.

The people of the Lower Neolithic phase lived in houses whose walls were made of water-worn stones taken from the river bed. No trace of mortar is noticeable in the remains and it seems that "dry walling" was the method of construction. The wall in the lowest level was only two stones thick and about 50 cm wide. This thickness increases to 65 cm in the middle layers. Floors were not laid or strengthened in any way in the lower levels and they were trampled smooth by use. These construc-tional details sharply differ from those discovered at Çayönü or Çatal Hüyük. The lithic industry recovered comprises tools made of black obsidian and the types include awls, daggers, tanged lance-heads, scrapers and "slugs". Some sickle blades, mostly made of chert, were also present. Other stone objects collected include a number of roughly shaped but smoothly hollowed stones, some of which may have served

as dishes, portions of a stone lamp, and a seal of green stone with primitive linear pattern. Bone tools are rarely recovered and traces of fragmentary human burials ascribable to Level XXVIII were noticed. Pottery
is consistently present from the earliest layers and comprises a monochrome, black faced, burnished pottery with black, grey or chocolate
surface colour. Among the types discovered are bowls, basins, jars and
dishes. Some improvement in technique and finish is noticeable in the
pottery of higher levels and short incised designs have been noted in the
pottery of Levels XXVIII and XXVII.

The upper Neolithic phase of Mersin is characterised by a change in
architectural details but the chipped stone industry shows little or no
change in technique except for the fact that lance-heads are represented by one specimen only and sickle blades become more numerous
than in the preceding levels. This may perhaps indicate a shift in emphasis from hunting to an economy based more on harvesting of cereal
plants. Miniature celts of green stone continue to appear and bone tools
now include spatulæ and needles. Another new tool characteristic of the
uppermost Neolithic levels is termed a "hand chisel" by Garstang. In
each case, this tool is made of a water-worn pebble of roundish section,
tapering naturally towards one end having been worked upon and gradually flattened and finished with a narrow cutting edge. Intra-mural burial
was practised. This feature is also shared by the contemporary culture
in the Konya plain. A single burial was discovered below the floor of a
room where the skeleton lay on its back with skull turned to the right
and the legs drawn up in contracted position. Funeral offerings included
personal ornaments like stone bracelets and disk-shaped beads of shell
and offerings in vases. The black burnished pottery of the lower Neolithic
phase continues to occur but the shapes now include large flat-bottomed
dishes along with basins and bowls.

Tarsus

A similar situation, as noticed at Mersin, obtained in the excavations
at Gözlü Kule, Tarsus, where Neolithic levels were encountered at the
base of the mound but could not be investigated properly due to a high
water table. Characteristic Neolithic pottery, obsidian flakes and parts of
a wall were noticed in a restricted area of 1·25 sq m (Goldman, 1956:5).
The pottery recovered comprises hand-made Dark Burnished ware with
such shapes as hole-mouthed jars together with light gritty wares with
big jars having narrow necks. Both the wares can be fairly well paralleled
at other Cilician and north Syrian sites and both wares are present at
Mersin (Mellink in Goldman, 1956:70) and in Amuq phases A-E.

Mellink observes that Tarsus pottery begins somewhere in the range of Amuq A-B. Dark Burnished sherds have also been picked up from such other sites as Tarmil, Samşi, and Tatarli in Cilicia (Seton-Williams, 1954:128).

References

ANGEL, J. LAWRENCE. (1971). Early Neolithic Skeletons from Çatal Hüyük: Demography and Pathology. *Anatolian Stud.*, **21**, 77-98.

BAILOR, PERRY A. (1962). The Chipped Stone Industry of Çatal Hüyük. *Anatolian Stud.*, **12**, 67-110.

BIERNOFF, D. C. (1964). Prehistoric Settlement in Muğla Vilayet. *Anatolian Stud.*, **14**, 33-35.

BORDAZ, JACQUES (1965). Suberde Excavations 1964. *Anatolian Stud.*, **15**, 30-32.

BORDAZ, JACQUES (1966). Recent Archæological Research in Turkey—Suberde. *Anatolian Stud.*, **16**, 32-33.

BORDAZ, JACQUES (1968). The Suberde Excavations, Southwestern Turkey: An Interim Report. *Turk. Arkeol. Derg.*, **17** (2), 43-71.

BRAIDWOOD, R. J., ÇAMBEL, H. AND WATSON, P. J. (1969). Prehistoric Investigations in Southeastern Turkey. *Science, N.Y.*, **164**, 1275-76.

BRAIDWOOD, R. J., ÇAMBEL, H., REDMAN, CHARLES L. AND WATSON, P. J. (1971). Beginnings of Village-Farming Communities in Southeastern Turkey. *Proc. Natn. Acad. Sci. U.S.A.*, **68** (6), 1236-40.

BURNHAM, HAROLD B. (1965). Çatal Hüyük—The Textiles and Twined Fabric. *Anatolian Stud.*, **15**, 169-74.

ÇAMBEL, H. AND BRAIDWOOD, R. J. (1970). An Early Farming Village in Turkey. *Scient. Am.*, **222** (3), 51-56.

CRANE, H. R. AND GRIFFIN, JAMES B. (1968). University of Michigan Radiocarbon Dates XII. *Radiocarbon*, **10** (1), 108-9.

FRENCH, D. H. (1965). Early Pottery Sites from Western Anatolia. *Bull. Inst. Archæol.*, **5**, 15-24.

FRENCH, D. H. (1968). Excavations at Can Hasan. *Anatolian Stud.*, **18**, 45-53.

GARSTANG, JOHN (1953). *Prehistoric Mersin*. Oxford: The Clarendon Press.

GOLDMAN, HETTY (1956). *Excavations at Gozlu Kule, Tarsus, Vol. II*. Princeton: University Press.

HELBAEK, HANS (1963). Textiles from Çatal Hüyük. *Archæology*, **16** (1), 39-46.

HELBAEK, HANS (1964). First Impressions of the Çatal Hüyük Plant Husbandry. *Anatolian Stud.*, **14**, 121-24.

LLOYD, SETON (1956). *Early Anatolia*. Harmondsworth: Penguin Books.

MELLAART, JAMES (1959). Excavations at Hacilar, Second Preliminary Report 1958. *Anatolian Stud.*, **9**, 51-66.

MELLAART, JAMES (1960). Excavations at Hacilar, Third Preliminary Report 1959. *Anatolian Stud.*, **10**, 83-104.

MELLAART, JAMES (1961*a*). Excavations at Hacilar, Fourth Preliminary Report 1960. *Anatolian Stud.*, **11**, 39-76.

MELLAART, JAMES (1961*b*). Early Cultures of South Anatolian Plateau. *Anatolian Stud.*, **11**, 159-84.

MELLAART, JAMES (1961*c*). By Neolithic Artists of 7500 Years Ago—Statuettes from Hacilar, Unique for Quantity, Variety, Beauty, and Preservation. *Ill. Lond. News*, **1961**, 229-31.

MELLAART, JAMES (1961*d*). Two Thousand Years of Hacilar—Starting from Over Nine Thousand Years Ago: Excavations in Turkey which Throw Light on the Earliest Anatolia. *Ill. Lond. News*, **1961**, 588-91.

MELLAART, JAMES (1961*e*). Hacilar: A Neolithic Village Site. *Scien. Am.*, **205** (2), 86-97.

MELLAART, JAMES (1962*a*) Excavations at Çatal Hüyük; First Preliminary Report 1961. *Anatolian Stud.*, **12**, 41-66.

MELLAART, JAMES (1962*b*). A 7th-6th Millennium Township of Southern Anatolia, Larger than Pre-Pottery Jericho: First Excavations at Çatal Hüyük. Part I. *Ill. Lond. News*, **1962**, 934-36.

MELLAART, JAMES (1962*c*). The Earliest Frescoes Yet Found on a Man-Made Wall: Remarkable Discoveries in the Excavations at Anatolian Çatal Hüyük. Part II. *Ill. Lond. News*, **1962**, 976-78.

MELLAART, JAMES (1963*a*). Excavations at Çatal Hüyük, Second Preliminary Report. *Anatolian Stud.*, **13**, 43-104.

MELLAART, JAMES (1963*b*). Çatal Hüyük in Anatolia: Excavations which Revolutionise the History of Earliest Civilisations. Part I, The Stone Sculptures. *Ill. Lond. News*, **1963**, 118-21.

MELLAART, JAMES (1963*c*). Çatal Hüyük in Anatolia: Excavations which Revolutionise the History of Earliest Civilisation. Part II, Shrines and Buildings. *Ill. Lond. News*, **1963**, 160-64.

MELLART, JAMES (1963*d*). Deities and Shrines of Neolithic Anatolia, Excavations at Çatal Hüyük 1962. *Archæology*, **16** (1), 29-38.

MELLAART, JAMES (1964). Excavations at Çatal Hüyük 1963: Third Preliminary Report. *Anatolian Stud.*, **14**, 39-120.

MELLAART, JAMES (1965). Çatal Hüyük, A Neolithic City in Anatolia. *Proc. Brit. Academy*, **51**, 201-13.

MELLAART, JAMES (1966). Excavations at Çatal Hüyük, 1965. *Anatolian Stud.*, **16**, 165-190.

MELLAART, JAMES (1967). *Çatal Hüyük*. London: Thames and Hudson.

MELLAART, JAMES (1970). *Excavations at Hacilar*. 2 Volumes. Edinburgh: University Press.

MELLAART, JAMES (1972). Anatolian Settlement Patterns, *Man, Settlement and Urbanism* (P. J. Ucko, Ruth Tringham and G. W. Dimbleby, eds). London: Duckworth. pp. 279-84.

MELLINK, MACHTELD J. (1955-1971). Archæology in Asia Minor. *Am. J. Archæol.*, **59-75**.

NANDRIS, JOHN G. (1969). Early Neothermal Sites in the Near East and Anatolia. *Memoria Antiquitatis*, **1**, 11-66.

PERKINS JR. DEXTER AND DALY, PATRICIA (1968). A Hunter's Village in Neolithic Turkey. *Scient. Am.* **219** (5), 96-106.

PERKINS JR. DEXTER (1969). Fauna of Çatal Hüyük: Evidence of Early Cattle Domestication in Anatolia. *Science, N.Y.*, **164**, 177-79.

RENFREW, COLIN; DIXON, J. E. AND CANN, J. R. (1966). Obsidian and Early Cultural Contact in the Near East. *Proc. Prehist. Soc.*, **32**, 30-72.

RENFREW, COLIN; DIXON, J. E. AND CANN, J. R. (1968). Further Analysis of Near Eastern Obsidian. *Proc. Prehist. Soc.*, **34**, 319-31.

RENFREW, JANE M. (1968). A Note on the Neolithic Grain From Can Hasan. *Anatolian Stud.*, **18**, 55-56.

RALPH, ELIZABETH K. AND STUKENRATH, JR. R. (1962). University of Pennsylvania Radiocarbon Dates V. *Radiocarbon*, **4**, 145-46.

REDMAN, CHARLES L. (1971). Changes in an Early Farming Community in Southeast Anatolia, *Seminar Papers on the Explanation of Culture Change*. Sheffield.

RYDER, M. L. (1965). Report of Textiles from Çatal Hüyük. *Anatolian Stud.*, **15**, 175-76.

SETON-WILLIAMS, M. V. (1954). Cilician Survey. *Anatolian Stud.*, **4**, 121-74.

SOLECKI, RALPH S. (1964). An Archæological Reconnaissance in the Beyşehir-Suğla Area of Southwestern Turkey. *Turk. Arkeol. Derg.*, **13** (1), 129-48.

STUCKENRATH JR. R. AND RALPH, ELIZABETH K. (1965). University of Pennsylvania Radiocarbon Dates VIII. *Radiocarbon*, **7**, 191-94.

TODD, IAN A. (1965). Surface finds from Various Sites. *Anatolian Stud.*, **15**, 34.

TODD, IAN A. (1966a). Ilicapinar-Cihanbeyli. *Anatolian Stud.*, **16**, 44-48.

TODD, IAN A. (1966b) Aşikli Hüyük—A Protoneolithic Site in Central Anatolia. *Anatolian Stud.*, **16**, 139-63.

TODD, IAN A. (1968). The Dating of Aşikli Hüyük in Central Anatolia. *Am. J. Archæol.*, **72**, 157-58.

TODD, IAN A. AND GIORGIO, PASQUARE (1965). The Chipped Stone Industry of Avla Dağ. *Anatolian Stud.*, **15**, 95-112.

4. Iraq

Ever since the discovery of the first Palæolithic implement by Dorothy Garrod in the cave of Hazar Merd near Suleimaniyah in 1928, Iraq has been known to be the habitat of Pleistocene man. However, no work was done for the subsequent two decades and it was only after 1948 that we began to know about the early prehistory of this country. The discovery of Middle Palæolithic artefacts at Barda Balka near Chemchemal by 'Asil in 1949 ('Asil, 1949), the subsequent excavation of this open-air settlement in 1951 by Wright Jr. and Howe (1951; Frazer, 1953) and the excavation of Shanidar cave in the Rowanduz area by Ralph Solecki (1952) amply demonstrate that the Zagros range was inhabited from Middle Palæolithic to Neolithic times. The excavations at Jarmo in 1948 and 1950-51, at Karim Shahir in 1951 and at Zawi Chemi Shanidar in 1951, 1956 and 1960 provide valuable data for understanding the transition from food-collecting to the food-producing era. This phase has been termed "Proto-Neolithic" by the Soleckis (Solecki and Solecki, 1963:58). According to them this phase belongs to

> that stage of human development which witnessed the beginnings of a village life and a shift away from a subsistence based entirely on hunting and gathering in favour of one over which man exercised more control.

However, the Braidwoods distinguish two stages in this transition. They call the first stage the "Era of Incipient Agriculture and Animal Domestication" which they define as follows:

> those assemblages—either from caves or from open sites—which include items suggesting incipient food-production but without traces of established village settlements (Braidwood and Braidwood, 1953: 282).

This stage, according to them, can be identified at Zawi Chemi Shanidar, Karim Shahir, M'Lefaat and Gird Chai. The second stage is designated "the Era of Early Village Farming Communities" represented by the assemblage discovered at Jarmo (Braidwood and Howe, 1960:182). It is during this stage that the art of making earthenware

111

vessels is attested for the first time in Iraq. Braidwood believes, however, that in the present state of research in the prehistory of Iraq, the transition from the first era to the second is as yet imperfectly understood. This is demonstrated by a chronological gap of 2000 years in the radiocarbon dates from the sites belonging to the two stages noted above. On techno-typological grounds he places the assemblage of Qara Chiwar, an un-excavated site overlooking a stretch of the Tang Chai between Karim Shahir and Jarmo, in the transitional period. The cultural assemblage of the sites of the "era of Incipient Cultivation" is as follows:

Karim Shahir

The first trace of a partly sedentary society comes from Karim Shahir situated about 2 km east of Jarmo, on the right bank of the Cham Gawra river in the valley of Chemchemal, Kirkuk Liwa. The site is approxi-mately 160 by 70 m in extent of which a 550 sq. m area was investigated by Braidwood and his team in March-May, 1951 (Braidwood, 1951a, b; Braidwood and Braidwood, 1953; Braidwood and Howe, 1960). The inhabitants of Karim Shahir probably lived in encampments as no formal architecture was found. In the principal and well-defined level were found erratic stones strewn all over the surface but it was not possible to comprehend any hut plan. These may perhaps represent stone floorings of irregular shape. The existence of clusters of hearth stones and of a pit probably used for storage has been suspected (Braidwood, 1951a: 102).

The tool-kit of Karim Shahir people contained microlithic tools pre-dominantly of chipped flint and obsidian was virtually absent. Among the microliths recovered, notched blades and flakes account for no less than 70% of the tools. Other types collected include bladelets, end-scrapers, burins and a few extremely dubious geometric microliths (Braidwood and Howe, 1960:52-53). The heavy tools recovered comprise nearly three dozen chipped celts with polished butts, milling stone fragments (both mortar and quern type) and ground stone rings. Personal ornaments included bracelets, beads and pendants. A noteworthy feature was the discovery of 2 tiny lightly baked but rather shapeless clay figurines.

The presence of chipped celts with polished bits, querns, mortars, sickle-blades and chipped and ground hoes suggests that Karim Shahir folk practised incipient agriculture. That the people had an abundant supply of meat is suggested by the fact that "almost half of the bones were of species which were at least potentially domesticable, if not domesti-cated" (Braidwood, 1951a). There is no radiocarbon date for this site but the collection seems to be typologically older than Jarmo.

M'Lefaat

The second settlement ascribable to the "Era of Incipient Cultivation" was located at M'Lefaat, a small mound measuring 90 by 120 m. It is situated on a natural hill above the terrace overlooking the Khazir river, immediately north of the Erbil-Mosul road, on the border of the piedmont with the foothills zone. Three trenches were laid out by Broman and an area more than 60 sq. m was investigated. These soundings revealed 5 levels with a cultural deposit of over 1·5 m indicating that M'Lefaat may have been a settlement of some degree of permanence.

The site has furnished evidence of rudimentary architecture. Traces of circular pit-dwellings have been suspected (Braidwood, 1956) and the foundation of a stone wall, 15 cm thick, was discovered. Two well-marked floors with concentrations of stones and a hearth depression were also noted from soundings III and I respectively. The tool-kit of M'Lefaat contained a chipped stone industry, ground stone tools, bone tools, about two dozen fragments of figurines and a simple clay bead. The chipped flint tools recovered comprise backed and notched bladelets, end-scrapers, pyramidal bladelet cores and polyhedral flake cores. Obsidian accounts for only 6 pieces found in situ (Braidwood and Howe, 1960:51). The ground stone industry findings include ground and polished celts, mortars, pestles, querns, rubbing stones and hammerstones. Bone tools are represented by the discovery of several awls and pierced pendants of clam shell.

The M'Lefaat industry compares well with Karim Shahir and Gird Chai but two points deserve mention. In the first place, the polished stone tools of M'Lefaat were better made than those of Karim-Shahir. Secondly, no decorative stones like beads, pendants and bracelets have been found at M'Lefaat. Braidwood believes that this settlement represents "a very elemental form of settled village life" (Braidwood, 1954: 133; Braidwood and Howe, 1960:27).

Gird Chai

Another occupation settlement measuring 60 by 90 m was located on a gravel hill overlooking the Zab river from its left bank and about 1 km west of Girdemamik village. The crown of the mound was tested in six small trenches and a total area of 45 sq. m was investigated to an average depth of about one metre (Braidwood and Howe, 1960:28, 54). The deposit was found to be disturbed by Islamic pits hence the evidence obtained is not conclusive.

The soundings at Gird Chai yielded flint tools comprising a quantity of pyramidal blade cores, backed and notched bladelets, numerous scrapers and three burins. Only eight pieces of obsidian were recorded from the dig besides five pieces from the surface. Ground stone tools were rarely found present *in situ* but such types as chipped celts, rubbing and grinding stone fragments were collected from the surface. The chipped celts recall those from Karim Shahir rather than M'Lefaat. No trace of architecture or any decorative stones was found.

Zawi Chemi Shanidar

A similar pre-ceramic settlement with traces of rudimentary archi-tecture was located at Shanidar cave (Layer B1) and at Zawi Chemi, an open-air site, situated on the second terrace of the Greater Zab river, about 4 km from the Shanidar cave in Erbil Liwa. The cave site was ex-cavated for four field seasons and yielded a cultural deposit of 14 m divisible into four layers, labelled from top to bottom A, B, C and D, with cultural, chronological and stratigraphical breaks between each of these layers (Solecki, 1963). Of these, Layer A yielded a mixed assem-blage of Neolithic and historical periods. However, Layer B, divided into B1 and B2, is important in the present context. Layer B1 is proto-Neolithic and is contemporary with the basal layer at Zawi Chemi. Layer B2 is Mesolithic or very late Upper Palæolithic. Layer C is Upper Palæolithic (Baradostian) and the last layer belongs to the Middle Palæo-lithic (Mousterian) period. The settlement of Zawi Chemi measures 215 by 275 m and it was tested in 1956-7 (Solecki, 1957, 1958) and again in 1960 (Rose Solecki, 1961). The cultural deposit of 1·5 m is divisible into two occupation layers, having an Iron Age assemblage on the top (Layer A) and an early Neolithic settlement at the bottom (Layer B).

That the first occupants of Zawi Chemi lived in some sort of perma-nent architecture is indicated by the presence of a curved and crude wall made of ordinary field stones and river pebbles. The structure was dis-covered at the bottom of Layer B at a depth of 1·10 to 1·50 m. A similar wall of compact loamy clay set in with heavy boulders was exposed in the corresponding levels in the Shanidar cave (Solecki, 1957:168). Near the base of the structure at Zawi Chemi was found some reddened earth and charcoal representing perhaps, part of a hearth. Also, some storage pits have been reported from Layer B1 at the cave site.

The ground stone industry of the Zawi Chemi people recovered in-cludes saddle querns, over a hundred mullers or hand grinding stones, cylindrical pestles and chipped stone celts—all indicative of a heavy dependence on plant food in their economy (Solecki, 1958:105). This fact was also attested by the discovery of a flat, crescent haft made of the rib-bone of a large animal (Solecki and Solecki, 1963:60). It had a shallow

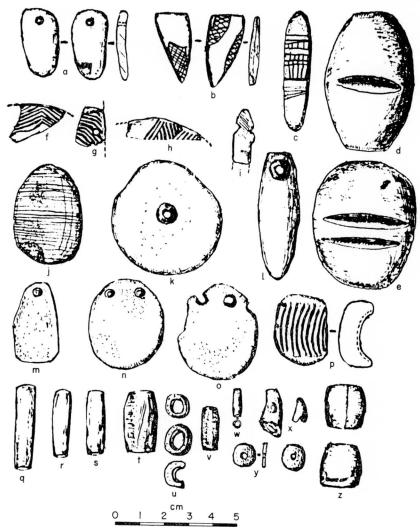

FIG. 45. Zawi Chemi Shanidar: Pendants, beads, and other objects from the proto-Neolithic layers at Shanidar Cave (a-d) and Zawi Chemi Shanidar Village (e-z).

wedge-shaped groove along the inner or concave edge suggesting that flint blades were once fitted into this groove. This artefact seems to have been a knife or sickle used to cut grasses. A similar triangular bone haft was also discovered from the corresponding level (Layer B1) at Shanidar cave. It had a flint blade fixed into one of the grooves with some bitumen-like substance still in position. Apart from the haft, Zawi Chemi yielded a good number of backed blades which may have been used in other similar sickles. Other types of microliths collected comprise notched blades, scrapers, lunates, borers, burins and sub-triangular points. Bone tools comprising many awls and polishers were particularly common finds at this site and pieces of bone decorated with incised designs were also recorded. Among the personal ornaments recovered mention may be made of small circular and large barrel-shaped beads of steatite. Tubular, barrel-shaped and flattened rectangular beads of bird-bones were common discoveries. Double-holed ovate pendants of marble and bone have also been recorded. In a preliminary study of the faunal remains Perkins Jr. (1960, 1964) states that the people largely depended upon sheep, bezoar and red deer for their meat supply. Bone of these animals account for 90% of the total collection of bones from both the sites. An important piece of evidence is the fact that sheep were domesticated at Zawi Chemi at the beginning of the 9th millennium BC. Also identified have been bones of red sheep, wild boar, fallow deer, roe deer, wolf, jackal, tawny fox, Syrian brown bear, marten, beaver, gerbil, land tortoise, land snail and riverine clam. In addition, there were large numbers of unidentified rodent bones recovered from both sites but fish bones were rare.

The Zawi Chemi collection is comparable to that of Karim Shahir and M'Lefaat although it lacks the "sophistication" of Karim Shahir, such as clay figurines and ground stone rings. However, personal ornaments like beads and pendants were found at both sites. It is worth noting that, at Zawi Chemi, clay objects are totally absent and obsidian is practically non-existent as only one piece of this material was found. The chronology of this collection is based on two radiocarbon dates, one from each site. The charcoal sample (W 681) coming from a depth of 1·2 m (well within Layer B) at Zawi Chemi, gives a date of 8900 ± 300 BC (Solecki and Meyer, 1958:1446). This is corroborated by another date of 8650 ± 300 BC of a sample (W 667) from the comparable levels (B1) at Shanidar cave. Thus it seems reasonable to believe that this culture flourished in the first half of the 9th millennium BC. An interesting feature is the discovery of 28 human burials associated with the proto-Neolithic (B1) layer at Shanidar cave. Of these, 26 were found in a cemetery group (Solecki, 1963:182). Rose L. Solecki suggests that it "probably developed out of a Zarzi type culture such as found on the bottom of Layer B" in this cave (Rose Solecki, 1961:125).

Jarmo

As noted above, the next phase of human development is represented by the "Era of Primary Village Farming Efficiency". The Braidwoods define this era as follows:

> As was foreshadowed, however, our working definition for the beginning of this era would be the establishment of permanent village sites. Such sites yield assemblages pertinent to a basic farming economy and are manifest in one or more levels of stable architectural activity. The persisting village is thus the hall-mark of the beginning of our era. For all practical purposes, the era ends with the close of the Halafian phase, or with the materials we judge to by typologically equivalent with the end of the Halafian phase (Braidwood and Braidwood, 1953:288).

Perhaps the best example of a primary village farming community in Iraq is represented by the village site of Jarmo situated on a hilltop overlooking the Wadi of Cham Gawra, 12 km east of Chemchemal. This settlement was discovered by Nasir al Nakshabandi, Inspector of Antiquities, Iraq, and was excavated by Robert J. Braidwood in the spring of 1948 and again in 1950-51 and 1954-55. The site measures 90 by 140 m and has a cultural deposit of 7 m divisible into 15 building levels. During three field seasons Braidwood investigated nearly 1400 sq. m of this settlement (Braidwood, 1951a, 1956, 1967, Linda Braidwood, 1951; Braidwood and Braidwood, 1950, 1951; Braidwood and Howe, 1960).

Three season's field-work at the largely aceramic mound of Jarmo reveals that the people lived in several roomed rectilinear mud-walled (*tauf*) houses. In the uppermost levels the *tauf* walls usually had stone foundations. The size of rooms greatly varied within each house complex. Thus one house of Level 5 in Operation II was found to have been divided into seven rectilinear spaces. This house had a big room measuring 5·6 by 2·2 m but other rooms measured only 2 m by 1·5 m. It is tempting to conclude that the bigger rooms were used for living while the smaller ones were meant for storage. One of the rooms was provided with an oven complete with chimney, with provision for firing it from the courtyard. The floors were made of clean mud packed over beds of reeds. Another house complex exposed in 1955 had walls over a metre and a half thick (Braidwood, 1956) and portions of elaborate stone foundations were uncovered near the surface. These houses were built in contiguity at least on two sides and it is supposed that the open area on the remaining two sides may have been relatively large. However, there is no indication of anything approaching roads.

The tool-kit of the Jarmo people contained implements of flint and obsidian—the latter was found in considerable quantity, accounting for 40% of the total collection, and shows a flourishing trade in this material took place during this period. However, flint still appeared very fre-

E

quently in the collection. The chipped stone industry found contains many microliths, mostly of obsidian, but such geometric shapes as triangles and trapezes are found present in the upper levels only. Blunted back blades are found throughout the levels but are extremely rare while sickle blades are found abundantly and many of them still bear traces of bitumen indicating that these were hafted in wooden or bone handles and used as sickles. In fact, in one intact sickle, four blades were found. In this case, all traces of the haft had vanished but the blades were found in a concentric curve, as originally set in the sickle. Linda Braidwood (1951), who has studied the microlithic industry, suggests that the industry is essentially the same throughout all the levels.

The recovered ground stone tools of Jarmo comprise celts, querns and rubbing stones, mortars and pestles—all present in sizable numbers. Large pierced balls, believed to have been used as digging weights, loom-weights or mace-heads, are found comparatively rarely. The yield of bone tools includes awls, pins, needles and spoons. Other bone objects collected comprise simple rings, made by cutting long bones transversely, and bone beads, cylindrical in shape. Among the ground stone industry, mention must be made of the recovery of stone bowls of which over 1000 fragments comprising perhaps 350 vessels were recorded in the 1950-51 season alone. These bowls were made of marble and the stone worked in such a way that the natural veins of the stone added to the decorative effect by making horizontal bands or oblique lines of various colours which was more pleasing to the eye and demonstrates the high æsthetic sense of the Neolithic artisans. The shapes produced include inverted truncated conical forms with flared lips; spherical or ellipsoid forms and low carinated bowls. These bowls are present in all the levels of the site and well ante-date the discovery of the potter's art.

As noted above, pottery makes its appearance in the upper one-third deposit of the site. The Jarmo pottery was handmade, vegetable-tempered, buff to orange in colour and frequently exhibited a darkened unoxidized core on a clean break. Potsherds from the earlier strata have a burnished surface, often over a red slip, or a painted decoration. Curiously enough, the ceramic technique shows a gradual decline in the subsequent strata where the fabric was coarser and softer than the earlier group and the surface decoration gradually disappeared. Painted motifs gave place to incised decoration though the latter feature is found in limited quantity (Braidwood and Howe, 1960:44). Nevertheless, once the art of potting had been discovered, it was pursued with enthusiasm. In the 1950-51 season, a total of 204 potsherds representing perhaps no less than 35 vessels, were recorded in the exposure of floors 5-3. The uppermost floors of the same operation yielded approximately 12,000 potsherds. This has led Braidwood and Howe (1960:43) to argue that

in its own simple fashion, the earliest Jarmo pottery shows technical compe-
tence in potting and it is not at all supposed that it represents the fumbling
beginnings of a new craft.

The painted sherds from the earlier levels have been compared with
Hassuna archaic painted ware and Caldwell and Matson (in Braidwood
and Howe, 1960:77) stress

"the commonality of the potting tradition of the later Jarmo pottery with
that of Ali Agha and basal Tell Hassunah".

However, Mortensen (1964:32, f.n.14) believes that the archaic
painted sherds

show greater similarities to the group of archaic painted sherds known from
Guran, than to the Hassunan archaic painted ware.

Braidwood agrees that the Jarmo pottery is not Hassuna*. Among other
containers, mention must be made of baskets because impressions of
woven matting or baskets have been found and it is suggested that baskets
were waterproofed by bitumen.

The personal ornaments of the Jarmo people were made of stone,
bone and clay, comprising beads, pendants and bracelets. Cylindrical,
barrel and flattened biconical beads of stone occur frequently and other
types such as collared barrel beads can be found. The presence of cylindrical beads of bone has already been noted. Beads of clay are common
discoveries and include spherical, barrel, flattened eliptical, and flattened diamond forms. Double pierced "toggle" beads of clay are present
and any stone pendants found are usually simple. Marble bracelets recovered were generally well-made and ovoid or round in cross-section.
Of these, no less than 225 complete specimens have been recorded
from the dig.

Small objects of clay are common at the site and as many as 5000
figurines or animals or human beings, have been recorded. Of these,
horned animal figurines and "double winged bases" seem to occur only
in the upper levels. Simple human figures are found in the lower levels
becoming more complex in the upper strata. However, most of the figures
were not carefully modelled and were lightly baked with a few of these
having their surface coated with red ochre. This feature may confirm the
ritual use of such objects. Three flat circular objects of stone with a hole
in the centre taken to be "spindle whorls" and supposed to be used in

*Information from Dr Joan Oates.

spinning (Braidwood and Braidwood, 1951:994, Fig. 12) were recovered. However, this observation is at variance with the earlier statement of Braidwood and Braidwood (1950:193) that "the lack of spindle whorls in either clay or stone might be noted".

Jarmo did not yield any ritual burial in the full sense of the term. In an earlier publication, the excavators reported (Braidwood and Braidwood, 1950:194).

> there were several flexed sub-floor burials at Jarmo. No grave-goods appeared with them. The skeletons were themselves in too fragmentary a condition for restoration.

However, in a subsequent publication Braidwood and Howe (1960:46) state

> few if any clearly intentional burials appeared in the Jarmo exposures. In most cases we suspected accidental death due to roof cave-in and in no case were a standardized burial position and *Beigaben* manifested.

Braidwood suspects that there was probably a cemetery somewhere outside the immediate village precincts.

The flora and fauna of Neolithic Jarmo have been studied by Helbaek and Reed respectively. The indirect evidence of cultivation such as the presence of sickles, polished stone celts, querns, pestles and mortars, has been supported by the positive evidence for the presence of cereals at Jarmo. Two types of wheat, found to be present at this site, bear close resemblance to their present-day counterparts in that area. Also, two-row barley was grown. Among the non-cereal food plants, the field-pea, lentil and blue vetchling are found to be present. On the basis of osteo-logical evidence Reed believes that the goat had already been domesti-cated at Jarmo while the pig was in the process of domestication. Remains of wild pigs only were recorded from the lower, pre-creamic levels but bones of domestic pigs along with those of the wild ones were recovered from the upper levels with pottery (Reed, 1969:371). However, the hunting of pig, sheep and gazelle and collection of such food as pistachio and acorn suggest that Jarmo people practised mixed economy based on hunting, food collecting and limited domestication of animals and plants.

The absolute chronology of Jarmo has been a matter of controversy. Radiocarbon determination of archæological samples from this settle-ment are not consistent. There are now 12 radiocarbon dates from this site (Braidwood and Howe, 1960:159) which fall within a time-span of 3310 ± 450 BC to 9300 ± 300 BC. However, Braidwood suggests that the earliest determinations of Jarmo (W 665, 9250 ± 200 BC and W 657:

9300 ± 300 BC) "must be ignored on the ground that they are too early" (Braidwood and Howe, 1960:158-59). On the other hand, four other samples (W 607, W 651, W 652 and H 551-491) give dates from 7090 ± 250 BC to 6000 ± 200 BC on the Libby half-life (Braidwood, 1967) which seem to be generally consistent for a Neolithic settlement like Jarmo in view of the fact that such dates have been obtained from comparable settlements in the Kermanshah plain. However, for the present the radio-carbon dates from Jarmo vary from 4950 BC to 7090 BC (leaving aside the two earlier dates of 9250 BC and 9300 BC mentioned above) covering a time-span of well over 2000 years. And of course these "mean" dates do not cover either the beginning or the end of the settlement. Thus these dates are at variance with the conventional archæological estimates for the Jarmo settlement. Braidwood and Howe (1960:40) argue that:

> the total duration of Jarmo may not have been long. We learned in neigh-bouring villages that 15 years is probably a generous average allowance for the life of a casually built house with sun-dried mud walls and mud finished roof. If *each* of the 16 floors mentioned above means a separate architectural renovation (which each probably does not), the total duration might still be only about 250 years *minimum*.

Braidwood assigns a "probable true general date" of Jarmo to about 6750 BC.

The population estimates for the Jarmo village have again been a matter of speculation. Earlier, Braidwood believed that the living area of 3.2 acres occupied by the Jarmo people may originally have contained about 50 houses to account for a population of perhaps 300 people (Braidwood, 1951a:103). This estimate has now been revised by the same author when he states that the total number of houses probably did not exceed 25 and the village population amounted to no more than 150 people (Braidwood and Howe, 1960:43, Braidwood, 1960:143).

Shimshara

Mention may be made in this context of the Danish excavations at Tell Shimshara located on the right bank of the Lesser Zab in the Dasht-i-Bitwain, a wide, grassy valley south of Rania. The 19 m high mound of Shimshara measures *c*. 60 m at the base but a southern extension of the mound, measuring about 13 m in height, increases the total length of the tell to more than 330 m. Excavation was started at this site by the Iraqi Directorate General of Antiquities in 1956 and a Danish Expedition led by Harald Ingholt investigated the top of the mound in 1957 (Ingholt, 1957; Mortensen, 1962; 1970). The excavation was continued by the former institution in 1958-59 but was mainly devoted to the later periods.

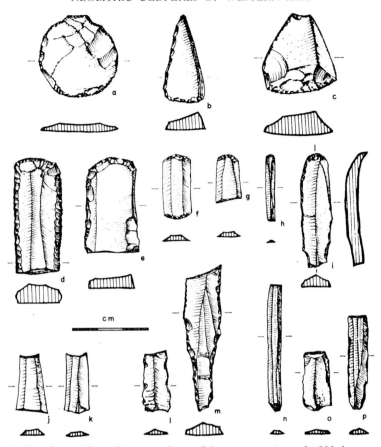

FIG. 46. Shimshara: Chipped stone tools, *a-c* flake scrapers; *d-p* end-of-blade scrapers.

It was in a section through the upper part of the tell that 16 levels (numbered from the top downward), representing a cultural deposit of 8 m below the top of the mound, were distinguished. The upper three levels are Islamic in character and are datable to the 12th-14th centuries AD. Levels 4 to 8 represent Hurrian deposits, and are partly contemporary with a hoard of tablets datable to the reign of Shamshi-Adad I, found in a monumental building exposed at the same site in the first season's work. Levels 9-16 are "prehistoric" in nature and are the subject of our investigation in the present context. This assemblage represents an aceramic Neolithic culture in the earliest three levels which have yielded vestiges of a sedentary culture represented by houses with walls of packed mud. Pottery makes its appearance only in Level 13. In an earlier study it was claimed that Shimshara fills a gap between the two well known cultures of Jarmo and Hassuna (Braidwood and Howe, 1960:161) but the study of Shimshara material reveals that virtually none of this material is "Hassuna" nor the flints *true* "Jarmo". The cultural assemblage of Shimshara is as follows:

The first settlers of Shimshara lived in mud-walled houses, traces of which were encountered in the earliest level (Level 16) at the site. These were comprised of floors, surrounded by fragmentary rectilinear walls on 3 sides. Towards the north, a wall with semi-circular buttresses was discovered. The walls, preserved to a height of 55·60 cm, had been heavily destroyed by fire. Owing to the limited nature of the dig, it was not possible to determine whether the walls were built of packed mud (*tauf*) or mud-bricks, but the latter seem to be more likely as traces of rectangular mud-slabs were visible in the sections. In Levels 15-14, these structures had stone foundations. That the Level 13 village of Shimshara was destroyed by a heavy fire is proved by the damaged conditions of the objects found on the floors of this level. The intensity of this fire can be gauged by the fact that pieces of bone were found to be calcified, stone objects were seriously cracked and several obsidian blades and implements were partly melted. However, it seems that there is no cultural break in the sequence and the people rebuilt their houses after this extensive damage. Curiously enough, no walls were encountered in Levels 13-9 but floors were traced in almost every level. Immovable storage basins and ovens were found to be built into the floors of Levels 13-12 and Level 9. The ovens have typological resemblances with those discovered at Jarmo and Tepe Guran.

The chipped stone industry was made of flint and obsidian. Most of the material used for flaking was obsidian and less than 15% was flint. A study of the obsidian by Colin Renfrew (in Mortensen, 1970:139-42), reveals that it has been brought from two different sources, one in Eastern Anatolia and the other in the volcanic crater of Nemrut Dağ on Lake Van, more than 300 km northwest of Shimshara. Contrary to this, the flint seems to be local. The principal types recovered include thin and narrow blades with almost parallel sides, flakes, end-of-blade scrapers, and borers. Some of the plain blades have sheen on one or both edges. A few trapezoid microliths and some burins were found in the lower levels. The number and distribution of the above mentioned types throughout the levels represent an unbroken tradition for the chipped stone industry. A unique type of tool is an obsidian dagger with a length of 35·5 cm reported from Level 13 (Mortensen, 1970: Fig. 30). The main features of the Shimshara chipped stone industry are summed up by Mortensen (1970:42-43) in the following words:

The chipped stone industry is based almost entirely on blades, constituting more than 85% of the total bulk of material. It seems that most cores, core fragments, flakes and small chips are débitage left over from the preparation of blades and blade implements. Only very few tools were deliberately made from flakes: 1 borer, 3 scrapers and 9 out of 12 burins. All other implements were based on an excellent blade technique characterized by a preponderance of thin and narrow blades with almost parallel sides. More than a third of the blades are microblades (cf. p. 28), but since geometric microliths were rare at Shimshara (Fig. 33) the industry can hardly be described as microlithic. On the contrary, several implements were prepared on very long blades.

He further observes that the chipped stone industry of Shimshara is

unrelated to the industry found at Hassuna/Samarra sites on the Mesopotamian plain. The material is slightly similar to the Jarmo industry, but the similarity is not so close that we can show a traditional developmental relationship between Jarmo and Shimshara. The resemblance may as well be due to a mutual functional background. (Mortensen, 1970: 46).

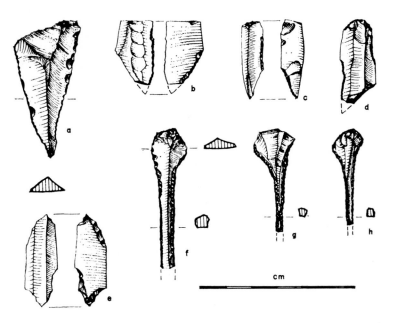

FIG. 47. Shimshara: Chipped tools of obsidian, *a* flake borer; *b-e* blade borers with semi-steep retouch; *f-h* blade borers with steep retouch.

The recovered ground and polished stone industry of Shimshara comprises vessels, ornaments (bracelets, beads, studs and pendants) and
domestic utensils like celts, circular stone discs, polishers, querns and
one specimen of each pestle and hammerstone. Fourteen fragments of
bowls (leaving aside the unidentifiable fragments) representing five main
types, all made of pink or cream coloured marble, have been recorded.
The predominant type is an inverted, truncated, conical form with flaring
rim (Mortensen, 1970:57, Fig. 48). Most of these bowl fragments came
from Level 12 to Level 10 and one specimen each has been reported
from Levels 15-13. No example was recorded from the earliest level.
Since pottery makes its appearance only in Level 13, it seems reasonably
certain that these bowls antedate the discovery of the potter's craft.

Among the personal ornaments discovered were bracelets of white
marble with an average diameter of 7-10 cm and a thickness of 0·8-1·8
cm. These are circular, oval or ovoid in section. They have been reported
from almost every level in the prehistoric assemblage but are predominant in Level 10. A couple of cylindrical beads of pinkish marble
have also been reported. Of these, one comes from Level 15 and the
other is unstratified. Besides these, a small group of studs (one of obsidian, two of white or grey marble, and three of serpentine) have been
recorded. These are confined, however, to the upper three levels of the
prehistoric assemblage. Three pendants, all made of grey or greenish
slate, have been found from the upper three levels. After a comparative
study of similar objects from other earlier and contemporary sites in the
Zagros region, Mortensen observes that while bracelets and bowls show
a close relationship to similar types at Karim Shahir, Jarmo, Guran and
Mohammad Jaffar and Ali Kosh phases in the Deh Luran plain, the studs
or nails have resemblance with later sites such as Hassuna, Matarrah and
Nineveh. This is in perfect accord with the stratigraphic position of
these antiquities at Shimshara itself.

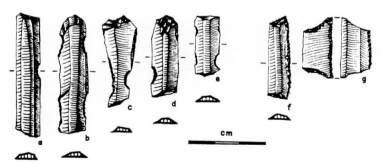

Fig. 48. Shimshara: Chipped stone tools, *a-e* notched blades; *f-g* geometric microliths.

The polished stone celts recorded comprise two main types—i.e. axes with rounded butts and slightly curved sides and adzes with rounded butts and irregularly curved sides. These celts show uneven distribution inasmuch as out of six specimens recorded, five came from Level 13 and the remaining one is unstratified. Other stone objects found include three oval querns with shallow central troughs and an oval grinding slab with two flat smoothed surfaces all coming from the earliest level at the site. Also, one specimen each of a circular hammerstone and a small pebble came from Levels 13 and 10 respectively. Three circular discs made of greyish or greenish slate with diameter of 6-8 cm and thickness of 0·6-0·9 cm were recorded from the earliest level. These were presumably used as spindle whorls. This observation is confirmed by the discovery of a biconical spindle-whorl of terracotta found in Level 9 (Mortensen, 1970:123). It has a height of 2·6 cm and a diameter of 4·3 cm. Mortensen observes that this type is common in the Hassuna period. As well as this, an impression of textile was discovered on the inner side of an undecorated standard ware sherd found on floor 13. An examination of the imprint reveals that the textile was made in plain weave (i.e. a simple over-and-under weave). Impressions of a very fine fabric have also been found on two small clay balls at Jarmo (Braidwood and Howe, 1960:46, 138) and at Çatal Hüyük in southern Anatolia (Mellaart, 1963; Helbaek, 1963).

Fig. 49. Shimshara: Bowl of polished marble.

The yield of bone objects of Shimshara comprises three lancet-shaped
handles made of metacarpus or metatarsus of red deer, all coming from
Level 13. These objects have V-shaped grooves cut into both ends of the
lower edge and Mortensen suggests that these grooves may have been
used for insertion of flint or obsidian blades and that the implements
may have been lancet-shaped knives with two cutting edges, one at each
end. Similar bone handles with grooves have been reported from several
sites but the objects in question are unique in that they have two edges
instead of one. Four bone points, made of red deer split radius, classified
here as awls, have also been recorded. Of these one each came from
Levels 16, 12, 11 and 10. Other bone objects collected include two
small pins, one each from Levels 14 and 10 and a highly polished pendant,
again from Level 10.

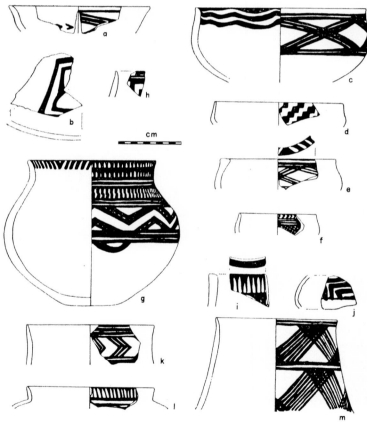

Fig. 50. Shimshara: Samarra Painted Fine Ware, selection of typical vessel shapes.

As noted earlier, the earliest three levels of Shimshara are aceramic and pottery is present only in Levels 13-9. But, like Jarmo, once the art of potting was introduced, it was pursued with full vigour. It may be remarked here that Shimshara pottery is relatively late while nothing earlier than Samarra had been found in the Rania plain so far. Shimshara yielded a variety of Samarra pottery which is related to that of Matarrah and Tell Es-Sawwan. This pottery is divisible into three main types such as coarse ware, standard ware and fine ware. These three groups have been further sub-divided by Mortensen into as many as 11 ceramic industries.

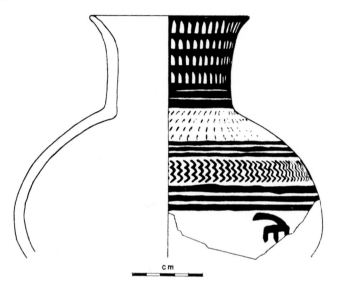

FIG. 51. Shimshara: Samarra Painted-and-incised Standard Ware, collared globular jar.

As noted above, the prehistoric levels at Shimshara were investigated in a very limited area for one field season only. Hence we do not know much about the contemporary flora and fauna or the economic background of the Neolithic communities. However, in the well documented report of the limited archæological material, Mortensen tries to establish the relative chronology of the early village-farming culture of northeastern Mesopotamia. On the basis of ceramic evidence he makes two important observations (Mortensen, 1970:129).

1. Since Samarra ware occurs in Shimshara 13-9, these levels are comparable to the younger part of the Hassuna sequence and to the upper phase of Matarrah.

2. The absence of Halaf ware known from several other sites in the Dokan valley reveals that Shimshara was no longer inhabited when Halaf pottery was introduced in this area.

A few words will follow about the relative chronology of Shimshara and the advent of the ceramic art at this site. True, the origins of Samarra ware are imperfectly understood for the present, however, the stratigraphic position of this ware is well documented at the type-site of Hassuna where it appears only from the middle levels onwards. But at Shimshara, this ware is consistently present from the beginning to the end of the pottery-bearing deposits (Levels 13-9). Thus Mortensen is right in equating this deposit to the younger Hassunan phase. But it seems that the material comparable to the archaic Hassuna is totally absent in the Zagros.

The absolute chronology of Shimshara remains undecided as yet. The four radiocarbon dates from this site (falling between 8080 BC to 5350 BC) are obviously too high (Mortensen, 1970:136, 143-44). However, barring the single date of 8080 BC (K 981) from Level 10, the other three dates show an internal consistency among themselves. Thus while one sample (K 951) from Level 13 gives a date of 5990 BC, the other (K 972) from Level 11 is dated to 5870 BC. The latest Neolithic phase (Level 9) is dated to 5350 BC (K 960). If we take into account the dates from other sites in Deh Luran and Kermanshah regions, and those of Tell Es-Sawwan, then the dates from Shimshara do make sense and perhaps may not be so far removed in time.

Hassuna

Although relics of a culture anterior to most of the well-known historical cultures of northern Mesopotamia were known from the deep soundings of the Nineveh test-shaft as early as 1931-32 (Mallowan, 1933), this assemblage was only placed in a proper chronological scheme by the discovery and excavations at Hassuna, which gives Hassuna culture its name. The prehistoric mound of Hassuna is situated 8 km northeast of Shura and 35 km due south of Mosul and measures 200 by 150 m rising to a height of 7 m. The site was discovered by Sayid Fuad Safar in 1942 and a test-excavation was done in the spring of 1943. A second season of six weeks was carried out in the following spring and a total area of 2500 sq. m (representing approximately one-tenth area of the mound) was investigated (Lloyd and Safar, 1945).

The excavation brought to light a culture-sequence ranging in date from the sixth millennium BC to the Assyrian period. This sequence is divisible into 15 levels (numbered from the bottom upwards), the first two of which represent Hassuna culture. Samarran pottery makes its appearance in Level III and continues in varying proportions up to Level VIII where it merges into the Lower Halaf levels. It is appropriate here to remark that Samarra ware, first identified more than half a century ago on the type-site of Samarra, was believed to represent a distinct culture. However, from the mid-forties it has been argued that the Samarra type of material was neither a "culture" nor an assemblage but "little more than a style of painted pottery" (Braidwood *et al.* 1944:65; Braidwood in Lloyd and Safar, 1945:258-59; Braidwood, 1952: 4; Leslie in Braidwood, 1952:65-66). This argument persisted as late as 1965 when Takey Dabbagh wrote that the so-called Samarran ware is a derivative Hassuna fabric and it "is a ceramic style rather than a ceramic ware". However, the individualistic traits of this ware consistently present throughout the long period of its survival were noted in the Hassuna excavations by Seton Lloyd who observed:

> From the first arrival of the Samarran pottery to its ultimate disappearance there was no perceptible sign of its style or material being in any way in-fluenced by the indigeneous Hassuna potters (Lloyd and Safar, 1945: 261).

The recent excavations by the Iraq Directorate General of Antiquities at Tell Es-Sawwan and at Choga Mami by Oates (1970) have yielded fresh evidence which gives new dimensions to this problem and have forced us to reconsider this issue afresh. The introduction of such new traits as the mud-brick architecture, use of irrigation techniques for the cultiva-tion of grains, a distinct method of the disposal of the dead and above all, the presence of the characteristic pottery—all help to demonstrate that Samarran assemblage represents a separate culture rather than a derivative of the Hassunan complex.

Returning to the consideration of the Hassuna culture, the first settlers of Hassuna, represented in Level Ia and designated "Neolithic" by the excavators, were apparently herdsmen and hunters rather than farmers. In spite of a careful search, no post-holes could be located but it is believed that the people lived in semi-permanent encampments and in the cultural deposit of one metre there is believed to be the existence of three successive camp-sites. Archæological traces of their material culture constitute a sequence of hearths, obsidian lanceheads, sling ammunition, implements for dressing skins and great quantities of animal bones. Large stone celts (termed "handaxes" by the excavators) were presumably used as hoes for breaking the ground. The recovery of sickle blades began in large numbers with the first "adobe" walls. The pottery in-cluded both coarse and burnished ware. Lloyd believes that the whole material of Level Ia should be treated as one distinct assemblage mainly because the succeeding phase witnesses a series of innovations in the way of living. It is being increasingly felt by a number of scholars that there may be a gap between Levels Ia and Ib at Hassuna and as will be seen below, traces of an antecedent culture have been identified in the recent excavations at Umm-Dabaghiyah, 26 km west of Hatra.

The main assemblage, represented in Levels Ib-V, shows a phenomenal improvement in the way of living and is marked by a series of innovations. The settlers were no longer herdsmen and hunters and Hassuna was now a permanent village of an agricultural community. The people lived in adobe* houses and the architecture became more planned and improved in each succeeding level. It is from Level III onwards that one begins to encounter several roomed buildings with walls made of lumps of mud of irregular sizes and the gaps filled with smaller lumps. The wall-faces had been smoothed with plaster and the thickness of the walls varied from 20 to 45 cm. A characteristic feature of the Hassunan houses was the presence of great spherical grain-bins, built of clay, coated outside with bitumen or white gypsum and sunk in the house-floors. No less than 30 grain-bins ranging in diameter from 60 cm to 1·50 m were found in Sounding I. One bin in a house of Level III contained two human skeletons "whose disposition suggested that they had been thrown in the bin without ceremony". The best preserved group of buildings was found in Level IV in which case one almost complete house comprised about 8 rooms grouped around a courtyard. Another house uncovered in Level V consisted of 9 rooms clustered around a central court.

This new period saw a considerable improvement in the potter's art and three ceramic industries, viz. Hassuna Archaic, Hassuna Standard and Samarra ware, are used during this period. The first recordings of ceramic ware seem to be restricted to the lower levels while Samarra Ware occurs from Level III onward. Hassuna Standard ware has been classified, on the basis of its surface decoration, into three sub-classes, viz. Standard painted, incised, and painted-and-incised. Of these, Standard incised is the principal ware and is consistently present in large numbers from Level Ib to Level VI. Standard painted ware makes its appearance in Level Ic but becomes prolific in the succeeding levels. Standard painted-and-incised ware also appears at these levels but is numerically less significant than the first two.

All the Hassuna pottery was handmade and there is no indication of the use of any kind of wheel or *tournette*. The common shapes for all the

*The use of the term "adobe" has been criticised by some scholars. "Adobe" is the Spanish name for mud-brick but the structures of Hassuna are made of packed mud rather than mud-brick.

wares were jars and bowls but "husking trays" (flat-bottomed oval dishes, usually 60 cm long and 40 cm wide, with slightly outward sloping sides, about 15 cm high and with the whole inner surface corrugated with deep grooves) in straw-tempered ware and long "milk-jars" (almost vertical sided oval vessels with lug-handles) again in coarse ware, are the diagnostic pottery-types of the Hassuna culture. The "husking trays" make their appearance in Level II and continue to occur up to the end of the Hassuna occupation. The globular jars with straight necks appear in Level Ic and continue in the later levels.

Among the stone objects recovered from Hassuna, were large polished stone celts found with a heavy coating of bitumen, called by the excavators "hoes". These tools are typical of Hassuna and are mainly found in the camp-site levels. They are missing from Matarrah (except for a solitary specimen) or any other site of this culture. Flint and obsidian tools have been recorded from all the levels of Hassuna deposits. These tools have not been studied in detail but published illustrations indicated that blades and tanged lance-heads of obsidian and arrowheads of chert are confined to Level Ia only. Flint toothed sickles occur in upper levels and a large section of a complete sickle with flakes still set in the original bitumen was found in Room 17 of Level II. Another example of the same type of sickle, but which was better preserved, was noted in Level III. These tools, together with the stone "hoes" and grain bins suggest that Hassunan folk practised agriculture for their subsistence. It is suggested that flour was ground between two flat-sided basalt rubbing stones and bread was baked in clay ovens differing only slightly from the modern Arab *tanour*.

The personal ornaments of the Hassunan folk included beads of shell and turquoise, pendants of limestone and malachite and amulets of limestone. Turquoise, considered to be rare in the early periods in Mesopotamia, has been found in the recent excavations at Tell-Es-Sawwan. Other minerals found in all levels include red ochrous paint, antimony and malachite. Double core shaped spindle-whorls of terracotta occur in all levels and suggest that spinning and weaving was an established industry. Some idea of the religious beliefs of these people can be obtained by their burial practices and the presence of symbolic clay figurines of "mother goddesses". The dead—both adult and children—were buried below the house-floors in the habitation area. A dozen infant burials have been recorded from Level Ib upwards. In one burial in Level II, two infants were found buried in a tall sided incised bowl. The skeletal remains of these infants were examined by Aziz and Jaroslav (1966) who believe that the two individuals were of identical age and both of female sex. The mode of burial in one jar indicates that death was simultaneous and the individuals were probably twins. Some of the infants were provided with small drinking cups placed by the side of the dead body. The adults were buried in a fully contracted position with the head towards the north and no grave-goods. Such a burial was found beneath the floor of Room 6 in Level Ic and another adult skeleton was found in the first camp-site (Level Ia). Three human skulls from this site were examined by Coon (1950) who observes that the remains represent rather heavy boned, prognathus and large-toothed Mediterraneans and they fit into the same racial category as the Eridu crania. Not many "mother goddess" figurines were recovered but an unbaked mother goddess figurine (Lloyd and Safar, 1945: pl. XVIII, 2) is remarkable for its skilful modelling.

The animal bones collected from Hassuna have not been studied fully as yet but a preliminary examination indicated the presence of toad, rat or similar animal, ox, ass, sheep and/or goat, wild pig, hare and possibly gazelle (Lloyd and Safar, 1945:284). A radiocarbon sample from Level V (W 660), is dated to 5090±200 BC on the Libby half-life. Another sample from Level Ia (W 609) is clearly out of context (Rubin and Corrinne, 1960:182-83).

Umm Dabaghiyah

Before examining other sites of the Hassuna/Samarra complex, mention must be made of the recent work at Umm Dabaghiyah which has yielded remains of a seemingly partly antecedent culture, previously unknown. This small agricultural settlement is situated in a marginal farming area, 26 km west of Hatra in the north-central Jazira. The settlement measures 100 by 85 m and has a depth of just under 4 m. Thirteen squares, each of 5 m, were opened by Kirkbride (1972). Three of them were carried down in part to bed-rock and remains of 12 building phases were recorded. The earliest settlers of Umm Dabaghiyah lived in houses made of packed mud or *tauf* without stone foundations and the front walls were covered with plaster, and sometimes painted red. The structures of Phases 12 (basal) and 11 were of irregular curving plan and small, single-roomed but rectangular buildings are seen in the upper phases.

The pottery from the earliest phases (12-5) seems to be of better quality, better fired and tempered than that of the later period. This pottery was chaff or straw-tempered and primitive throughout and all the vessels were hand-made by the coil-technique. The slip, usually cream or whitish, was used for the medium and finer wares. The pottery has burnished, painted, incised and applied decoration with shapes including high-sided bowls, "double ogee" of Hassuna Ia and plain husking trays. Two sherds of the proper husking-trays were found in the later levels.

FIG. 52. Umm Dabaghiyah: Two rectangular houses. Copyright: Diana Kirkbride.

The chipped stone industry recorded is made of flint and obsidian, the former in far larger proportions than the latter; no less than 3400 pieces were counted, the majority of which were débitage. The types found include fine blades, sickle-blades with sheen, borers made on both flakes and blades, end-scrapers, small flake scrapers and blade cores. Side-blow blade-flakes, all of obsidian, are relatively scarce finds in the lower levels but increase from Phase 4 upwards. They are noted at Jarmo and Hassuna. A few arrowheads were recovered and these are similar to those at Byblos (Ancien) and Ramad II. None of the hoes, characteristic of Hassuna Ia, have been found present at this site.

The small finds of Dabaghiyah include well made bone tools consisting of awls, points and spatula. Spindle-whorls, pot-lids, basket linings and mortars—all of gypsum—and grinders of both gypsum and hard sandstone have been recorded. Axe-heads made of various hard stones like

a

b

c

Fig. 53. Umm Dabaghiyah: Three vessels of "double ogee" type. Copyright: Diana Kirkbride.

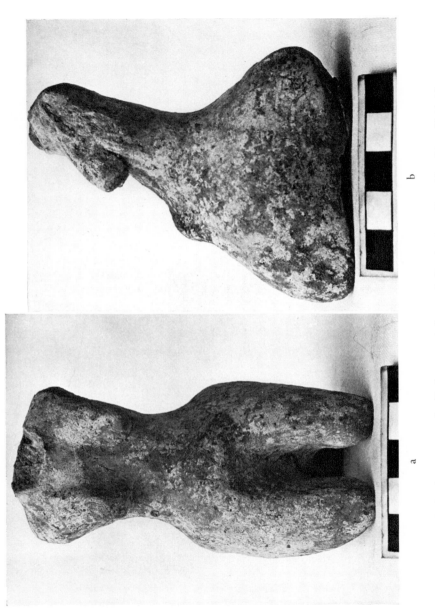

a   b

Fig. 54. Umm Dabaghiyah: Terracotta female figurine, (a) front and (b) side view. Copyright: Diana Kirkbride.

basalt occur and baked clay missiles with a point at each end were recorded in large numbers. Record of a single bead of dentalium points to trade connections with the Mediterranean coast rather than the Gulf. Noteworthy finds include three female figurines, all incomplete and coming from below Phase 5. A considerable number of animal bones were found throughout all the levels and plant impressions have been found on a mud-brick pavement of Phase 5. The excavator believes that Umm Dabaghiyah resembles the early cultures represented by Hassuna Ia, Gird Ali Agha, basal Matarrah and Thalthat-2 Levels XV and XVI. She observes that the culture takes us back a step earlier into the antecedents of Hassuna, but this remains to be proved in another season's work. In a recent study of the plant remains from Umm Dabaghiyah, Helbaek (1972b) has identified grains of emmer, einkorn, naked barley and hulled barley and concludes that agriculture was practised at this site. Umm Dabaghiyah is not an isolated site in the Jazira as in an exploration of 87 sites in this area, as many as 40 were found to be Hassuna/Samarra.

Yarim Tepe

Recently another prehistoric settlement with typical Hassunan pottery and antiquities has been excavated by Russian archæologists at Yarim Tepe, situated about 7 km southwest of Tell Afar (Mosul province) on the banks of the little river 'Ibra (Merpert and Munchajev, 1969). The site consists of six mounds of different sizes, three each on either bank of the river. Of these, mound N3 is the biggest and it measures 250 m in diameter and rises to a height of 9 m. However, the Hassunan assemblage has been exposed on mound N1 which is about 130 m in diameter and 4·50 m in height, and is located on the eastern bank of the river. In all, 750 sq. m area of the mound was investigated in March-May 1969 and the total deposit of 6 m is divisible into eight occupation levels which essentially represent one culture i.e. Hassuna. This culture covers an area of 1·5 h at this site.

The excavators exposed more than an hundred rooms of the Hassuna culture. Their size varies from 3·50 m by 3·00 m to 1·50 m by 1 m. They found some single-roomed houses but multi-roomed houses were more frequent. The biggest house recovered measured 14 m by 6 m. The houses, situated very close to each other, were divided by narrow, long passages or streets. The rooms had clay walls but the use of unbaked bricks in upper levels has been suspected. The floors were made of rammed clay and domed ovens of '*tanour*' type, 70 to 80 cm in diameter, have been noticed.

The pottery from Yarim Tepe closely resembles that from Hassuna itself. Hassuna Standard with the three familiar techniques of decoration, incision, painting and combined painting-and-incision, is the main ceramic industry. The types recorded include big storage jars, round, or flat-bottomed open bowls, jars, jugs and goblets. The find of interest is a tetrapod—one of the first in a Hassuna ceramic complex (Merpert and Munchajev, 1969: 128). Samarra pottery, with its specific style of painting occurs mixed with the main Hassuna levels but becomes prolific in the upper strata. Stone and gypsum vessels are also found to be present.

The yield for the ground stone industry includes grinding stones, mortars and polished hammer-stones, while the chipped stone industry is made of flakes, blades and broken cores of flint and obsidian. It is important to note that flint is an uncommon find at Yarim Tepe while obsidian is more abundant. Bone implements included needles, polishers and handles. Spindle-whorls, sling pellets and 16 human figurines representing standing women with high long coiffure, elongated eyes, thin waist and wide hips, complete the terracotta inventory. Among the personal ornaments recovered were two big flat beads of chalcedony and a large pebble bead. Two clay cover discs with loops on the back and regular incisions on the surface have been taken to be primitive seals. This observation is strengthened by the fact that a seal of red stone with some incised lines on the surface and a loop on the back, was found in room 77 (Level V). The excavated animal bones comprise bones of wild pig, large wild bull, gazelle, domestic pig, goat and sheep. The site also yielded bones of domestic cow.

The succeeding culture at Yarim Tepe is Halafian identified on Mound 2. After a cultural break of several centuries, the site was again inhabited for a short period during Sassanian times.

Matarrah

Another settlement basically of Samarra culture (earlier claimed to be a somewhat impoverished southern variant of the normal Hassunan assemblage) has been located at Matarrah, situated 34 km south of Kirkuk and about 3 km west of the Baghdad-Kirkuk road. The mound is roughly ovoid in plan, about 200 m in diameter and rising to a height of 8 m; only the upper half represents occupational debris, the lower half being a small natural hill. The site was tested by Braidwood and his team (Braidwood, Braidwood, Smith and Leslie, 1952) in March-April, 1948. Fourteen trenches were dug and more than 200 sq. m of the settlement was investigated. Vestiges of the Samarra culture, with a poor representation of the Hassunan assemblage at the base, were recovered. The cultural deposit of 4 m has been sub-divided into two phases; viz. upper phase and lower phase. The upper phase is marked by the appearance of Samarra ware which forms the basis of this classification.

A careful perusal of the Matarrah report reveals that no architecture of the lower phase could be recorded but a house of operation IX, first floor, consisted of 4 to 6 rooms with walls of packed mud or *tauf*. Stratigraphically, they are assignable to the upper sub-phase (Samarra ware phase). Another house in the second floor of the same cutting and assignable to the same sub-phase, had 4 rooms, the largest of which measured 3·5 by 2 m; the smallest being 2 m by 1 m only. The houses had horse-shoe shaped ovens, constructed of clay.

The ceramic wares of Matarrah have been classified by Leslie as coarse simple ware, fine simple ware and Samarra ware. Such characteristic shapes as the "husking trays" have been identified in the first two wares. A few proper "milk jars" of Hassuna type and large jars with shoulders low on the body (erroneously called "milk-jars" in the original report: *cf.* Braidwood and Howe, 1960:36), are fairly common discoveries in these wares. All the pottery was hand-made. Among the small antiquities recovered were 199 sling missiles with an average size of 54 x 31 mm; 46 spindle-whorls of biconical shape; a single clay scraper, a long tubular bead and an anthropomorphic female figurine from the surface—all made of terracotta.* Animal figurines are found to be more numerous. Two clay nails and a knob-like object were also recorded.

The chipped stone industry yield of Matarrah was comparatively poor and included 722 pieces of flint and 94 pieces of obsidian representing about 40 % of the total excavated material.† Of these, only 5 % of the tools had definite retouch. Sickle blades, identified by their glossy sheen, are found and have a coating of bitumen. Other tools included 3 borers, 1 knife and some blades—all of flint. The only type found in obsidian was a simple blade, other pieces being waste chips. Like the chipped stones, the ground stone industry is poorly represented. The discoveries comprised a solitary celt, a large hoe-like implement, some large mortars and globular rubbers, 2 borers and 6 stone nails. An important addition from Matarrah is a collection of 40 stone beads, most of which came from the upper sub-phase. These are made of limestone, chalcedony, calcareous shale, carnelian and soapstone. A complete necklace was found in association with a burial. Twelve beads of shell and four beads of bone were also found. The bone industry included awls, needles and gauges.

---

*This number represents only the half of the antiquities which are in the possession of the Oriental Institute, Chicago.
†The remainder 40% of the pieces are in Baghdad and 20% of the material was left at the site itself.

As at Hassuna, the dead were buried in the habitation area, under the house-floors, but most of the excavated burials are ascribable to the upper level (Samarra level). The adults were buried in flexed position with offerings but unlike Hassuna, a newly-born infant was found in a grave-pit instead of a burial jar. A multiple burial contained the remains of four individuals. The bones had been dismembered and thrown into the pit without any orientation. A radiocarbon sample (W 623) is dated to 5620 ± 250 BC on the Libby half-life (Rubin and Corrinne, 1960:182-3).

Nineveh

Before proceeding to examine the newly-excavated Samarran material from Tell Es-Sawwan and Choga Mami, it is appropriate to review the assemblages from other Hassunan settlements known before the excavations at the type-site in 1943-44. The pottery and other published antiquities from these sites have been studied by Perkins (1949: fifth printing, 1968) who has tried to build up a comparative stratigraphy for prehistoric northern Mesopotamia. The most important site with pre-Halaf pottery is Nineveh, situated not far from Mosul. A pit measuring approximately 20 m by 16 m was dug to a depth of 27·5 m on the northwestern side of the temple. The assemblage which is comparable to the Hassuna culture is Ninevite 1 (lowermost phase) and Ninevite 2 (which is sub-divided into 3 sub-phases, IIa, IIb and IIc. Of these, Levels IIa and IIb belong to the Hassuna period). Due to the limited nature of the dig no traces of architecture were found but hut-settlements have been noted in Nin-1. The same type of architecture continues in Nin-2 which is, in fact, a continuation of the earlier phase. The first trace of stone walling appears in Nin-3 and loose burnt bricks are met with in Nin-4, both phases belonging to the post-Hassuna context. The major industry, furnishing data for correlation with other sites, is pottery. Ninevite 1 ware recorded includes painted wares, incised pottery, incised-and-painted ware and burnished wares. The main shapes recovered are bowls with variants (high necked deep bowl with wide mouth, squat bowls with straight or everted rims and deep bowls with incurving sides) and flat, wide-mouthed dishes. Similarities with Samarra ware are found present in the succeeding Nin-2 phase. Seven types, common to the Samarran pottery occur at Nineveh and many characteristic designs accompanying these shapes, are also found there.

The excavated material culture of Hassunan phase comprises implements of flint and obsidian, ground stone axes, bone implements, spindle whorls of baked clay and terracotta human figurines. The principal shapes found in flint tools are flakes, scrapers, knives and blades with serrated edges. A number of blades bear traces of bitumen—a fact also recorded from other sites. Obsidian is found present in sizable quantity but is not as common as flint. Mallowan believes it to be of Vannic origin (Mallowan, 1933:143). Ground axe heads or celts of serpentine, diorite and hard sandstone are fairly common finds. Hemispherical, circular and biconical spindle whorls, decorated with incised nickings, are recovered in good number. An important element, perhaps a survival from the earlier stone-working tradition of Jarmo, is the presence of one or two fragments of exceedingly hard sandstone bowls in Nin-1 and fragments of alabaster are reported from Nin-2. Bone implements are common at Nineveh and several specimens of awls and needles have been recorded from Nin-2 and Nin-3 levels. Terracotta figures include a headless human figure from Nin-2 and several examples of miniature clay dogs.

Tall Arpachiyah

Another prehistoric site is Tall Arpachiyah, a small compact mound rising to a height of 5 m, about 6 km from the Tigris river in Mosul Liwa. The settlement covers an area of 67 m in diameter but how much of it was occupied in prehistoric times is not known. Excavations conducted in 1933 (Mallowan and Rose, 1935) revealed the existence of 10 building levels numbered from the top downward. The analysis of ceramic data and other antiquities leads the excavators to conclude that the main pre-historic culture represented here is Halaf but pottery-sherds comparable to those of Nin-1 were found below the lowest building level (TT-10). Mallowan suspects the existence of at least five more occupation levels below this point. Numerous celts and many thousand flint and obsidian knives and scrapers have been recorded from the bottom of the well in TT-10. An important feature at Arpachiyah is that obsidian is as common as flint,* although it is a much rarer find at Nineveh, not very far from Arpachiyah. Mallowan remarks that no examples of Samarra ware were found in the lowest levels which antedate TT-10 at this site.

Chagar Bazar

Some non-Halaf pottery was found in association with the Halaf assemblage at the base of the impressive mound of Chagar Bazar, situated 25 km due south of 'Amuda and 40 km southwest of Kamichlie in the drainage basin of the Khabur river in Syria. A test-pit was sunk by Mallowan in 1934-35 (Mallowan, 1936) at the northwestern end of the

*Dr. Joan Oates informs me that there are large quantities of obsidian at all Halaf sites.

mound and natural soil was struck at a depth of 15 m. Once again no level belonging wholly to the pre-Halaf horizon could be distinguished and Halaf pottery was recorded from the earliest settlement. The non-Halaf pottery comprised sherds of burnished black ware and rough incised ware. Diagnostic Hassuna traits are absent here but the presence of burnished pottery together with some Samarran sherds* indicate an overlap with the Samarra culture. However, Perkins, while agreeing with Mallowan that the first settlement belongs to the Halaf period, remarks that the "non-Halaf wares may perhaps represent an earlier deposit, made by semi-nomadic peoples wandering in the area" (Perkins, 1968:12). A similar situation prevails at Tell Halaf also in the Khabur drainage basin and at Tepe Gawra near Arpachiyah. At the former site, a thick-walled and badly fired pottery has been found in the pre-Halaf levels and the existence of such a deposit has been suspected at the latter site (Perkins, 1968:13).

Baghouz

Perhaps it is well to remember that Samarra pottery has been recorded from as far west as Baghouz, a small settlement on the Mesopotamian bank of the Euphrates, near Abu Kemal in Syria, at a distance of 275 km west of the type-site of Samarra. This oval mound, measuring 100 x 60 m and with a cultural deposit of 2 m was tested in a 25 m long and 2 m wide trench by Du Mesnil Du Buisson (1948), Associate Director of the Yale expedition at Dura-Europos. Mud-brick architecture and knives of tabular flint together with blades of obsidian have been reported. These are associated circumstantially with typical Samarra pottery. A collection of 53 sherds from this site has been studied by Braidwood and his associates (Braidwood, Braidwood, Tulane and Perkins, 1944) who have presented a master-chart of the painted motifs on the Samarra pottery.

Tell Es-Sawwan

The prehistoric settlement of Tell Es-Sawwan (Mound of Flints) is situated on the eastern bank of the Tigris, 11 km downstream of Samarra. It comprises 3 mounds (mounds A, B, and C; mound B being the highest) covering an ovoid area of 230 m from north to south and 110 m from east to west. The extant height of the mound is 3·5 m above the surrounding plain. As early as 1911 its importance was realised by Herzfeld. It was

*Ann Perkins does not agree with the identification of these sherds as "Samarra Ware" by Mallowan (cf. Perkins, 1968: 11).

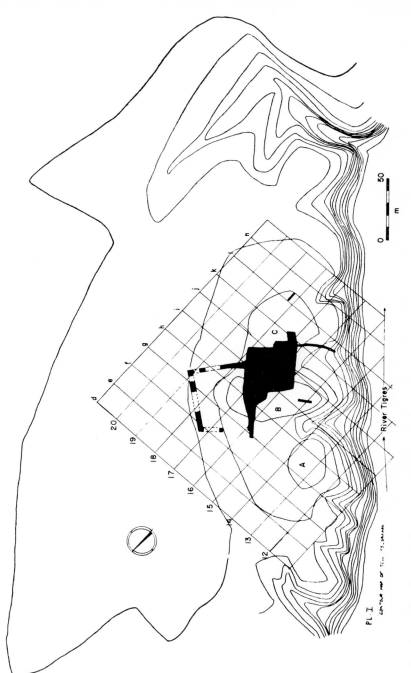

Pl. I

CONTOUR MAP OF TELL ES-SAWWAN

Fig. 55. Tell Es-Sawwan: Contour map of the mound.

later inspected by the Directorate of Antiquities, Iraq, in 1948 and work was started by Al-Soof in 1964 which lasted for 6 field seasons*. The prehistoric squence at Tell Es-Sawwan is divisible into five main building levels,† all belonging to the Samarran culture. Level III (numbered from bottom upward) has been divided into two sub-phases :‡ A and B. The upper sub-phase (IIIB) is characterised by the widespread use of *juss*. The material culture of the Es-Sawwan people, as can be reconstructed on the basis of the preliminary reports, is described below.

The first settlers of Es-Sawwan were Samarran folk who lived in permanent houses with walls made of moulded mud-bricks (*libn*) and plastered over with mud. Well preserved walls of large rectangular bricks resting on the virgin soil have been found in a trench on Mound C. Two large architectural units with a notably regular ground plan and separated by a lane, have been discovered. Of these one unit comprises as many as 14 rooms and probably more than one courtyard. Similar architecture is seen in the succeeding level (Level II). The houses of Level III are probably smaller and some new features have been noted, such as external buttresses at junctions of the walls and three circular grain bins or silos made of gypsum and with a diameter of 1-2 m. A noteworthy feature of this level is the discovery of a defence system, previously unknown in any other contemporary or earlier site in Iraq. The defences constituted an artificial ditch, 2·5 m wide and 3 m deep, cut into the natural conglomerate and enclosing three sides of Mound B. This ditch was traced in 5 trenches. It was dominated on its inside by a thick buttressed mud-brick wall. The stratigraphic position of this ditch and the wall is not clear. It has been claimed that it was excavated during an early phase of Level I and that it remained open during the subsequent two levels. The massive buttressed wall lining the ditch on the perimeter of Mound B was investigated by Al-Soof in the fourth season who concludes that it

*A summary report of each field season's work has been presented by El-Wailley (1963-67) and Salman (1969). Preliminary reports of the first four seasons' work have been presented by El-Wailley and Al-Soof (1965), Al-A'dami (1968), Wahida (1967) and Al-Soof (1968) respectively. The chipped stones of the upper 2 levels have been studied by Al-Tekriti (1968) and the animal remains of Level III have been examined by Flannery and Wheeler (1967). Carbonised grains and seeds discovered in 1964 have been studied by Helbaek (1964) who draws important conclusions about the economy of the people.
†There has been some confusion in the numbering of these levels. In the first two seasons, these levels were numbered from bottom upward but in the third season's dig, the order was reversed and these were renumbered from the top downward. Hence Level V became Level I (Wahida, 1967: 168, 1968: 58). The original method of numbering was resumed again by Al-Soof (1968: 4) in the fourth season. In the present work, we have followed the method of numbering from bottom upward and consequently Level I here would mean the earliest deposit and Level V, the latest.
‡Al-Soof (1968:10) suspects an additional sub-phase in Level III.

was originally constructed in the first phase (A) of Level III and was subsequently reinforced in places and sometimes coated with *juss*.

The architectural remains of Level IV comprise two types of buildings: i.e. private houses, and some large structures claimed to have been granaries though this is not universally accepted. These structures were made of mud-bricks measuring 60 to 100 cm in length, 30 to 34 cm in width and 6 to 9 cm thickness. The average size of the mud-bricks was approximately 80 by 30 by 8 cm. A class of buildings excavated during the third and fourth seasons, on the northeastern side of the mound has been claimed to be granaries. But a number of agricultural implements such as querns, pestles, part of a sickle consisting of 4 flint blades stuck together with bitumen, flint sling balls and unworked pebbles found in these buildings suggest them to be ordinary residential houses rather than granaries. This area was surrounded by a mud-brick wall which was probably built in Level III and was in use during the following level. Again, a T-shaped building uncovered in the second season is believed to have been constructed for religious purposes, or as a temple, but this building is the same as others in Levels III and IV. Structures of the last phase (Level V) have largely been washed away by constant erosion but a group of four rooms belonging to a single building have been excavated. As in the preceding levels, the walls are made of sun-dried bricks (*libn*), and the floor was paved with a thin layer of gypsum. This plastering covered the extant portions of the walls which stand to a height of 5 to 10 cm. Like those in the preceding phase, four circular basins, made of gypsum with an average diameter of 70 cm, were discovered but these were found to be empty.

The pottery of Es-Sawwan is not fully published but that of the upper two levels has been studied by Wahida (1967, 172) and it comprises a number of ceramic wares such as coarse ware, semi-coarse ware, plain ware, incised, painted, and painted-incised wares. The designs, where present, comprise the familiar Samarran motifs. Hassuna standard wares are absent in both these levels and in general from the whole site. There is only a very small amount of genuine Hassuna pottery—some painted and some incised; but 73 Halaf sherds have been reported from this deposit.

The stone artefacts include a disc-shaped polisher, 2 celts of black stone and some small balls—all coming from the uppermost level. Other objects recovered comprise a large number of querns, flint sickles, polishers, pestles or pounders, hoes and hammers, and sling bullets. Flint and obsidian tools of the upper two levels have been studied by Al-Tekriti (1968) who observes that the flint industry was confined to the manufacture of small blade tools. However, such other types as borers, scrapers and points have also been reported although in small numbers.

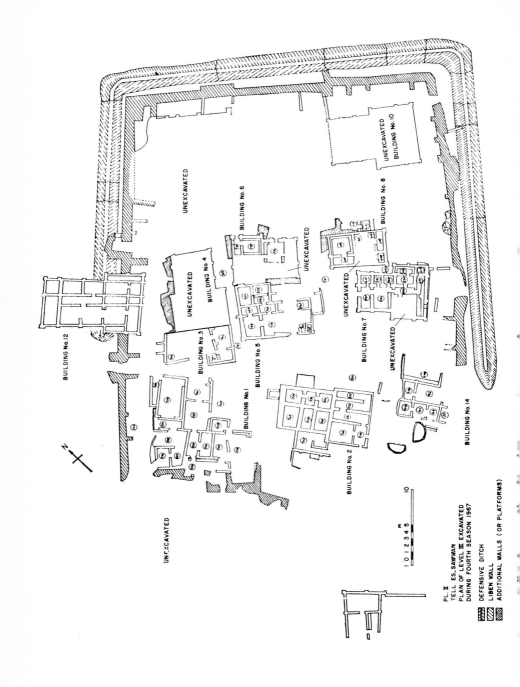

PL. II
TELL ES-SAWWAN
PLAN OF LEVEL III EXCAVATED
DURING FOURTH SEASON 1967

▨ DEFENSIVE DITCH
▨ LIBEN WALL
▨ ADDITIONAL WALLS (OR PLATFORMS)

BUILDING No.12

BUILDING No.4

BUILDING No.6

BUILDING No.3

BUILDING No.1

BUILDING No.5

BUILDING No.8

BUILDING No.7

BUILDING No.10

BUILDING No.2

BUILDING No.14

UNEXCAVATED

UNEXCAVATED

UNEXCAVATED

UNEXCAVATED

UNEXCAVATED

UNEXCAVATED

m
10 1 2 3 4 5   10

The last named tool-type has been further classified into straight points, shouldered points and curved points which are somewhat similar to the drill points found at Shanidar cave. Other types recorded include backed blades and sickle blades with sheen. The blade industry is found to be present in obsidian but the tendency towards re-chipping and re-using the same tools indicates that the supply of obsidian was limited at Es-Sawwan. Bone tools found in the upper levels were awls. Two dentalium beads found in the third season imply contact with the Arabian Gulf.

Among the characteristic antiquities of Es-Sawwan, was a large collection of bowls and statuettes made of alabaster, mostly found in association with child-burials in Level I. Some of them are exquisitely carved and show a high degree of workmanship. Other finds include stamp seals in baked clay found in the fourth season. They are engraved with parallel and intersected lines. A flat, oblong seal of black stone, with intersected incisions was found in the fifth season. These are amongst the earliest seals discovered in Mesopotamia and are comparable with those obtained from Hassuna and Yarim Tepe. Among the terracotta figures of interest is a squatting male with a pronounced sexual organ found in the second season.

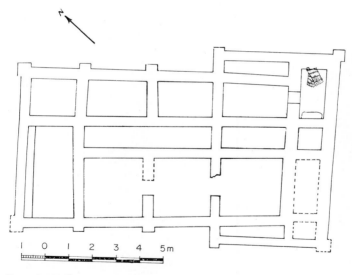

Fig. 57. Tell-Es Sawwan: Temple (?) Level IV.

An important addition to our knowledge is the reported occurrence of copper at Es-Sawwan. Three beads and a small natural piece of copper were found on the floor of building No. 3 in Level II and a very small

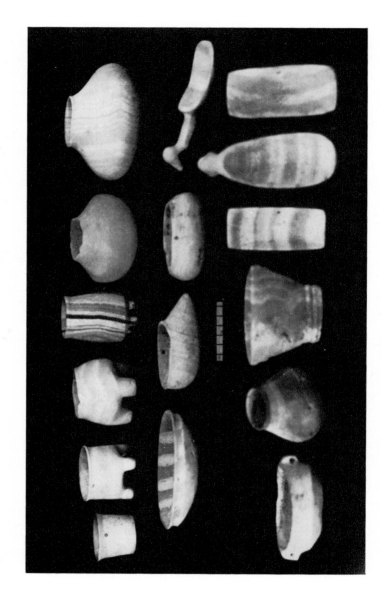

Fig. 58. Tell Es-Sawwan: Stone vessels and statuettes found in various graves.

knife with a hole bored at one end was discovered from Level I (earliest) inside a grave in Room 142 (El Wailley and Al-Soof, 1965:28; Al-A'dami, 1968:59). A large number of burials, both of children and adults, have been uncovered at this site. One hundred and thirty burials of the earliest phase, comprising remains mostly of infants, more rarely of adults, were discovered in the first season. These graves contained offerings in pottery vessels together with statuettes, and alabaster vessels, carnelian and turquoise beads and flint blades etc. An unusually large number of infant burials were discovered under buildings 3 and 4 in the second season. This has led the excavators to believe that these were perhaps "mortuary buildings" (Al A'dami, 1968). These buildings did not yield any household debris or agricultural implements—a fact which supports the above hypothesis.

The practice of burial under house-floors was continued in the succeeding phase and 16 Samarran graves were exposed by Al-Soof (1968) in the fourth season. The adults were buried in ovoid pits in the fully contracted position on the right side, with the head to the east, facing north. In one case the entire body was wrapped with matting and coated with bitumen. The deceased were provided with offerings in pottery bowls placed under the head. Children were buried in globular jars or in wide, shallow bowls. A study of the animal bones and carbonised grains and seeds from this site, has considerably helped in the reconstruction of the economy of the people. The Samarran folk at Es-Sawwan practised a mixed economy based on simple irrigated agriculture, herding and hunting. Great masses of osteological remains were obtained during the first, fourth and fifth seasons. In a preliminary study, Bökönyi (in Al-Soof, 1968:15) has identified bones of birds, fish, hare, rodent, wolf, onager, fallow deer, gazelle, aurochs and domestic sheep and goat. Of these, sheep, goat and gazelle played an important part in the economy. Fish constituted a significant proportion of the diet during Level III. Animal bones of this level have been studied by Flannery and Wheeler (1967) who have identified domestic sheep and goat, ox, gazelle, fallow deer, wild cat, fish and mussels.

Small deposits of carbonised grains and seeds found in the moat were examined by Helbaek (1964) who has identified emmer, einkorn, and bread wheat; six-row naked barley, six-row and two-row hulled barley; goat-face grass and linseed. The presence and size of the linseed at this site leads Helbaek to argue (1964:47) that irrigation was practised. He observes:

Judging from Tell Es-Sawwan's nearness to the river we may take it that some sort of irrigation was employed, an assumption that is supported by the presence and size of the linseed which cannot be grown in such a climate without artificial watering. But on the other hand, the poor size of the cereal grains makes it improbable that regular canalization was instituted at the time. Most probably agriculture was conducted on the basis of the seasonal flood of the river, spill pools were exploited, run-off checked in favourable spots by primitive damming—generally the activities which we may visualise as the forerunners of the later full-fledged canal irrigation.

The chronology of Es-Sawwan is based on three radiocarbon dates. Thus while one sample (P 855) from the earliest level gives a date of 5506 ± 73 BC, two samples (P 856, P 857) from Level III have been dated to 5349 ± 86 BC and 4858 ± 82 BC respectively on the Libby half-life (El-Wailley and Al Soof, 1965: 19).

Choga Mami

Proceeding southeast from Es-Sawwan, one encounters a number of Samarran sites in the region northeast of Baghdad. Surface exploration of well over 50 sites near Mandali in Diyala Liwa and Badra in Kut Liwa by Oates (1966a, b) resulted in the discovery of several Samarran sites. An earlier assemblage is represented at Tamerkhan, situated just north of Mandali, which yielded surface material comprising ground stone tools, flint tools and pottery, comparable to the assemblages of Jarmo, Sarab*, Guran and Ali Kosh. The second group of sites include Choga Mami and Serik Kabir, located within 2 km of Tamerkhan. These yielded Samarra, Hajji Muhammad and later Ubaid style pottery together with one Hassuna sherd and flint implements resembling those from Jarmo. Recent excavations at Choga Mami (Oates, 1969a, c, d) revealed, among other things, remains of a true Samarran village with four building levels, adding further weight to the hypothesis that the Samarran assemblage may represent a separate culture rather than a variant of Hassuna. Oates observes that Hassuna is essentially a culture of the rainfed northern plain, while Samarra flourished as a culture in its own right on the fringes of the alluvium (1969d:134-35). The site is situated on the edge of the rainfall zone and provides a meeting-ground for northern and southern pottery traditions i.e. Samarra Ware from the north and Hajji Muhammad ware from the south, the latter though in limited quantity. The excavation has furnished evidence of canal irrigation at such an early date, its existence already postulated on the basis of the presence of certain types of grain at Tell Es-Sawwan. Choga Mami has also produced a new class of

*Braidwood believes that this collection is certainly earlier than the Sarab inventory (Oates, 1966a: 4).

terracotta human figurines, hitherto unknown from the early cultures of Mesopotamia.

The large neolithic village of Choga Mami, representing the eastern limit of Samarran settlements, covers an area of 350 by 150 m and rises to a height of 2 to 5 m. Excavations conducted between December 1967 and February 1968 uncovered the remains of four building levels numbered from the top downwards. As at Sawwan the first settlers lived in permanent houses made of cigar-shaped mud-bricks 60-90 cm in length and 12-18 cm in diameter. The walls were coated with mud-plaster. A house of the earliest levels comprised as many as 12 rooms, all of small size, measuring 1·50-2 m in length. This house had massive buttressed walls, a feature also noticed at Es-Sawwan. A high-necked incised jar, buried in the floor of Room 7 in this house contained fragmentary remains of an infant burial. The structures of the succeeding level (Level II) were similar to those described above and impressions of a large quantity or reed matting and tiny rectangular compartments measuring 2·15 m by 0·15 m were presumably used as storage bins. Structures of the last building phase (Level I) are not so well-preserved and have virtually disappeared in some portions of the mound due to soil-erosion. However, a few relatively thin and fragmentary walls, ascribable to this period, have been noted.

The pottery of Choga Mami is divisible into two categories. The first is Samarra ware found in the earliest levels at the site. It is associated with a wide variety of incised pottery together with plain and coarse wares and burnished pottery which is less common but occurs in all levels. The normal Samarra painted ware is well finished and tempered with grit. This ware closely compares with Samarra pottery from Es-Sawwan, Hassuna, Matarrah and Baghouz. Associated with this assemblage are a large number of rather unusual ceramic objects, termed "ladles". They consist of a small cup, usually with a wide, shallow longitudinal groove and a long tapering handle. Most of these are painted. These objects continued to occur in the transitional phase as well.

The next group of pottery which is stratigraphically later than the classical Samarra ware is termed "Transitional pottery". Commenting upon this, Oates (1969a:137) remarks:

> It seems not unreasonable to suggest that this pottery does actually represent some as yet undefined transitional stage between the classical Samarra repertoire, which it follows without break, and the early Ubaid materials in the south. In actual fabric and general appearance the obvious connections are with al-Ubaid 2, Hajji Muhammad, but on specific analogies the closest affinities would appear to lie with the earlier Eridu ceramic. I have already

(b)

(a)

Fig. 59.   Choga Mami: *a–d* Terracotta heads of the Samarra period.

←(c)

(d) ↓

felt that there exists some generic link between Samarra and Eridu and Choga Mami seems to represent one of the intermediate stages in this, perhaps collateral development.

Five Hajji Muhammad sherds have been recorded from the latest transitional levels at the site.

The chipped stone industry recorded is made of flint and obsidian. Of these, flint is predominant and accounts for 90% of the tools while obsidian represents the remaining 10%. The yield of common tool-types includes sickle blades and awls or drills. The sickle blades have silica gloss on their edges and 60% of them retain traces of bitumen used for hafting. The workmanship of these tools seems to be superior to that of Matarrah and some awls or drills compare with those at Jarmo. The ground stone tools recovered include a number of rubbers, pounders, grinders, mortars and querns. Like Matarrah, celts are rare and only 2 specimens were recorded. One ground stone sickle and one possible hoe or chopping tool were found in the Samarran levels.

As noted above, Choga Mami yielded a new class of terracotta human figurines. These are mostly depicted standing with the hands at the waist. They have large buttocks and exaggerated feet. They are found mostly in fragmentary condition and the excavator observes that the different limbs were modelled separately and were subsequently joined together with a surface slip. The head was attached to the body on a cylindrical peg-like neck. These figurines are elaborately decorated and the facial ornaments usually consist of two nose plugs and a single lip plug at the right side of the mouth. Some figurines have three vertical strokes on either cheek which presumably indicate tattooing. Their typical features are the "coffee-bean" eyes sometimes with attractively painted eye-lashes and the scalloped hair-line. Some bird-like examples have elongated head-dresses, reminiscent of the much more stylised "lizard headed" Ubaid figurines from Ur and Eridu (Oates, 1969c) but they differ radically from the majority of terracotta figurines found at the otherwise comparable site of Es-Sawwan. Other clay objects found at Choga Mami include small studs of various shapes from both Samarran and post-Samarran levels. A large number of clay beads have been recorded. They are round, pearshaped, oblong, biconical, conical and cylindrical in shape. Some of the round and biconical examples were covered with red ochre. Other personal objects recovered from various levels at the site include 55 circular beads of shell, a marble pendant, a pendant and a toggle each of chalcedony and one ground obsidian amulet. Bone tools recorded comprise 10 awls, 2 gauges, 2 spatulæ, and 2 needles. Five cowrie-shell beads were also recorded but dentalium shells, which are

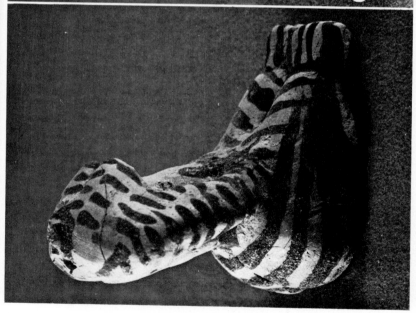

Fig. 60. Choga Mami: A seated female figure, 7 cm high.

common at Sawwan, are conspicuous by their absence at Choga Mami.

Preliminary study of the faunal remains from Choga Mami shows that domesticated sheep, goat, pig and dog are present in the Samarran level. An important addition to our knowledge is that domesticated cattle are definitely present though rare (Oates, 1969a:140). Bones of wild animals like roe-deer, fallow-deer, fox, gazelle, wild pig, wolf, onager and large wild cat have also been recorded. Botanical specimens recorded comprise emmer, hexaploid wheat, six-row barley and a small number of einkorn (Field, 1969). In a recent study Helbaek (1972a) has identified grains of einkorn, emmer, bread wheat, wild barley, two-row barley,

FIG. 61. Choga Mami: A painted and well-fired terracotta head from surface, 4·8 cm high.

naked six-row barley, hulled six-row barley and lentil. He concludes that agriculture was employed from the earliest levels explored so far. The discovery of the presence of six-row barley and large seeds of lentil indicate that irrigation was practised. This fact is also corroborated by archæological evidence. A series of water channels have been identified when cutting a section against the northern side of the mound. However, on the basis of palæobotanical studies, Helbaek (1972*a*:40) argues that

> such grain sizes as can be ascertained seem to indicate that the irrigation technique had not yet reached perfection but that some areas were higher than others and that therefore the water was unevenly distributed.

A single radiocarbon sample (BM 483) from the Transitional Samarra/ Hajji Muhammad phase has been dated to 4896 ± 182 BC on the Libby half-life (Oates, 1972).

Southern Mesopotamia

Eridu Culture

The first known settlers in southern Mesopotamia are the village folk of Eridu, the modern site of Abu Sharain, situated south southwest of Ur. Some of the significant contributions of the Eridu excavations include the discovery of a new culture pre-dating the Al-'Ubaid culture and the exposition of a new series of prehistoric temples, 14 in number, superceding one another and all built of sun-dried bricks ('Al Asil, 1950). The earliest of these goes back to the "Eridu" phase where it is a modest single room shrine measuring 3 m². The Eridu culture (or 'Ubaid 1 culture as it is now called), is characterised by a fine, monochrome, usually chocolate-coloured pottery decorated with small rectilinear patterns between horizontal lines. It was made of a well-tempered buff or reddish clay covered with a light slip and the shapes included shallow dishes with slightly rounded bottom, deep bowls with tall, straight sides and tall, graceful goblets with everted rim. This pottery continued to be in use from the bottom of the "hut sounding" to Level XVI. This ware is believed to have connections with Samarra decorative styles—a feature which leads Oates (1960:42) to observe that there may be a common ancestor for Eridu and Samarra wares. Such characteristic shapes as the Hassunan "husking trays" and "milk jars" have parallels in Eridu Levels XIX, XVII, and XV. Minor objects exclusively associated with it were large baked clay beads of doubtful purpose (Lloyd and Safar, 1948:125).

A 7 m² shaft dug in this mound, called the "hut sounding", contained 15 strata. In Level X a large portion of a hut built of reeds and plastered on both sides with clay was discovered. The hut had formed an annexe to a brick built house. A circular clay oven was discovered in this hut. Finds from this hut include a basin of a greenish ware, the upper part of a large jar, a bowl and net weights in the form of clay discs (Safar, 1950). The excavators believe that "the culture arrived fully fledged and continued in full virility until supplanted by that of Al Ubiad about Level XIII" (Lloyd and Safar, 1948:125). The animal bones recovered from Level XIII of the "hut sounding" corresponding with Levels XI-IX of the "temple sounding" at the same site and ascribable to the "Early Ubaid" phase, have been examined by Flannery and Wright (1966). These comprise bones of wild onager, and a single unfused proximal tibia that may be from a sheep, goat or gazelle. The lack of sheep and goat bones is significant in view of the fact that a similar situation obtains at Ras al 'Amiya, situated between the Tigris and the Euphrates where cattle bones greatly outnumber those of the smaller ungulates.

An earlier phase of the well known Ubaid culture in Mesopotamia has been distinguished by the appearance of a new class of pottery first identified at Qala'at Hajji Muhammad, situated southwest of Warka on the right bank of the Euphrates. This ware is a light buff pottery with the wide bowl as a characteristic shape, and painted in dark purplish black paint with dark and reserved triangles. The excavators of Eridu consider this ware as a connecting link between the Eridu ware (pre-Ubaid) and the Ubaid ware. However, Oates (1960:39) does not believe that the different phases at Eridu necessarily constitute different cultural elements and argues that Hajji Muhammad is an integral part of what had previously been called the earliest Ubaid ceramic (Levels XII-VIII).

Ras al 'Amiya

Another prehistoric settlement of southern Mesopotamia was accidentally discovered while digging a canal at Ras al 'Amiya, located about 8 km north of Kish and 32 km northeast of Hilla, at a point midway between the rivers Tigris and the Euphrates. The site was excavated in May-June 1960 (Stronach, 1961) and the results indicate that this settlement provides a link in transition from the Hajji Muhammad phase to the later Ubaid times. This prehistoric settlement covers an oval area of seven acres and the cultural deposit has been divided into five building levels numbered from the top downward. No architectural remains were noticed in the earliest two levels but traces of human habitation include a fine mixture of sherds in a sandy layer in Level V and circular ovens with a diameter of 1·80 m in Level IV. The third level yielded good architectural remains comprising four courtyards of varying sizes and more than 20 rooms with several large bread ovens. The use of mud-bricks, instead of *tauf* is noticed in the succeeding level (Level II). However, the bricks are exceptionally crude and constitute thin, large slabs of sun-dried mud. The structures of the latest phase are badly denuded but small rooms 2 m by 2 m in size and with walls 20-60 cm in thickness, were identified. The excavator believes that the total life-span of Ras al'Amiya is little more than a hundred years and the site was deserted by its inhabitants for an unknown reason.

The recovered pottery of Ras al 'Amiya is divided into heavy, ordinary and fine wares on the basis of the fineness of the fabric and the shapes include bowls, dishes, jars, beakers and a number of vases of distinctive type. The majority of the vessels have buff or cream slip both on the exterior and the interior and vessels of finest quality have burnished surface. The painting has been executed in an enormous variety of colours like purplish black, yellow, brown, brick red to dark violet and lightest to darkest green, but true polychromy never occurs (Stronach, 1961 :109). Only one type of paint was applied to any given vessel. The painted motifs include typical Hajji Muhammad patterns such as zig-zag in reserve, reserved triangles and running petal patterns.

The yield of chipped stone industry includes blades of flint and ob-sidian, some with serrated edges and a few of them with silica sheen. In at least three examples, the blades still possess traces of bitumen. The recovered ground stone industry is made of stone axes, a pair of pendants, a small disc bead of white limestone and three small balls of rock-crystal. A number of rough stone pestles and mortars complete the ground stone inventory. Bone tools were not very popular as only one point and 4 needles of this material have been recorded. Ras al 'Amiya did not yield any terracotta human figures but other terracotta objects comprise spindle-whorls of plain, biconical and flat disc types, and two animal figures of which one is a dog. A series of curved nail-shaped mullers, believed by some to be large decorative wall cones, provide an important link with the earliest Ubaid levels at Eridu. The excavator considers Ras al 'Amiya contemporary with Eridu XI. The animal remains are under study and cattle and sheep are believed to have been domesticated. The chance discovery of this site demonstrates that many more prehistoric settlements still lie buried under the thick alluvium deposits of southern Mesopotamia.

References

ABDUL-AZIZ, N. H. AND JAROSLAV (1966). Twins from Tell Hassuna. *Sumer*, **22** (1-2), 45-50.

AL 'ASIL, NAJI (1949). Barda Balka. *Sumer*, **5** (2), 205-6.

AL 'ASIL, NAJI (1950). Recent Archæological Activities in Iraq. *Sumer* **6** (1), 3-5.

AL-A'DAMI, K. H. (1968). Excavations at Tell Es-Sawwan (second season). *Sumer*, **24** (1-2), 57-98.

AL-SOOF, BEHNAM ABU (1968). Tell Es-Sawwan Excavations of the Fourth Season. *Sumer*, **24** (1-2), 3-16.

AL-TEKRITI, ABDUL QADIR (1968). The Flint and Obsidian Implements of Tell Es-Sawwan. *Sumer*, **24** (1-2), 53-55.

BRAIDWOOD, LINDA S. (1951). Preliminary Notes on the Jarmo Flint and Obsidian Industry. *Sumer*, **7** (2), 105-6.

BRAIDWOOD, ROBERT J. (1951*a*). A Preliminary Note on the Prehistoric Investigations in Iraqi Kurdistan 1950-51. *Sumer*, **7** (2), 99-104.

BRAIDWOOD, ROBERT J. (1951*b*). From Cave to Village in Prehistoric Iraq. *Bull. Am. Sch. Orient. Res.*, **124**, 12-18.

BRAIDWOOD, ROBERT J. (1954). The Iraq-Jarmo Project, Season 1954-55. *Sumer*, **10** (2), 120-38.

BRAIDWOOD, ROBERT J. (1955). The Earliest Village Materials of Syro-Cilicia. *Proc. Prehist. Soc.*, **21,** 72-6.

BRAIDWOOD, ROBERT J. (1956). The World's First Farming Villages. *Ill. Lond. News*, **1956,** 410-11.

BRAIDWOOD, ROBERT J. (1960). The Agricultural Revolution. *Scient. Am.*, **203,** (3), 130-48.

BRAIDWOOD, ROBERT J. (1967). A Note on the Present Status of Radio-active Carbon Age Determination. *Sumer*, **23** (1-2), 39-44.

BRAIDWOOD, R. J. AND BRAIDWOOD, LINDA S. (1950). Jarmo: A Village of Early Farmers in Iraq. *Antiquity*, **24,** 189-95.

BRAIDWOOD, ROBERT J. AND BRAIDWOOD, LINDA S. (1951). Discovering the World's Earliest Village Community: The Claims of Jarmo as the Cradle of Civilization. *Ill. Lond. News*, **1951,** 992-5.

BRAIDWOOD, R. J. AND BRAIDWOOD, LINDA S. (1953). The Earliest Village Communities of South Western Asia. *J. Wld. Hist.*, **1,** 278-310.

BRAIDWOOD, R. J. AND HOWE, BRUCE (1960). *Prehistoric Investigations in Iraqi Kurdistan* (SAOC No. 31). Chicago: Universtiy of Chicago Press.

BRAIDWOOD, R. J., BRAIDWOOD, LINDA S., TULANE, EDNA AND PERKINS, A. L. (1944). New Chalcolithic Material of Samarran Type and its Implictaions. *J. Nr. East. Stud.*, **3,** 47-72.

BRAIDWOOD, R. J., BRAIDWOOD, LINDA, SMITH JAMES G. AND LESLIE, CHARLES (1952). Matarrah: A Southern Variant of the Hassuna Assemblage, Excavated in 1948. *J. Nr. East. Stud.*, **11,** 1-71.

CAMPBELL THOMPSON R. AND MALLOWAN, M. E. L. (1933) The British Museum Excavations at Nineveh 1931-32. *Annls Archæol. Anthrop.*, *Liverpool*, **20,** 70-186.

COON, C. S. (1950). Three skulls from Tell Hassuna. *Sumer*, **6** (1), 93-6.

DABBAGH, TAKEY. (1965). Hassuna Pottery. *Sumer*, **21** (1-2), 93-112.

DU MESNIL DU BUISSON. (1948) *Baghouz, L'Ancienne Corsôté.* Leiden: Brill, E. J.

EL-WAILLEY, FAISAL (1963). Foreword. *Sumer,* **19** (1-2), 1-7.

EL-WAILLEY, FAISAL (1964). Foreword. *Sumer,* **20** (1-2), 1-8.

EL-WAILLEY, FAISAL (1965). Foreword. *Sumer,* **21** (1-2), 4.

EL-WAILLEY, FAISAL (1966). Tell Es-Sawwan. *Sumer,* **22** (2), A-J.

EL-WAILLEY, FAISAL (1967). Foreword. *Sumer,* **23** (1-2), A-J.

EL-WAILLEY, FAISAL AND AL-SOOF, BEHNAM ABU (1965). The Excavations at Tell Es-Sawwan: First Preliminary Report (1964). *Sumer,* **21** (1-2), 17-32.

FIELD, BARBARA S. (1969). Botanical Remains from Choga Mami. *Sumer,* **25** (1-2), 138-39.

FLANNERY, KENT V. AND WHEELER, JANE C. (1967). Animal Remains from Tell Es-Sawwan Level III (Samarra Period). *Sumer,* **23,** 179-82.

FLANNERY, KENT V. AND WRIGHT, HENRY T. (1966). Fanual Remains from the "Hut Sounding" at Eridu, Iraq. *Sumer,* **22** (1-2), 61-4.

FRAZER, F. C. (1953). Animal Bones from Barda Balka. *Sumer,* **9** (1). 106-107.

HELBAEK, HANS (1963). Textiles from Çatal Hüyük. *Archæology,* **16** (1), 39-46.

HELBAEK, HANS (1964). Early Hassunan Vegetable Food at Es-Sawwan, Near Samarra. *Sumer,* **20** (1-2), 45-48.

HELBAEK, HANS (1972a). Samarran Irrigation Agriculture at Choga Mami in Iraq. *Iraq,* **34** (1), 35-48.

HELBAEK, HANS (1972b). Traces of Plants in the Early Ceramic Site of Umm Dabaghiyah. *Iraq,* **34** (1), 17-19.

INGHOLT, HARALD (1957). Danish Dokan Expedition. *Sumer,* **13** (1-2), 214-5.

KIRKBRIDE, DIANA (1972). Umm Dabaghiyah 1971: A Preliminary Report. *Iraq,* **34** (1), 3-15.

LLOYD, SETON AND SAFAR, FUAD (1945). Tell Hassuna: Excavations by the Iraq Government Directorate General of Antiquities in 1943 and 1944. *J. Nr. East. Stud.,* **4,** 255-89.

LLOYD, SETON AND SAFAR, FUAD. (1948). Eridu: A Preliminary Communication on the second season's Excavation 1947-48. *Sumer,* **4** (2), 115-27.

MALLOWAN, M. E. L. (1933). The Prehistoric Sondage of Nineveh 1931-2. *Annls Archæol. Anthrop., Liverpool,* **20** (1933), 71-186.

MALLOWAN, M. E. L. (1936). The Excavations at Tall Chagar Bazar and an Archæological survey of the Habur Region 1934-5. *Iraq,* **3,** 1-86.

MALLOWEN, M. E. L. AND ROSE, J. C. (1935). Prehistoric Assyria: The Excavations at Tall Arpachiyah. *Iraq,* **2** (1), 1 ff.

MERPERT, NICOLAI AND MUNCHAJEV, RAUF (1969). Excavations at Yarim Tepe. *Sumer,* **25** (1-2), 125-32.

MELLAART, JAMES (1963). Çatal Hüyük in Anatolia. *Ill. Lond. News,* **1963,** 196-8.

MORTENSEN, PEDER (1962). On the Chronology of the Early Village Farming Communities in Northern Iraq. *Sumer,* **18** (1-2), 73-80.

MORTENSEN, PEDER (1964). Additional Remarks on the Chronology of Early Village-Farming Communities in the Zagros Area. *Sumer*, **20** (1-2), 28-36.

MORTENSEN, PEDER (1970) *Tell Shimshara: The Hassuna Period*. København: Kommissionaèr Munksgaard.

OATES, JOAN (1960). Ur and Eridu: The Prehistory. *Iraq*, **22**, 32-50.

OATES, JOAN (1966a). Prehistoric Investigations Near Mandali, Iraq. *Iraq*, **30** (1), 1-20.

OATES, JOAN (1966b). First Preliminary Report on a Survey in the Region of Mandali and Badra. *Sumer*, **22**, (1-2), 51-58.

OATES, JOAN (1969a). Choga Mami 1967-68: A Preliminary Report. *Iraq*, **31** (2), 115-52.

OATES, JOAN (1969b). New Perspectives from Iraq. *Ill. Lond. News*, **1969**, 30-31.

OATES, JOAN (1969c). Goddess of Choga Mami. *Ill. Lond. News*, **1969**, 28-9.

OATES, JOAN (1969d). Excavations at Choga Mami. *Sumer*, **25** (1-2), 133-7.

OATES, JOAN (1970). Prehistoric Settlement Patterns in Mesopotamia. *Seminar Paper on Settlement Patterns and Urbanisation*. London: December, (1970).

OATES, JOAN (1972). A radiocarbon Date from Choga Mami. *Iraq*, **34** (1), 49-53.

PERKINS, ANN LOUISE (1949). *The Comparative Archæology of Early Mesopotamia*. (SAOC No. 25). Fifth Printing, 1968. Chicago: University of Chicago Press.

PERKINS, DEXTER JR. (1960). The Faunal Remains of Shanidar cave and Zawi Chemi Shanidar: 1960 Season. *Sumer*, **16** (1-2), 77-8.

PERKINS, DEXTER JR. (1964). Prehistoric Fauna from Shanidar Cave, Iraq. *Science, N.Y.*, **144**, 1565-6.

REED, CHARLES A. (1969). The Pattern of Animal Domestication in the Prehistoric Near East, *Domestication and Exploitation of Plants and Animals*. (P. J. Ucko and G. W. Dimbleby, eds). London: Duckworth, pp. 361-80.

RUBIN, MEYER AND CORRINNE, ALEXANDER (1960). U.S. Geological Survey Radiocarbon Dates V. *Radiocarbon*, **2**, 182-4.

SAFAR, FUAD (1950). Eridu: A Preliminary Report on the Third Season's Excavation 1948-49. *Sumer*, **6** (1), 27-38.

SALMAN, ISA (1969). Foreword. *Sumer*, **25**, c-d.

SOLECKI, RALPH S. (1952). Notes on a Brief Archæological Reconnaissance of cave sites in the Rowanduz District of Iraq. *Sumer*, **8** (1), 37-48.

SOLECKI, RALPH S. (1957). The 1956 Season at Shanidar. *Sumer*, **13** (1-2), 165-71.

SOLECKI, RALPH S. (1958). The 1956-57 Season at Shanidar, Iraq. *Sumer*, **14** (1-2), 104-108.

SOLECKI, RALPH S. (1963). Prehistory in Shanidar Valley, Northern Iraq. *Science, N.Y.*, **139**, 179-93.

SOLECKI, RALPH S. AND ROSE, L. (1963). Two Bone Hafts From Northern Iraq. *Antiquity*, **37**, 58-60.

SOLECKI, RALPH S. AND RUBIN MEYER (1958). Dating of Zawi Chemi, An Early Village Site at Shanidar, Northern Iraq. *Science, N.Y.*, **127**, 1446.

SOLECKI, ROSE L. (1961). The 1960 Season at Zawi Chemi Shanidar. *Sumer*, **17** (1-2), 124-5.

STRONACH, D. (1961). The Excavations at Ras Al 'Amiya. *Iraq*, **23** (2), 95-138.

TAUBER, HENRIK (1968). Copenhagen Radiocarbon Dates IX. *Radiocarbon*, **10** (2), 322-3.

WAHIDA, GHANIM. (1967). The Excavations of the Third Season at Tell Es-Sawwan, 1966. *Sumer*, **23** (1-2), 167-78.

WRIGHT JR. H. E. AND HOWE, BRUCE. (1951). Preliminary Report on Soundings at Barda Balka. *Sumer*, **7** (2). 107-118.

5. Iran

The first relics of Stone Age man were found in Iran in the Spring of 1949 when Ghirshman (1954:27) explored a cave at Tang-i-Pabda in the Bakhtiari mountains, northeast of Shustar. In the same year Coon (1951) located several caves containing implements and excavated four of them, viz. Tamtama cave overlooking Lake Reza 'iyeh; Bisitun, about 50 km east of Kermanshah; Belt Cave, overlooking the Caspian Sea in the north; and a rockshelter at Khunik in Khurasan. The tools obtained from these caves range in date from Levalloiso-Mousterian to Neolithic times. Of these, Blet Cave or Ghar-i-Kamarband, situated 8 km west of Behshahr and 6 km from the shore line, has yielded artefacts showing transition from the food-gathering to the food-producing stage. The habitational deposit of well over 4 m in this cave has been divided into 28 levels, the upper 9 of which are Neolithic in character. Levels 10-28 represent Mesolithic deposit. The Neolithic culture comprised full ground celts, querns, mortars, pestles and pierced ground stones. Braidwood suggests that the last named tool may have been used as a dibble weight (Braidwood, 1952: 552). Bone tools such as needles, awls, spatulae and fleshers (all dominant in late Neolithic levels) are also found. Plain blades and sickle-blades—the latter attesting the harvesting of crops—have been recorded in increasing numbers with the growth of the Neolithic settlement. A software pottery was unquestionably in use in Level 7 although a single sherd, believed to be intrusive, has been recorded from Level 10 (Coon, 1951: 78). Goats and sheep are the first domesticated animals to be found and they were predominantly premature at the time of slaughter. Ox and pig were domesticated a little later. Both these facts have been substantiated by the controlled excavations in Deh Luran. A charred bone sample collected from Levels 6 through 10 (with its mean located at Level 9) gives a date of 6135 BC on the Libby half-life for the beginning of the Neolithic Culture (Coon, 1951:31).

An analysis of the artefacts and animal bones leads Coon to distinguish the following 3 stages in the transition from the food-gathering to the food-producing economy:

1. The first settlers of Belt Cave were hunters of Mesolithic times.

Their principal prey were gazelle and ox but they also hunted wild sheep and goat. However, they began to domesticate the two last named animals towards the close of this period.

2. In early Neolithic times, before the adoption of cereal culture, pottery-making, weaving and the use of stone axes, the Belt cave people kept both sheep and goats as animals for slaughter.

3. In the third stage, they adopted cereal culture, pottery-making, weaving and the use of stone axes. They also domesticated the ox and the pig during this period.

However, because of the paucity of material from artefacts in the first three levels (Levels 8, 9 and 10) of the Neolithic deposits, Braidwood suspects a gap in the continued human occupation between the Meso-lithic and Neolithic levels. Such a hiatus is also indicated by the widely divergent radiocarbon dates from the two levels. Thus while the last phase of the Mesolithic culture (Level 11) gives a date of 8160 BC, the succeeding Neolithic level is dated to 6135 BC only, leaving a gap of more than 2000 years.

The discoveries made by Ghirshman and Coon have been actively pursued by several prehistorians during the last two decades. Thus while Braidwood and his team explored the environs of Kermanshah, careful work in Khuzistan has been done by Hole, Flannery and Neely, and the regions southwest of Lake Reza 'iyeh have been explored by Dyson, Young and Burney. Also Mortensen, Smith and Young have sounded several sites in different parts of Luristan. Each of these excavated sites has added invaluable data in understanding the way of life of the pre-historic communities, and the surveys of Adams in Khuzistan, of Solecki in the Lake Reza 'iyeh region and Goff in Luristan have helped in knowing about the settlement patterns and the density of population in each period.

The distribution of these newly-discovered sites on the prehistoric map of Iran suggests the existence of three clusters of sites each with its own diagnostic traits, like architecture and ceramics, although having contacts with each other. These clusters are:

1. The Plains of Kermanshah.
2. The Plains of Khuzistan.
3. The area southwest of Lake Reza 'iyeh in Azerbaijan.

A description of the cultural assemblage of each of the three zones follows:

The Kermanshah Group

The first group of partially settled cultures has been identified by Robert J. Braidwood in the environs of Kermanshah in central-western

Iran. Surface exploration of the river valleys west of Kermanshah, Shahabad, Shiam, Zibri and parts of Mahidasht plains undertaken in 1959-60 resulted in the discovery of well over 250 open sites, rock-shelters and caves which have yielded artefacts from Acheulian handaxes to antiquities of the late Uruk or protoliterate periods. Of these, 6 sites, viz. Gar Kobeh, Gar Warwasi, Tepe Asiab, Tepe Sarab, Tepe Siabid and Tepe Deshawar have been sounded. The material from these furnishes invaluable data regarding the earliest settlement but remains largely unpublished except for short notes (Braidwood, 1960a:695-696; 1960b:214-218; 1961:3-7; Braidwood, Howe and Reed, 1961: 2008-2010).

Of the 6 excavated sites, Gar Kobeh yielded tools of Mousterian industry which has been dated to 38,000 BC. Gar Warwasi is a rock-shelter which has yielded Baradostian and Zarzian type tools. These two industries have been dated to 23,000 BC and 8500 BC respectively. As these cultures represent only a hunting and food-gathering stage, they do not concern us in the present context. Among the remaining four sites, Tepe Asiab furnishes evidence of semi-permanent settlement while Tepe Sarab is possibly a permanent settlement (Bökönyi, 1970) with most of the concomitants of Neolithic culture and hence both these sites may be examined here in detail.

Tepe Asiab

The small mound of Tepe Asiab is situated at a distance of 6 km east of Kermanshah, overlooking the Kara Su river. It contains the vestiges of a semi-permanent settlement of food-collectors. Limited soundings revealed part of a roughly round and shallow basin with an estimated diameter of well over 10 m. This basin is believed to be a semi-subterranean domestic structure. However, no post-holes or any other evidence has been obtained to suggest the existence of any roofing arrangement.

The collection of artefacts for Asiab includes a flint industry comparable to that of Karim Shahir. The main tool-types recovered are small blades, blade cores, microliths, numerous irregular flake tools, coarse scraping tools and a curious type of chipped stone tool with thin ovoid form which superficially resembles the Eskimo "Ulu" (Braidwood, 1960: 695-96). Some of the blades have sheen and may have been used as sickle-blades. Coarse ground stone objects and fragments of stone bowls were also picked up. The smaller objects comprised beads, pendants,and bracelets of marble. Numerous small clay objects including a few figurines have been recorded. Of these figurines, a human figure with plaque-like face, deserves special mention. Evidence for the disposal of the dead was obtained by the discovery of two human burials with traces of red ochre (Braidwood *et al.*, 1961 :2008-10).

The earliest settlers of Asiab collected quantities of clam shells from the Kara Su river which flows at the base of the hill on which the site lies. The people supplemented their diet by meat and a wide range of animal bones, especially of wild boars, has been collected in the excavations. This evidence together with the sheen on some blades led Braidwood to suggest that the Asiab Culture was based on intensive collecting and may have been on the verge of achieving food production. A large amount of coprolites have been collected and if on examination they turn out to be human, they will provide valuable clues regarding the diet of the Asiab people. No radiocarbon date is yet available for the Asiab assemblage but on the basis of its typological resemblance with that of Karim Shahir, Braidwood suggests a date between 10,000 to 7000 BC for the Asiab settlement which on comparative grounds seems to be too early. He also thinks that Asiab is probably a bit more advanced (and hence slightly later?) than Karim Shahir.

Tepe Sarab

The next phase of the early food-collecting culture of this region has been identified on the small mound of Tepe Sarab about 7 km east northeast of Kermanshah. Study of animal bones from the small soundings made at this site indicates that the settlement was occupied permanently (all the year round) (Bökönyi, 1970) and the people lived in pit-like depressions similar to those found at Asiab. However, the pits at Sarab are comparatively smaller in size. Again, there is no trace of post-holes or other evidence to give any clue for roofing. No mud-walled architecture has been noted. An important advancement over the Asiab assemblage is the manufacture of pottery at Sarab. Pottery is present in small quantity and comprises plain as well as painted ware, both usually showing traces of burnishing. The shapes are simple as expected in this early stage of ceramic art. The main type is a bowl of medium size and ovoid in plan. Flint tools have been recorded but have not been published as yet. This stone industry has been compared with the Jarmo assemblage and it is believed to have somewhat less variety. Stone bowls and bracelets occur as at Asiab. Like Jarmo a large number of clay objects like figurines, "nails", "plugs" and balls have been recorded. Particular mention must be made of a mother goddess figure, the now famous "Sarab Venus" for its skilful modelling. Clay animal figures include a wild boar figure showing realistic modelling.

FIG. 63. Type 6 site. The site was subjected to ...

The economy of the Sarab people is difficult to reconstruct unless definitive reports on relevant samples are forthcoming. There is no firm indication of the presence of wheat or barley but among the excavated animal bones, goat is believed to be domesticated (Braidwood *et al.*, 1961:2008-2010). Food was considerably supplemented by hunting and collection as indicated by large numbers of animal bones and snail shells. The latter include shells of local land snail, *Helix Salomonica*, as at Jarmo.

The Sarab assemblage has been compared with that of Jarmo and some common traits between the two cultures such as the occurrence of a large number of clay objects, the domestication of goat and the collection of land snail, have been noted. On the other hand there is no proof for the presence of cereals and architecture like those at Jarmo. Braidwood suggests that Sarab is perhaps more developed but not necessarily later in date than Jarmo. Three charcoal samples from different levels of Sarab have been run by the University of Pennsylvania Radiocarbon Laboratory. These samples (P 465, 466, 467) give dates of 5655 BC, 6006 BC and 5694 BC respectively on the Libby half-life (Stuckenrath, Jr., 1963: 91-92).

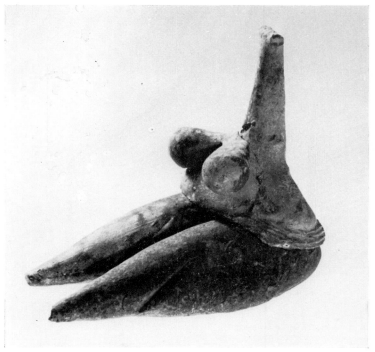

FIG. 63. Tepe Sarab: The "Venus".

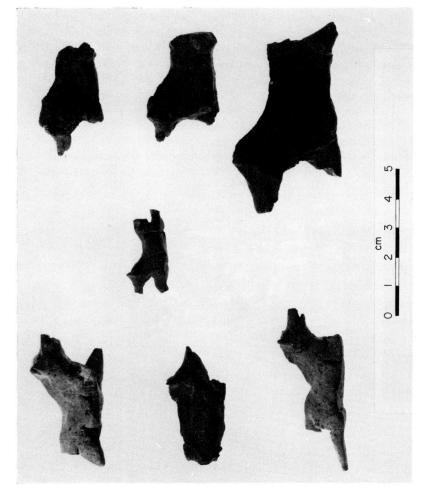

Fig. 64. Tepe Sarab: Clay figurines of animals.

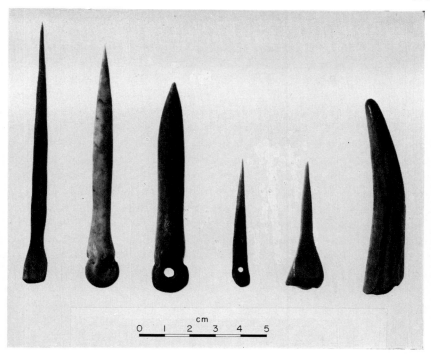

cm
0 1 2 3 4 5

FIG. 65. Tepe Sarab: Bone tools.

That the Kermanshah region continued to be inhabited in later times is proved by the results of a 5-day sounding at Tepe Siabid (Braidwood, 1960a:695-96) some 10 km east northeast of Kermanshah and not far from Sarab. The site yielded painted pottery and flint comparable to that of Tepe Giyan and Halaf. Braidwood thinks that the Siabid assemblage does not immediately follow that of Sarab and he suspects a typological (and perhaps chronological) gap between the two assemblages. A date between 5000 to 6000 BC has been suggested for the Siabid assemblage. But a single sample (P 442) from Level I at the site gives a date of 3865 BC (Stuckenrath, Jr., 1963:91). Other dates also suggest that this is too early. Another mound, Tepe Deshawar, 7 km east of Kermanshah, was also sounded and yielded late Uruk pottery and some stamp clay jar sealings.

Ganj Dareh Tepe

Moving further east, but well within the Kermanshah district one encounters the Neolithic settlement of Ganj Dareh Tepe ("Mound of the

Treasure Valley''). Ganj Dareh is situated at an altitude of nearly 1400 m in the Gamas Ab Valley near the town of Hasrin. The mound is oval in ground plan and conical in profile measuring about 40 m at its maximum width. The settlement has been under excavation by Philip L. Smith of the University of Montreal for three field seasons. The occupational deposit of 8 m is essentially Neolithic as no post-Neolithic assemblages has been found on the site, although the uppermost layers have been disturbed by several Islamic burials. This cultural deposit has been divided into five occupational levels (or perhaps six; Smith, 1968:158-60) numbered from the top downwards. After the preliminary sounding in 1965 Ganj Dareh was believed to be an early aceramic Neolithic site with solid architecture going back to the 9th millennium BC (Young and Smith, 1966:388-89; Smith 1967:139) but a small quantity of pottery was found in the subsequent field seasons. The second season's work (1969) yielded more pottery and fragments of large storage jars have been recorded from the upper four levels of the site. No trace of pottery has been found in the basal level so far but it must be borne in mind that the lowest levels still remain to be probed thoroughly. A definitive report of the excavations is not available for the present but on the basis of preliminary accounts the position may be summarised as follows.

Our knowledge regarding the houses and habitations of the first settlers of Ganj Dareh is extremely scanty owing to the limited area excavated so far. The limited excavation of the basal level did not yield any trace of permanent architecture although the people probably lived in temporary huts and encampments. The next four levels are represented by solid mud-brick rectilinear architecture. The clearance of a 144 sq. m area of Level D has brought to light a series of small rooms, alcoves or cubicles built of straw-tempered long plano-convex bricks laid between layers of mud mortar with the extant walls rising to a height of 60 cm and coated with mud plaster both from inside and outside. In addition to the brick walls there is an unusual type of walling which constitutes alternating layers of mud and fine plaster, built up in strips and then coated with plaster on both faces. This method of construction has not been noted from any other Neolithic site of this region. Most of the rooms are rectangular in plan and very small in size. Some of these are round and silo-like also. The houses are of cluster-type and are built against each other with no paths or lanes between them. The small size of the rooms and the absence of doorways and any other sign of domestic occupation like ovens or hearths suggests that these were perhaps storage places rather than living rooms. Clay containers as well as small domed bins of plaster-like mud were found in several rooms built against the walls. Smith

(1970:179) believes that the living areas may perhaps be found on the flanks of the mound. This village was destroyed by fire.

Fɪɢ. 66. Ganj Dareh Tepe: General view of the mound at the beginning of the 1971 season showing the central excavated area.

In the following two building levels (Level c and b) houses again with rectangular rooms were constructed of mud-brick as well as *chineh*. The walls were occasionally coated with white plaster (Smith, 1968:159). The mud-brick architecture continues in the last 1·5 m deposit represented by Level A but the bricks are no longer oval in shape and they are now smaller in size. The rooms had plastered floors. This level is badly eroded and disturbed by roots, animal burrows and recent Islamic graves.

As mentioned above, no pottery was found in the initial sounding of the site and the culture was believed to be aceramic. However, a small quantity of pottery was found in the subsequent field-season from the "burned village" level (Level D) at a depth of 5 m. A very friable but almost intact gourd-shaped vessel was found in a corner of a room. More chaff-tempered sherds of large bowls or jars were found in another building and a storage jar, about 80 cm high, with very thick walls was obtained from another part of the same village. It is suggested that these vessels were originally sun-dried only and they owe their preservation to secondary baking when the village was subsequently burned (Smith, 1968:159). It may be noted that pottery makes its appearance in Level D for the first time and no trace of this industry has been found in the basal one metre deposit which is still inadequately investigated.

The stone industry of Ganj Dareh represents a blade-flake tradition and is essentially made of flint. The tool types recovered include parallel sided blades, backed bladelets, nibbled blades, side and end-scrapers and some fine cylindrical cone choppers. The stone industry was taken to be non-geometric but a few geometric microliths (trapezes and segments of circles) have been reported in the third seasons' dig (Smith, 1970:179). Preliminary observation reveals that there are no important morphological changes in the chipped stone tools from the base to the top (Smith, 1968:159). A chipped axe or pick has been recorded, but no polished stone tools have been found. A number of worked bone implements like perforators, awls and sawn pieces have also been reported.

That the Neolithic man of Ganj Dareh harvested grain is indicated by well defined areas of polish on some blades. This observation is further supported by the recovery of large numbers of mortars, pestles and rubbers from different levels of the site. The stone industry is believed to resemble that of Tepe Guran, Asiab and Sarab. A curious feature of the Ganj Dareh stone industry is the complete absence of obsidian. Not a single piece has been recorded in three season's work. Does it mean that Ganj Dareh remained isolated and did not participate in the Near Eastern obsidian trade, so characteristic during this period?

Clay animal figurines are abundant, especially in Level D. Some of these are fairly naturalistic and probably represent goats and/or sheep. Several human figurines have also been recorded. A tiny delicately modelled female with pointed head and prominent breasts, and a "stalky-headed" female figure found in the third season are of particular interest. Another important addition to our knowledge, is the evidence regarding the disposal of the dead. In all, 26 human skeletons (most of them coming from Level D) had been excavated up to the end of the third field season. The adults were buried in flexed and extended positions and the infant burials were found in sub-floor cubicles. In one case three extended skeletons (an adult, an adolescent and a child), were found together inside a curious elongated "sarcophagus" made of mud-bricks and covered with a kind of mud roof (Smith, 1972:167).

Fɪɢ. 67. Ganj Dareh Tepe: Several of the small cubicles of Level D, constructed from plano-convex bricks.

A good amount of vegetal material has been retrieved by flotation technique in the last two seasons. Their study is likely to reveal many new facts regarding Neolithic man's economy. The faunal remains have been studied by Dexter Perkins Jr. who believes that at least goat was domesticated. This observation is supported by the discovery of hoof prints of goat or sheep on a number of oval-shaped bricks from Level D. Apparently the animals had walked over the bricks while they were being sun-dried.

The absolute chronology of the Ganj Dareh Neolithic settlement is based on five radiocarbon dates from different levels. Of these, one sample (Gak 807), from the basal levels of the mound (Smith, 1968:158) gives a date of 8450 BC on the Libby half-life (Kunihiko Kigoshi, 1967: 61). Another sample from the same dig (Gak 994) coming from one metre higher than the former sample has been dated to 6960 BC. Three more samples (P 1484, 1485 and 1486) coming from Levels D, C, and B respectively, give dates of 7018 BC, 7289 BC and 6938 BC (Lawn, 1970: 579). These three dates together with the one noted above (Gak 994) give a time-bracket of approximately 400 years (7300 BC to 6900 BC) for the three levels (Levels D to B). In this context the date of 8450 BC given by the first sample (Gak 807) for the basal deposit seems to be unusually high as it leaves an unaccountable gap of more than a thousand years between Levels D and E. The site seems to have been deserted around 6800 BC.

Godin Tepe

Another Neolithic settlement has been located at Godin Tepe on the banks of the same river system (Gamas Ab) and shares the same geomorphological features as Ganj Dareh. Situated at an altitude of 1400 m, the site has at present habitational deposit spreading over an area of 15 h. Just how much of this was occupied during Neolithic times is not clear. The central citadel mound comprising nearly half of the site rises to a height of 26 m. The site was tested by T. Cuyler Young Jr. of the Royal Ontario Museum of the University of Toronto in 1965 and 1967 (Young and Smith, 1966:389-91; Young Jr., 1967:139-140, 1969). It was found to contain a continuous habitational deposit ranging in date from the middle of the 6th millennium BC to as late as 1600 BC. A violent earthquake caused the abandonment of the site for the subsequent 800 years. It was reoccupied in the 8th century BC. The last occupation belongs to the Islamic period. The cultural deposit has been divided into seven phases numbered from the top downwards.

The assemblage of the earliest phase (Phase VII) is relevant in the present context but our knowledge regarding this phase is extremely poor and is derived only from the two test-trenches dug in 1965. Extensive digging of the mound in 1968 and 1969 was confined to the later deposits only (Young, 1968:160-61, 1970:180-82).

The earliest occupants of Godin Tepe lived in houses made of chineh and manufactured pottery and stone tools. Remains of two building levels with secondary evidence of considerable chineh architecture has been noted. The pottery was handmade and straw-tempered, and was poorly fired resulting in a soft and fairly porous ware with grey core. The surface colour ranged from buff-pink to orange-red and the shapes included deep oval bowls with thin or thick walls. The stone tools recovered comprise parallel sided blades with extensive retouch. Like Ganj Dareh the culture is found to be devoid of obsidian and polished stone tools. No radiocarbon date is presently available but the pottery of Godin Tepe has been compared with that of Guran, Ali Kosh, Sarab and Hajji Firuz, and a tentative date of 5500 to 5000 BC has been suggested for this assemblage (Young and Smith, 1966:389-91).

The existence of a Neolithic assemblage over a deposit of Zarzian industry has been suspected in Ghar-i-Khar Cave ("Donkey Cave") situated in the limestone cliff face of Bisitun mountains in the same river valley (Gamas Ab). Thus grinding stones and worked stone bowls along with geometric microliths were found in an inconclusive sounding of the cave in 1965 (Young and Smith, 1966:386-391).

The Pish-i-Kuh region of central Luristan has been explored by Goff (1971:131-152) between 1963 and 1967 and the material obtained ranges in date from aceramic Neolithic to the Early Dynastic period, indicating once again the continuous habitation of the region through the ages. The aceramic levels are represented at Tepe Abdul Hosein (Goff and Pullar, 1970:199-200) situated over a huge spring in the southernmost part of the plain of Khawa, about 65 km east southeast of Ganj Dareh. This mound measures over 40 m in diameter and rises to a height of 6 m. The sides of the mound had been quarried away by the villagers, leaving open the lower strata. The exposed section reveals that pottery was confined in the upper one third deposit of the mound. The pre-pottery strata yielded a flint industry comprising backed blades, obliquely truncated blades, notched blades and finely prepared pencil-shaped blade cones. No geometric microlith or obsidian was found. The industry falls within the Ganj Dareh, Sarab and Asiab range. Traces of mud-brick walls and a series of well-defined charcoal bands have been noted in the section. Pottery comprising a coarse, heavy, straw-tempered red ware appears to be later in date than the main deposit described above.

Tepe Guran

Approximately 65 km due south of Kermanshah is the carefully excavated site of Tepe Guran. It is situated at an altitude of 950 m on the right bank of a little stream called Jazman Rud in the western part of the very fertile Hulailan Valley. The mound was located by Meldgaard in a survey of Luristan in 1962 and the excavations of the neolithic settlement were done by Mortensen in April-June of the subsequent year (Meldgaard, Mortensen and Thrane, 1964:97-133). Tepe Guran is a small mound measuring approximately 100 x 80 m. The cultural deposit of 8 m was sounded from the top to the bottom and 220 m³ of settlement deposit was investigated. This careful excavation brought to light 21 main layers numbered from the top A-V. Of these, Layers A-C yielded remains of Islamic and Luristan-Bronze periods and Layers D-V are Neolithic in character. The importance of Guran lies in the fact that it has yielded direct evidence of transition from the hut to house and from aceramic to the ceramic stage. In the controlled excavations, statistical principles were applied for different wares in the ceramic Neolithic levels and the data obtained have greatly helped in building the relative chronology of the Zagros group of ceramic Neolithic cultures.

FIG. 68. Tepe Guran: Fragmentary floors of white gypsum and of small pieces of feldspar laid in clay coloured with red ochre, joining lower part of wall with foundation stones.

The first settlers of Guran were primarily herdsmen and lived in wooden huts with rectilinear or slightly curved walls (Mortensen, 1964: 28-36). Well built mud-walled houses on stone foundations together with wooden huts appeared for the first time in Level P. Mud-walled houses were universal from Level M. upwards. These were built of oval, un-baked mud bricks and faced with straw-tempered mud plaster. The house-complex was divided into small rooms and walls had recesses for low mud benches or tables in the upper level of the Neolithic settlement. Walls as well as floors were faced with red or white gypsum during this period. Floors and courtyards began to be constructed by a kind of terrazzo technique with small pieces of white feldspar laid in clay coloured with red ochre (Meldgaard et al., 1964:111).

As noted above, Guran provides a good example of transition from the aceramic to the ceramic stage. The earliest three levels are devoid of any pottery and the first pottery fragments are reported in Level S. But once the art of potting was discovered, this craft was pursued with vigour. No less than five fabrics have been noted in the pottery of the ceramic Neolithic phase. These fabrics are as follows :—

1. Undecorated greyish brown ware—it is confined between Levels O and S. The main type is a coarsely modelled, thick-walled bowl with vertical or slightly curved sides and with flat or rounded rim.
2. Undecorated buff ware—this ware appeared for the first time in Level R and continued till the site was abandoned. The main type is an oval or circular bowl.
3. Archaic painted ware—it occurred in very limited quantity in Levels R-O. The shapes are bowls and beakers with curved or vertical sides and flat bases.
4. Standard painted ware—this ware first appeared in Level O and continued throughout in the Neolithic occupation. The painted motifs of oblique lines and other designs are executed in red ochre on the outer surface. Vessels with curved sides and flat base occurred in the earlier levels and are analogous to those from the pottery bearing horizon at Jarmo. These are replaced, in the upper levels, by those with out-curved sides and flat or rounded base and the decoration becomes more regular and finally changes to a "close pattern" style with obliquely arranged geometric decoration.
5. Red burnished ware—it is known from Levels H-D. The shapes comprise open bowls with flat or rounded base.

The yield of chipped stone industry of Guran comprises flake-blades of flint and obsidian. Only 5-10% of tools were made of obsidian, the rest being of flint. More than 80% of the tools showed no sign of retouch. Conical microblades and blades with gloss along the edges—the latter presumably used as sickle-blades—have been reported in large numbers. Other tools recovered include end-of-blade scrapers, borers, and partly retouched and notched blades. A few microliths such as lancets and trapezes have also been reported.

FIG. 69. Tepe Guran: Open courtyard with floor of feldspar laid in clay coloured with red ochre.

The ground stone industry collected comprises pestles, mortars, rubbing stones, palettes, slingstones, celts and grinding stones. It is note-worthy that tools like querns, rubbers, and sickle blades which are usually related to agriculture are absent in the lower levels (Mortensen, 1964: 30). This indicates that agriculture was perhaps unknown in the early

history of this site. It has been argued further that agriculture developed
little by little and its growth is perhaps concurrent with the growth of the
village manifest in the solid mud-walled houses.

Besides the earthenware pots noted above, marble was used for making
vessels. An intact semi-globular bowl of pink marble has been recorded.
The yield of the bone industry comprises awls, needles and spatulae. Other
small objects noted include nails, buttons, beads, pendants, figurines of
women and animals made of stone, bone and shell.

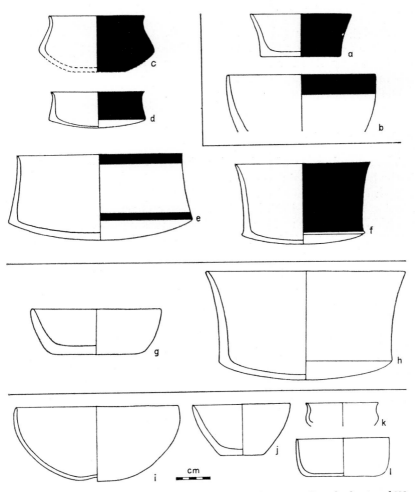

FIG. 70. Tepe Guran: Vessel types, a-b Archaic Painted Ware, c-f Standard-painted Ware,
g-h Undecorated buff Ware, i-l Red-burnished Ware.

G

Important evidence regarding the disposal of the dead has been recorded from the aceramic levels. A few single burials with skeletons in contracted position have been excavated from under the house floors. Grave-goods are extremely rare finds but two lancet-shaped microliths and some bones of perforated animal teeth have been found in one grave. Another grave yielded a single little bead of shell.

The absolute chronology of Tepe Guran rests on two radiocarbon determinations. Of these, one sample (K 1008) from the aceramic Neolithic levels (Level "U") gives a date of 6460 BC$\pm$200 years on the Libby half-life. Another sample (K 879) from Level H has been dated to 5810 BC$\pm$150 years (Tauber, 1968:322). As the Neolithic culture continued to flourish for four levels after Level H, a life-span of 300 years has been suggested for this deposit. Thus a time-bracket of 6500-5500 BC for the Neolithic culture of Guran suggested by Meldgaard et al. (1964: 104) seems to be perfectly logical.

Deh Luran Plain

The second group of early village farming cultures has been identified in the Deh Luran plain on the fringes of Khuzistan, about 110 km west of Dizful. Flints and sherds had been collected by the French Archæological Mission as early as 1903 but the Neolithic character of these sites was revealed in 1958-59 by the survey of the Iranian Prehistoric Project of the Oriental Institute, Chicago. A test-pit measuring 5 x 3 m was dug by Frank Hole and Kent V. Flannery at one of these sites, viz. Tepe Ali Kosh in the subsequent year (Hole, 1962; Hole and Flannery, 1962). During the same year Robert M. Adams surveyed the region around Susa and reported no less than 130 prehistoric sites (Adams, 1962). Ali Kosh was subsequently excavated by Hole and Flannery in the autumn of 1963 and two more mounds, Tepe Sabz and Tepe Musian "E" were tested simultaneously (Hole, Flannery and Neely, 1965).

The composite sequence of Tepe Ali Kosh and Tepe Sabz runs from c. 7500 BC* to 3700 BC and has been divided into seven successive phases (Hole and Flannery, 1967). The excavators took great pains in retrieving the carbonised seed and plant remains by such advanced methods as flotation and bouyancy technique and much care has been taken in the study of animal bones. This study has not only furnished fresh data regarding the history of domestication but has also given some idea about the ancient butchering practices and about the palæo-environment. But the excavations failed to reveal any traces of architectural remains i.e.

*Some scholars prefer a date around 7000 BC rather than 7500 BC.

how people lived. Similarly, no less than 31 radiocarbon samples from various levels have been dated but the dates are not always consistent because as many as 15 samples come from the "midden" area and hence these are less reliable. However, inferences have been drawn about the social organisation of the past societies on the basis of the knowledge of the palæo-environment, settlement patterns and population size; division of labour, craft specialisation and trade (Hole, 1968).

The studies in Deh Luran plain have shown that the era of early dry-farming and caprine domestication starting from around 7000 BC was gradually succeeded and replaced by the era of irrigation farming and cattle domestication which began around 5000 BC. The excavations revealed such significant facts as: the domestication of *capra* (goat) preceded that of cattle by no less than 2000 years in Deh Luran. (This feature was first of all noticed by Coon (1951) for the Belt Cave where the data was insufficient.) A similar situation prevails at Zawi Chemi Shanidar on the Greater Zab river where sheep were domesticated in the proto-Neolithic phase (Solecki, 1963:191; Perkins Jr., 1964).

This excavation also proved that native hammered copper was used even in aceramic levels although in limited quantity and stone bowls were made and used before the art of making pottery vessels was discovered in Deh Luran. Again, the site of Ali Kosh has given actual remains of matting which was previously known only from Çatal Hüyük in Anatolia.

As pointed out above, the composite sequence of seven phases in Deh Luran has been obtained from three sites. The first three phases have been noted at Tepe Ali Kosh ("the place where Ali was killed"). It is a low mound measuring 135 m in diameter and rises to a height of 4 m above the surrounding plain. It has a cultural deposit of 7 m, the lower 3 m of which have been buried in the subsequently deposited alluvium. The first two phases (Bus Mordeh and Ali Kosh) are aceramic and pottery appears in the third phase (Jaffar phase). The cultural assemblage of each phase is described below.

Bus Mordeh Phase

The first occupants of the valley lived in small mud-brick houses measuring no more than 2 x 2·5 m. These houses seem to have been better made than Guran and are comparable only with those at Ganj Dareh. The unfired bricks measure 25 x 15 x 10 cm. Floors were made of stamped mud or clay but no plaster is known as yet from this phase. The people practised a mixed economy based on intensive collection, cultivation, herding and even hunting in varying degrees. They collected seeds of a wide variety of annual legumes and wild grasses and planted emmer wheat and two-row hulled barley which may have been native to Khuzistan. Food was supplemented by other grasses like goat-face grass, rye grass and wild einkorn which perhaps came from outside Khuzistan. The cereals were harvested with flint sickles; were roasted and then threshed by grinding with flat-topped or saddle shaped grinding slabs of limestone. The people herded goat and sheep, the latter though in a much smaller ratio (goats were 10 times more numerous than sheep). A similarly high proportion of goats has been noted at Guran, Sarab and Jarmo (Hole, Flannery and Neely, 1969:344). Most of the goats were eaten while young. The Bus Mordeh people also hunted Persian gazelle, onager, wild ox or aurochs and wild boar. Aquatic resources like carp, catfish, mussel and water turtle were also exploited.

The collection of stone tools of the Bus Mordeh people comprises microliths which perhaps served as parts of composite hunting tools; blades, drills, end-scrapers and burins. Some heavy tools like pounders and small "picks" have also been reported. All these tools are essentially made of flint nodules which were brought from the Dawairij river. Obsidian was accounted for in only one per cent of the total collection and it came from the Lake Van region. The existence of containers for daily use is suggested by three fragments of bowls ground from soft stone. The personal ornaments recovered consist of small pendants of boar tusk, mussel shell, stone beads and small "buttons" of tusk and mother-of-pearl. A number of lightly baked figurines found resembling goats may have been used for magical purposes.

There is no evidence for the disposal of the dead. The only evidence of a secondary internment from Zone C1 (upper levels of the Bus Mordeh phase) comprising limb bones of three adult individuals is believed to be intrusive from the lower levels of the Ali Kosh phase (Hole et al., 1969: 248). On analogy with most of the hunting people today, Hole thinks that the social organisation of the Bus Mordeh people was based on patrilineal families. The permanence of the settlement indicates traditional rights to the land surrounding the site and the diversified economy suggests the division of the labour between two sexes (Hole, 1968: 260-61).

The excavators believe that on the basis of the comparable artefacts and their resemblances the Bus Mordeh phase is broadly contemporary with sites like Zawi Chemi Shanidar, Karim Shahir, Asiab and Ganj Dareh. Three radiocarbon samples from this phase give widely divergent dates. Thus while two samples (AK 91-525 and AK 94-691) give dates of 5430 BC and 5720 BC respectively; the third sample, (A 76-680) is dated to 7950 BC on Libby half-life (Hole et al, 1969:338). Unfortunately all three samples come from the "midden" area and hence are less reliable and should be treated with caution.

Ali Kosh Phase

The succeeding phase witnessed an all round prosperity in the life of the people. They now lived in multi-roomed houses. The size of the rooms increased to 3 x 3 m and the walls became up to a metre thick. The walls were still made of sun-dried mud-bricks which were comparatively large in size (40 x 25 x 10 cm). Walls were plastered with clay both from inside and outside and the house floors were made of stamped mud, surfaced with a layer of clean clay and topped with woven mats of reed. Cooking was done in the courtyards.

There was an increase in the domestication of plants like emmer wheat and two-row hulled barley and there was a gradual tapering off in the collection of small seeded wild legumes. The crops were still harvested with flint sickles and the grain was ground up on shallow grinding slabs using simple discoidal handstones. A new innovation was the use of pestle and mortar. The percentage of domesticated sheep increased from the preceding phase but goats still outnumbered sheep and were eaten while young. An interesting feature of this phase was the increase in the hunting of gazelle, onager and wild cattle although emmer wheat, hulled barley, sheep and goat had been fully domesticated and consequently their production increased. A set of new specialised tools like flint pebble choppers were used for chopping off the meat of the hunted animals.

The tool-kit of Ali Kosh people had flint blades, retouched into diagonal-ended and backed blades or into end of blade scrapers. These were struck from narrow, conical and bullet-shaped cores. Drills, reamers and burins were found to be present in this level and obsidian accounted for 2 % of the tools indicating an increase in the volume of trade. Awls and needles of bone were also recovered and there was an increase in the use of containers as "wicker" baskets waterproofed with asphalt and stone bowls were found in large numbers. Terracotta human figures were preserved in very fragmentary condition as well as goat-like figures which continued from the preceding phase. The people wore strings of beads of white stone discs, sea-shells and mussel-shell pendants. An important discovery was a tubular bead of native copper which had been cold hammered, cut with a chisel and rolled into shape.

The dead were buried with their personal ornaments in tightly flexed position under the house-floors. As noted above, there is evidence of secondary burial where limb bones of three adults had been buried after the decomposition of the flesh. We do not know what area of the mound was inhabited by the people during this phase but it has been inferred that the village was approximately a hectare in extent with an estimated density of population of 0·3 persons/sq. km. Ali Kosh assemblage is believed to be typologically contemporary with the pre-pottery levels of Jarmo and Guran. Nine samples, from both zones of this phase, have been tested by radiocarbon method. Of these, seven dates fall in a time-bracket of 5790 to 6475 BC while one sample from each gives a date of 6900 BC and 8000 BC, respectively. However, the excavators give a date of 6750-6000 BC for Ali Kosh phase.

Mohammad Jaffar Phase

This phase witnessed major innovations in subsistence pattern, architecture and artefacts in Deh Luran. Houses were made on solid foundation of river pebbles and the clay slab brick walls were not only plastered on both the faces but also painted in red ochre. The thickness of walls increased to one metre. Floors were still made of stamped mud of clean clay but were covered with reed mats.

The economy was still a mixed one and cultivation, herding, hunting and fishing constituted major ways for supplying food. Emmer wheat and two-row hulled barley, now known for more than a thousand years, were grown and the crops harvested with flint sickles. Herding of goat and sheep—both now osteologically highly domesticated—continued and the proportion of sheep increased towards the end of this phase. Both the animals were eaten young as in the preceding phases and only 40% of the herd reached the age of three years. Hunting of gazelle, onager, aurochs and wild pig continued and the butchering methods remained the same. Aquatic resources like carp, catfish, crabs, water-turtles and mussels still formed part of the diet. Flint tools like blades, reamers, drills, end-scrapers and bone awls and needles continued to be manufactured and used.

Perhaps the most striking innovation in the Jaffar phase was the art of making pottery vessels. Soft, friable and straw-tempered pots were made in the initial stages but once the ceramic art was discovered, it was pursued with full vigour. No less than three ceramic industries have been noted in this assemblage. The predominant shape is a bowl with variants. Some of the bowls had been decorated with geometric designs, like zig-zag, chevrons, pendant triangles and lozenges, executed in fugitive red paint. A few globular jars with dimpled base and constricted "hole-mouth" appear during the later part of this phase. Lightly baked human figures termed "mother-goddess" have been recorded. Personal ornaments recovered include lip plugs of asphalt besides beads and pendants already available in the Ali Kosh phase. Ritual objects discovered like "phalli" of limestone or alabaster have been taken to be the first real evidence of interaction between the Khuzistan steppe and the Tigris river region, as similar objects had been found in the graves of the earliest occupation at Tell-Es-Sawwan near Samarra.

There is a perceptible change in the burial rites performed by the people. The dead were no longer buried inside the house but taken away from the habitation area and buried in semi-flexed position, on the left side and facing left. The dead were provided with personal ornaments, food and drinks and red ochre. The village covered an area of one hectare in extent and the estimated population density increased to 1·0 person per sq. km. Hole believes that Mohammad Jaffar village had an estimated population of 270 persons probably composed of several lineages representing a self-sufficient egalitarian community (Hole, 1968:261-62).

Tepe Ali Kosh was now in contact with other contemporary sites and shared in the net-work of trade. Obsidian was imported from eastern Turkey, turquoise from north-eastern Iraq, specular hæmatite from Fars and sea-shells from the Persian Gulf (Hole et al., 1969:353). Radiocarbon dates from this phase are again inconsistent. Three samples examined give dates of 5270, 5870 and 6970 BC but the excavators assign a time-bracket of 6000-5600 BC for this phase.

The sequence of Deh Luran plain is now taken by Tepe Sabz where four phases i.e. Sabz, Khazineh, Mehmeh and Bayat, take the story from 5500 BC* down to 3700 BC. Two major innovations, i.e. the beginning of irrigation agriculture and the domestication of cattle in the beginning of Sabz phase pave the way for the rise of urban communities. This has been amply proved by the surveys of Robert M. Adams in Khuzistan. Thus he records only 34 sites of Susa A period in Khuzistan plain, all uniformly small mounds but in the immediately following phase the number of village sites suddenly increases to 102. This is largely due to the introduction of irrigation although dry-farming was still practised (Adams, 1962).

There is a suspected gap in the sequence between the end of the Mohammad Jaffar phase and the beginning of the Sabz phase. This gap seems to have been filled now by the recent excavations by Hole (1969: 171-172) at Choga Safid, about 160 km east of Dizful in the Deh Luran plain where three distinct intermediary phases have been encountered. Details of this excavation are not available but all the three phases are known to have yielded an unexpected variety of the local ceramic tradition marking the transition between the Mohammad Jaffar and the Sabz

*Recent evidence from Choga Safid must make Sabz much later.

phases. The uppermost sub-phase yielded red unpainted wares associated with well preserved houses founded with large stones. In this context mention must be made of the recent work at Tepe Farrukhabad on the banks of the Mehmeh river, 12 km south of the village of Deh Luran (Wright, 1969:172-73). This settlement is believed to have been founded around 5000 BC and remained under occupation more or less continuously till 3000 BC. Again, in a survey of Deh Luran plain in 1968-69, James Neely has recorded nearly 300 sites (Neely, 1970:202-203) ranging in date from Bus Mordeh phase to the Islamic period. A definitive publication of these researches will greatly help in understanding the culture-dynamics in the plains of Khuzistan.

Solduz Valley, South Western Azerbaijan

The third group of early village cultures has been identified in the Solduz segment of the Qadar river valley in southwestern Azerbaijan. Research carried out in this valley by R. H. Dyson Jr., T. C. Young and Charles Burney has given a culture sequence ranging in date from 6th millennium BC to the beginning of the historical period. Four sites, viz: Hasanlu, Hajji Firuz, Dalma Tepe and Pisdeli Tepe have been excavated. The work was started in 1956 when a test-trench was dug on the citadel mound at Hasanlu (Dyson Jr., 1960:132-34). This work was continued in the subsequent two field seasons and other mounds in the vicinity were also tapped at the same time. Thus Pisdeli Tepe was sounded in 1956 and Dalma Tepe was dug in 1958 and in 1959. Work was concluded at the last-named site in 1961 (Young Jr., 1962:707-709). Hajji Firuz was excavated by Charles Burney in 1958 and again by Young in 1961. Lower levels of this site have been further excavated by Dyson Jr. in 1968 (Dyson Jr., Muscarella and Voigt, 1969: 179-181).

The chronology of the Solduz valley has been reconstructed by the excavations at Hasanlu which has given a stratified sequence of super-imposed ceramic remains to a depth of more than 27 m (about 89 ft). This sequence has been divided into nine ceramic phases (numbered from the top downward) based on major shift in fabric, shape and style of the different wares. The existence of a tenth and the earliest phase has been suspected from sherds found out of position, but was never reached due to the high level of the water table. Excavations carried out at Pisdeli Tepe, Dalma Tepe and Hajji Firuz Tepe confirm the basic stratigraphy of Hasanlu. The pottery of the three earliest phases was named after the site where the best sample was obtained (Dyson Jr., 1969:39-47). The absolute chronology of these cultures has been fixed by series of no less than 50 radiocarbon dates run by the University of Pennsylvania. The assemblage of the three Neolithic cultures is described briefly in the following pages.

Hajji Firuz Culture

The type-site of this culture, Hajji Firuz is a small mound, lying about 2 km south of Hasanlu. Preliminary excavations undertaken by T. C. Young Jr. at this site brought to light remains of 4 building levels and parts of a 5th level were also excavated but natural soil could not be reached due to the high water table (Young Jr., 1962:707-09). The earliest building is now believed to have been made of mud-brick and not of packed mud (Persian *chineh*) as reported earlier. Irregularly shaped rooms were set around an open courtyard, and were provided with plaster floors (Dyson Jr., 1961:534-36). More details of architectural features have been obtained in the area-excavation of the site in 1968 when 10 5-metre squares were excavated on the eastern side of the mound (Dyson Jr. *et al.*, 1969:179-81). The latest Hajji Firuz level was found to be almost completely destroyed by fillings from the chalcolithic to recent times. Therefore, work was concentrated on the earlier two building levels. To the upper building level belonged two houses separated by a narrow alley. The earlier phase (third from the top) consisted of a complete house and parts of at least six other buildings. In both these levels, the houses were almost square and comprised a single room partially divided by a wall which extended only half-way across the building. The excavator argues that the partition-wall probably served to help support the roof enabling the builders to use shorter beams. The house in the upper building level contained two hearths, a series of bins and large storage jars in the cooking and storage area which was separated by a partition-wall. The house in the lower level contained only a single horse-shoe shaped hearth. The doorway of this house had a raised sill and a single step down to the inside door level.

Pottery has been obtained from all the five levels of this period and it is both plain and painted. It was crude, hand-made and straw-tempered, and fired at a low temperature making it very friable and easily broken when handled. The vessel-forms appear to have been oval rather than round. The shapes included large storage jars and shallow bowls. Pots were rarely painted but painting where present, was done in a kind of fugitive red paint. It comprised light red designs on a pinkish buff ground. Geometric motifs included zig-zags, triangles and lozenges.

Other small objects recorded at Hajji Firuz culture include clay spindle-whorls, bone awls and stone implements. Only a small quantity of chipped stones was found consisting of an equal amount of flint and obsidian.

Typologically they are divided into two groups i.e. flakes and blades. Other stone objects recovered include small celts and crude whetstones. Fragments of female figurines have been reported from the area excavations and they are in a style presently known only from Hajji Firuz. There is no positive evidence for the domestication of animals but domestication of plants is indirectly indicated (Young Jr., 1962:707-709). The stone celts and whetstones were probably used for primitive agriculture.

Evidence for the disposal of the dead comes from the discovery of four mass graves. These graves contain the bodily remains of no less than 51 individuals. Of these, three mass graves were sunk into the remains of walls of Level II suggesting *inter alia* that these graves were dug before the construction of the building of Level I. The 4th grave was found at the back of the main living room of the house excavated in 1968 (Dyson Jr. *et al.*, 1969:179-81). This burial comprised a bin which had been covered by a layer of hard packed clay. It contained the burial of at least 13 individuals (5 children and 8 adults). The bodies were presumably put into this tomb over a period of time and only the uppermost skeletons were fully articulated. The largest of the three graves excavated earlier contained remains of 17 individuals. Commenting upon these mass graves, Young observes that these represent the "earliest archæological documentation of human conflict" (1962:707-709). The dead were provided with funeral offerings of numerous small plain pots, clay spindle-whorls, some flint blades and ground stone celts. The bones in the grave excavated in 1968 were found to have been covered with red ochre. This grave yielded a small rectangular stone which had been carved with linear geometric designs.

The Hajji Firuz people seem to represent the first settlers of the Solduz valley as no assemblage earlier than Hajji Firuz has been reported so far. These pioneer farmers and herders settled in the region around Lake Reza 'iyeh establishing for the first time a series of permanent villages. Where they came from is difficult to decide, as at present we have little knowledge about this. Striking similarities have been noted between Hajji Firuz assemblage and Sarab assemblage (Young 1962:707-709). It has also been argued that the main ceramics of Hajji Firuz indicate at least a direction of influence if not actual origin from Hassuna culture in Mesopotamia (Dyson Jr., 1969:46).

The chronological position of Hajji Firuz culture has been fixed by two radiocarbon dates. A sample from Level II (P 502) gives a date of 4945 BC on the Libby half-life. Another sample (P 455) from stratum D-15, operation V is dated to 5319 BC (Stuckenrath Jr., 1963:90). Therefore a time bracket of 5500 BC to 5000 BC may perhaps not be out of place for Hajji Firuz culture.

Dalma Culture

Following Hajji Firuz is Dalma culture represented best at the type-site of Dalma Tepe nearly 5 km southwest of Hasanlu. The site was tested by Charles Burney in 1958 and 1959 and again by Young in 1961. Below the graves of second millennium BC were found two levels of Dalma culture (Dyson Jr., 1961:534-36) dated by radiocarbon to the second half of the 5th millennium BC. Here again, natural soil could not be reached due to the high level of the water table.

Details regarding architecture are not fully known but preliminary reports indicate that houses consist of small rooms around a courtyard. The walls are made of layers of packed mud or *chineh* (Young Jr., 1962: 707-709). The diagnostic trait of Dalma culture is its characteristic pottery which is divisible into three ceramic industries i.e. plain ware, surface impressed ware and painted ware. All were straw-tempered, hand-made and rather badly fired and very friable. Beaker with flared out or turned in rim was the common shape but shallow dishes and occasional "fruit-stand" have also been reported (Dyson Jr., 1961:534-36). The painted ware is remarkable in that the painting was executed with characteristic boldness and stylistic vigour. The interior of the vessels was covered with a maroon-red slip. The designs were painted on the exterior of the pot only in a purplish-black or maroon-black paint over a light pink or cream-slipped background (Young Jr., 1963:38-39). Only geometric motifs have been found, but the artist has "sought to explore almost every avenue of geometric design open to him" (Young Jr., 1963: 38). A remarkably well painted design can be seen on a pot where each half of the same vessel has been painted with two different motifs i.e. cross-hatched zig-zag pattern in one half and with rows of solid hanging triangles on the other. An unusual bowl painted with a "double W" pattern framed in a double crescent has been taken to be an import from other painted pottery cultures.

The impressed pottery from Dalma Tepe is represented by an assortment of fragments. The techniques used include impressing with tubes, combs, sticks and fingers. This pottery has been found above the stratum yielding the painted ware (Dyson Jr., 1961: 534-36). Such impressed pottery has not been found so far in Iran. Surface exploration of the adjoining region by the Hasanlu Project team suggests that while plain and surface impressed wares associated with the painted pottery occur in central western Iran as far south as the Khorramabad plain, little is known of the painted pottery itself beyond the limits of the Solduz Valley (Young Jr., 1962:707-709). The painted style is believed to be contemporary with two cultures—an Ubaid related grouping to the south in the central Zagros region and a second grouping in central Iran of Sialk II-III type (stretching from Yanik Tepe in northeastern Azerbaijan eastwards to Tepe Hissar (Dyson Jr., 1969:39-47).

The yield of stone artefacts of Dalma culture includes blades made of a wider variety of materials than in the preceding Hajji Firuz culture. Chert was the common material while obsidian became rare. Does this indicate that obsidian trade was on the decline during this period? Instead of obsidian, granite—a rather harder stone to work on—was used during this period for the manufacture of blades. A large loom weight and a spindle-whorl of clay recovered give clear indication of spinning and weaving.

Evidence regarding disposal of the dead in Dalma culture has been obtained for children only. Fourteen infant pot burials have been found below the house-floors. A radiocarbon sample (P 503) from the earlier two building levels gives a date of 4036 BC on the Libby half-life and 4428 BC on the higher half-life of carbon (Young Jr., 1962:707-709; Stuckenrath Jr., 1963:90).

The stratigraphic position of Dalma culture vis-a-vis Hajji Firuz culture was substantiated again in the excavation of Dalma Tepe in 1961 when below the lower building level of Dalma culture a stratum of loose wash dating to Hajji Firuz period was discovered before the water-table was encountered.

The origin of Dalma culture is a matter of speculation. Thus while Dyson (1969:39-47) thinks that the culture was derived from, or may have evolved from, the preceding Hajji Firuz culture, Young believes it to be an import. To quote Young:

> ...Nevertheless, it is clear from the two assemblages that the Dalma culture did not grow out of Hajji Firuz culture. There is therefore, a distinct possibility that Dalma ware is not native to this area of north-western Iran.

Pisdeli Culture

The third culture with an agricultural economy and with domesticated plants and animals in the Solduz Valley was identified at Pisdeli Tepe. The culture seems to be restricted to the southeastern corner of Lake Reza 'iyeh and is datable to the first half of the fourth millennium BC. Our knowledge regarding Pisdeli culture is scanty as it is based on a small sounding measuring only 2-metres square and excavated in 1957 (Dyson Jr., 1960:132-34). The culture is represented by a distinctive pottery known as "Pisdeli ware". Architectural details are not known but structures of mud-brick were observed though not excavated. Blades or knives of grey chert and black translucent obsidian have been reported.

Some of these blades have lustrous edges presumably because of their use as sickle blades. This indicates that harvesting, if not fully fledged agriculture, was practised by the people. A bone axe-like tool and awls of splintered long bones of animals have been reported. A clay animal figurine recovered probably represents a sheep. Spindle whorls of backed clay were found in the exposed strata as assignable to this culture but were not encountered in the limited dig. The animal bones recorded include those of cattle, sheep/goat and perhaps dog.

The Pisdeli pottery was handmade without exception and tempered with chopped straw or chaff. It varied in colour from red to buff or buff-green (Dyson and Young, 1960:19–28). It is divisible into two classes on the basis of surface treatment, i.e. plain ware and painted ware. Shapes in the plain ware comprised simple hemispherical bowls, small jars and flat open trays. The discovery of painted ware shapes was comparatively limited and was confined to deep hemispherical bowls and simple cups. There were no handles, spouts or lugs. Painting was always confined to the exterior of the pots and only in the upper half of the body. Six main design elements have been noted. These are:

1. horizontal lines of hanging loops;
2. solid painted triangles above and below a thick straight line;
3. small, stylised animals;
4. parallel horizontal lines;
5. a vertical panel of fine or heavy-lined diagonal cross-hatching and;
6. random dots between a border of straight lines (Dyson and Young, 1960:21).

A comparison of the painted motifs on Pisdeli pottery with those on the pottery of northern Ubaid sites, i.e. Tell Arpachiyah, Hassuna, Tepe Gawra, Nineveh and Nuzi leads the excavators to conclude that Pisdeli ware is the first documented incidence of pottery of pure "Ubaid" style in northern Iran. This comparison is not confined to the painted motifs alone. The animal figurine from Pisdeli is taken to be indistinguishable from those of Gawra XVII. The pottery has common elements with Tepe Giyan V C-D. Tepe Sialk III, Susa I and Bakun II in Iran and at Anau in Soviet Turkestan.

The absolute chronology of the Pisdeli assemblage is based on three consistent radiocarbon dates. Thus sample P 151 whose level is not indicated, gives a date of 3510 BC on the Libby half-life (Ralph, 1959: 45-58). Two other samples (P 504, 505) coming from Stratum 5 and Stratum 10 respectively, are dated to 3568 BC and 3688 BC on the same half-life (Stuckenrath Jr., 1963:89). Thus this assemblage may be placed in the first half of the 4th millennium BC.

The western part of Azerbaijan has been subjected to intensive archæo-logical explorations in recent years. Thus Ralph S. Solecki has located 18 caves, 7 rock-shelters, 4 tumuli and 38 Tepe (Solecki, 1969:189-90). The caves and rockshelters were devoid of any Palæolithic remains but of particular interest in the present context is the late Neolithic settle-ment at Tepe Seavan in the Ziweh valley, west of Reza 'iyeh. Ceramics ascribable to the Hajji Firuz and Dalma periods was found together with obsidian and chert fragments in two small sondages made at this site. Again explorations made in the valleys of the Ushnu and the Solduz rivers southwest of Reza 'iyeh by Kearton proved to be more rewarding as well over 250 sites of all periods from the late Palæolithic to the recent past were recorded (Kearton, 1969:186-87). No non-ceramic open-air site could be discovered but a "soft-ware" neolithic similar to that found at Hajji Firuz was found throughout western Azerbaijan.

Tepe Yahya

Leaving the three principal clusters of early village farming sites in Western Iran, one encounters another Neolithic settlement at Tepe Yahya in Southern Iran. This settlement is situated on the Kish-i-Shur river in the fertile Soghum Valley, 225 km south of Kirman and 30 km northeast of the town of Dolatabad. It was discovered by C. C. Lamberg-Karlovsky in August 1967 (Lamberg-Karlovsky, 1968:167-68; 1970b). The impressive mound of Tepe Yahya has a diameter of 180 m and rises to a height of 20 m above the surrounding plain. Vertical excavations done at this site during the last two field-seasons have revealed a culture-sequence ranging in date from the Neolithic to the Parthian-Sassanian period which has been divided into six periods* from the top to the base.

The Neolithic inhabitants of Tepe Yahya were the first occupants of the site to live in mud-brick houses and manufacture and use pottery and flint tools. The assemblage of this period is divisible into five superimposed architectural phases numbered A to E, without evidence of a strati-graphic hiatus between any two phases (Lamberg-Karlovsky, 1970b:111). Housewalls were made of thumb-impressed chaff-tempered mud-bricks of different sizes. They measured from 84-18 cm in length, 14-20 cm in width and 11-14 cm in thickness. They appear first in the earliest sub-phase and continue to be in use until the end of the Neolithic occupation. A dozen rooms excavated in the second season and ascribed to phase VIc are consistently small in size, measuring approximately 1·5 m². It is

---

*In the second field-season's work the excavator divided the cultural assemblage into eight periods but in the subsequent season he has revised this sequence and has regrouped the material into six periods (Lamberg-Karlovsky, 1970b: 5; 1971: 87-96).

likely that they were used for storage of grains although no direct evidence has been found to corroborate this suggestion.

Pottery was present right from the first habitation at the site. A coarse chaff-tempered "soft-ware" is consistently present in each level. Some of the pots bear red slip on the exterior. A bichrome painted ware with black and red painted geometric motifs makes its appearance in the second building level. This pottery has no parallel in this region for the present. The stone industry associated with this assemblage is entirely microlithic and made of different coloured flint. The typology of these tools and their percentage has not been worked out as yet. The occurrence of pestles and mortars in large numbers suggests the utilisation of cereals for food. However, direct evidence for agriculture has not been reported. The people made stone bowls for their daily use. Their artistic achievement is attested by the discovery of a female figurine made of green soapstone. This figurine measures 28 cm in height and was found resting on a bed of 30 flints, a bone spatula and three arrow straighteners on the floor of Room 7 ascribable to phase VID. It has been suggested that it represents the male phallus with the attributes of a female carved over it (Lamberg-Karlovsky, 1970b:113; Lamberg-Karlovsky and Meadow 1970:14) but this view has been criticised by Carter (1972:89) who believes that the hole drilled in the top of the head was a purely functional device for fixing the attachment of hair or headdress and it is not the terminus of "the urethra" as suggested by the excavators.

The chronology of the Neolithic settlement at Tepe Yahya is based on three radiocarbon determinations. The pottery-shapes recorded are comparable to those of Bakun BII and include such characteristic shapes as "milk-jars" which compare with similar vessels in Hassuna/Samarra assemblage. Two radiocarbon samples (Gx 1509, 1737) from phase VIA have been dated to 4120 ± 180 BC and 3620 ± 160 BC on the Libby half-life. Another sample (Gx 1728) from an earlier sub-phase (VIc) gives a date of 4660 ± 140 BC on the same half-life (Lamberg-Karlovsky, 1970b: Appendix). As virgin soil was reached below phase VIE, it is reasonable to give sufficient margin for the beginning of this culture. Earlier, the excavator suggested a time bracket of 4500 BC to 3800 BC but in the light of the subsequently obtained radiocarbon dates from phase VIc quoted above, it is quite likely that the beginning of the Neolithic settlement at Tepe Yahya may be earlier still. There is no cultural break between the end of the Neolithic and the beginning of the succeeding "Yahya culture and a direct continuity in pottery and architecture from the former to the latter period has been noted" (Lamberg-Karlovsky, 1970b:111).

The importance of Tepe Yahya lies in the fact that it represents the first Neolithic settlement in southern Iran discovered so far. This site is not an isolated settlement as other sites with typical chaff-tempered "soft-ware" have been located at Tepe Alash and Tepe Langar, 20 km north and 30 km southwest of Kirman respectively. A human burial of this culture has been recorded from the latter site. Another such settlement was located at Gholi Tepe, 10 km west of Dolatabad.

References

ADAMS, ROBERT M. (1962). Agriculture and Urban Life in Early Southwestern Iran. *Science, N.Y.*, **136**, 109-122.

BÖKÖNYI, S. (1970). Zoological Evidence for Seasonal or Permanent Occupation of Prehistoric Settlements. *Seminar Papers on Settlement Patterns and Urbanisation.*

BRAIDWOOD, R. J. (1952). Review of Cave Exploration in Iran 1949 by Carleton S. Coon. *Amer. Anthrop.*, **54**, (4), 551-553.

BRAIDWOOD, R. J. (1960a). Seeking the World's First Farmers in Persian Kurdistan: A Full-Scale Investigation of Prehistoric sites Near Kermanshah. *Ill. Lond. News*, **1960**, 695-696.

BRAIDWOOD, R. J. (1960b). Preliminary Investigations concerning the Origins of Food Production in Iranian Kurdistan. *J. Br. Ass. Advmt Sci.*, **17**, 214-8.

BRAIDWOOD, R. J. (1961). The Iranian Prehistoric Project. *Iranica Antiqua*, **1**, 3-7.

BRAIDWOOD, R. J., HOWE, B. AND REED, C. A. (1961). The Iranian Prehistoric Project. *Science, N.Y.*, **133**, 2008-2010.

CARTER, THERESA HOWARD (1972). Review of *Excavation at Tepe Yahya, Iran* 1967-1969, by C. C. Lamberg-Karlovsky. *Am. J. Archœol.*, **76** (1), 87-89.

COON, CARLETON S. (1951). *Cave Explorations in Iran* 1949. Philadelphia: University of Pennsylvania, The University Museum.

DYSON, ROBERT H. JR. (1960). Where the Golden Bowl of Hasanlu was Found: Excavations Near Lake Urmia which throw New Light on the Little-known Mannæans. *Ill. Lond. News*, **1960**, 132-134.

DYSON, ROBERT H. JR. (1961). Excavating the Mannæan Citadel of Hasanlu: And New Light on Several Millennia of Persian Azerbaizan. *Ill. Lond. News*, **1961**, 534-536.

DYSON, ROBERT H. JR. (1969). A Decade in Iran. *Expedition*, **11** (2), 39-47.

DYSON, ROBERT H. JR. AND YOUNG, T. CUYLER JR. (1960). The Solduz Valley, Iran: Pisdeli Tepe. *Antiquity*, **34**, 19-28.

DYSON, ROBERT H. JR., MUSCARELLA, OSCAR WHITE AND VOIGT, M. (1969). Hasanlu Project 1968: Hajji Firuz, Dinkha Tepe, Se Girdan, Qalatgeh. *Iran*, **7**, 179-181.

GHIRSHMAN, R. (1954). *Iran*, Harmondsworth: Penguin Books.

GOFF, CLARE L. (1971). Luristan Before the Iron Age. *Iran*, **9**, 131-152.

GOFF, CLARE AND PULLAR, JUDITH. (1970). Tepe Abdul Hosein. *Iran*, **8**, 199-200.

HOLE, F. (1962). Archæological Survey and Excavation in Iran 1961. *Science*, *N.Y.*, **137**, 524-526.

HOLE, F. (1968). Evidence of Social Organisation from Western Iran, 8000-4000 B.C. *New Perspectives in Archæology*. (Sally R. Binford and Lewis R. Binford, eds). Chicago: Aldine Press, pp. 245-266.

HOLE, F. (1969). Excavations at Choga Sefid. *Iran*, **7**, 171-172.

HOLE, FRANK AND FLANNERY, KENT V. (1962). Excavations at Ali Kosh, Iran, 1961). *Iranica Antiqua*, **2**, 97-148.

HOLE, FRANK AND FLANNERY, KENT V. (1967). The Pre-history of South-Western Iran: A Preliminary Report. *Proc. Prehist. Soc.*, **33**, 147-206.

HOLE, FRANK, FLANNERY, KENT V. AND NEELY, J. A. (1965). Early Agriculture and Animal Husbandry in Deh Luran, Iran. *Curr. Antrhop.*, **6** (1), 105-106.

HOLE, FRANK, FLANNERY, KENT V. AND NEELY, J. A. (1969). *Prehistory and Human Ecology of the Deh Luran Plain*. Ann Arbor: University of Michigan.

KEARTON, R. R. B. (1969). Survey in Azerbaijan. *Iran*, **7**, 186-187.

KUNIHIKO KIGOSHI (1967). Gakushuin Natural Radiocarbon Measurements VI. *Radiocarbon*, **9**, 61.

LAMBERG-KORLOVSKY, C. C. (1968). Survey and Excavations in the Kirman area. *Iran*, **6**, 167-168.

LAMBERG-KORLOVSKY, C. C. (1969). Excavations at Tepe Yahya. *Iran*, **7**, 184-186.

LAMBERG-KORLOVSKY, C. C. (1970*a*). Tepe Yahya. *Iran*, **8**, 197-199.

LAMBERG-KORLOVSKY, C. C. (1970*b*). *Excavations at Tepe Yahya, Iran, 1967-1969*. Progress Report I. Cambridge, Massachusetts: Peabody Museum: Harvard University.

LAMBERG-KORLOVSKY, C. C. (1971*a*). The Proto-Elamite Settlement at Tepe Yahya. *Iran*, **9**, 87-96.

LAMBERG-KORLOVSKY, C. C. (1971*b*). The Yahya Project: Tepe Yahya and Tepe Dasht-i-Deh. *Iran*, **9**, 182-183.

LAMBERG-KORLOVSKY, C. C. AND MEADOW, RICHARD H. (1970). A Unique Female Figurine: The Neolithic at Tepe Yahya. *Archæology*, **23**, 12-17.

LAWN, BARBARA (1970). University of Pennsylvania Radiocarbon Dates XIII. *Radiocarbon*, **12** (2), 579.

MELDGAARD, J., MORTENSEN, P. AND THRANE, H. (1964). Excavations at Tepe Guran, Luristan. *Acta Archæol.*, **34**, 97-133.

MORTENSEN, PEDER (1964). Additional Remarks on the Chronology of Early Village-Farming Communities. *Sumer*, **20**, 28-36.

NEELY, J. A. (1970). The Deh Luran Region. *Iran*, **8**, 202-203.

PERKINS, DEXTER JR. (1964). Prehistoric Fauna From Shanidar, Iraq. *Science*, *N.Y.*, **144**, 1565-66.

RALPH, ELIZABETH K. (1959). University of Pennsylvania Radiocarbon Dates III. *Radiocarbon*, **1**, 45-58.

SMITH, P. E. L. (1967). Excavations at Tepe Ganj-i-Dareh. *Iran*, **5,** 139.

SMITH, P. E. L. (1968). Excavations at Ganj Dareh Tepe. *Iran*, **6,** 158-160.

SMITH, P. E. L. (1970). Ganj Dareh Tepe. *Iran*, **8,** 178-180.

SMITH, P. E. L. (1972). Ganj Dareh Tepe. *Iran*, **10,** 165-168.

SOLECKI, RALPH S. (1963). Prehistory in Shanidar Valley, Northern Iraq. *Science, N. Y.*, **139,** 179-193.

SOLECKI, RALPH S. (1969). Survey in Western Azerbaijan. *Iran*, **7,** 189-90.

STUCKENRATH, ROBERT JR. (1963). University of Pennsylvania Radiocarbon Dates VI. *Radiocarbon*, **5,** 82-103.

TAUBER, HENRIK (1968). Copenhagen Radiocarbon Dates IX. *Radiocarbon*, **10** (2), 322.

WRIGHT, HENRY T. (1969). Excavations at Tepe Farukhabad. *Iran*, **7,** 172-173.

YOUNG, T. CUYLER, JR. (1962). Taking the History of the Hasanlu Area back another Five Thousand Years: Sixth and Fifth Millennium Settlements in the Solduz Valley, Persia. *Ill. Lond. News.* **1962,** 707-709.

YOUNG, T. CUYLER, JR. (1963). Dalma Painted Ware. *Expedition*, **5** (2), 38-39.

YOUNG, T. CUYLER, JR. (1967). Excavations at Godin Tepe. *Iran*, **5,** 139-140.

YOUNG, T. CUYLER, JR. (1968). Excavations at Godin Tepe. *Iran*, **6,** 160-161.

YOUNG, T. CUYLER, JR. (1969). *Excavations at Godin Tepe: First Preliminary Report.* Ontario: Royal Ontario Museum.

YOUNG, T. CUYLER, JR. (1970). Excavations at Godin Tepe. *Iran*, **8,** 180-182.

YOUNG, T. CUYLER, JR. AND SMITH, PHILIP E. L. (1966). Research in the Prehistory of Central Western Iran. *Science, N. Y.*, **153,** 386-391.

6. Summary

Architecture

The survey of the cultural assemblages of the earliest village-farming communities of western Asia presented in the preceding pages shows that the transition from the food-gathering to the food-producing stage was preceded by an era of intensive collection which may be dated to the beginning of the ninth millennium BC. This transition was a slow and long-drawn out process and was in no way uniform in all the parts of the foot-hill zone of the Fertile Crescent. An assured supply of food brought many changes in the life of the hitherto migratory or nomadic bands who gradually adopted a sedentary life. This change is noticeable in the archæological record in the form of permanent architecture (i.e. houses occupied all the year round) and the emergence of villages. No definite architectural trace is seen at Karim Shahir but the existence of some sort of permanent building is envisaged at Zawi Chemi in the form of crude walls of field-stones and river cobbles. Among other settlements of the 9th millennium BC Mureybit has yielded round buildings made of red clay walls. At almost every site the first settlers lived in flimsy huts but these soon changed to permanent structures of pisé, mud-brick or stone. This is clearly noticeable at such early sites as Ganj Dareh, Jericho and Guran and is apparent at later sites like Ramad, Bouqras, Suberde and Hassuna.

The earliest evidence for the use of mud-brick comes from Ganj Dareh in Iran where solid architecture goes back to the ninth millennium BC. Here, as on other sites of Neolithic culture, the first settlers lived in temporary huts but walls made of straw-tempered oval bricks and coated with white mud plaster have been noted from the succeeding levels. Again, some "brick shapes" have been identified in the Natufian levels at Beidha but the large buildings, discovered in the PPN levels at Nahal Oren, were made of boulders taken from the stream bed. Among the aceramic Neolithic sites of the Levant, Beidha yielded semi-subterranean houses comprising very small rooms with walls made of dry stones. Round or rectilinear houses made of plano-convex bricks have been discovered at PPNA Jericho and large, well-proportioned rooms with walls made of cigar-shaped bricks have been noted from the succeeding phase at this site. The inhabitants took much care to keep the houses clean and tidy as floors of flat thin stones have been observed at Nahal Oren. Walls and floors were covered with strong lime plaster at Beidha and floors were covered with gypsum plaster in the PPNB phase at Jericho.

Neolithic settlements in the Kermanshah and Deh Luran regions are not rich architecturally as they were excavated on a very limited scale but semi-subterranean depressions or pits, supposed to be for habitation, have been noted at Asiab and Sarab and small mud-brick houses with floors of stamped mud or clay have been discovered from the Bus Mordeh and Ali Kosh phases in Deh Luran. Several-roomed rectilinear mud-brick houses are present at Aceramic Jarmo and small rooms with walls of large mud-bricks have been discovered at Aceramic Hacilar. Among other early sites, Guran and Çayönü, both of which have mud-brick structures, have yielded beautiful floors made in the terrazzo technique. At the former site the floors are faced with red or white gypsum and the technique of making terrazzo floors at Çayönü has already been described (p. 84). By about 6500 BC, well-planned, carefully plastered mud-brick houses with elaborate decoration on the walls are seen at Çatal Hüyük and 1 m thick walls made of oblong flat bricks resting on stone foundations, presumably supporting the superstructure of two-storeyed buildings, have been exposed at Late Neolithic Hacilar. In Mesopotamia mud-brick does not occur in the Hassuna culture but its use is attested from the Samarra period onwards. By about the first half of the sixth millennium BC mud-brick was the principal building material both in Iraq and Iran and also at other sites in Turkey and the Levant. However, the shape and size of the bricks and the bonding technique differ at different sites. Thus while large, rectangular bricks are common on several sites in the Levant, loaf-shaped bricks were used at Munhata (Level IV). Bricks with hog-back outline, present at Jericho in the PPNA phase give way to flattened cigar-shaped bricks in the succeeding phase. Bricks similar to these were used at Choga Mami and at the nearby contemporary site of Es-Sawwan. A significant departure is the use of loaf-shaped lime-stone slabs at Mureybit. Here, the slabs were laid like ordinary bricks with red clay covering them. An element of town-planning with a defensive system is present at Jericho and a defensive system, though of much later date, has been suspected at Es-Sawwan.

In a recent paper, Flannery (1972) has raised the question of the house-plans and presents an interesting hypothesis. Circular, semi-subterranean huts with diameter ranging from 2·5-9 m have been found at Ain Mallaha. Similarly at Nahal Oren (Level II), 13 huts, 4-15 m in extent, have been exposed. Circular hut compounds with a floor space of 5-28 sq. m have been noted at Beidha. A few circular huts with stone foundations, 2·7-4 m in diameter, have been noted at Mureybit. Circular depressions, presumably used for habitation, have been discovered at Asiab and Sarab. These circular structures were gradually replaced by rectangular ones in the upper levels at Beidha and Mureybit. Flannery (1972:40) believes that between 7000 and 5000 BC over much of the Near East villages with rectangular houses replaced the circular hut compounds of the first sedentary communities. This change, according to him, is the result of the increased economic activity and the changed social system. He argues (Flannery, 1972:42). :

> It is not the "circular" or "rectangular" shape of the house which is crucial, but whether it is intended for a single individual or a family—in other words, whether the minimal unit of production and storage is a polygynous extended household or a (primarily) monogamous nuclear family.

Domestication of Plants

The transition from the nomadic to the settled life was largely the result of an economic revolution based on the domestication of plants like wheat and barley and of animals like sheep, goat, pig and cattle. The domestication and exploitation of plants and animals had a profound effect on the history of mankind; the people became sedentary and the assured supply of food gave rise to a rapid increase in the population. In the archæological record the presence of such artefacts as querns, grinding stones, bone hafts and sickle-blades is taken to indicate the collection of cereals for food. These have been recorded from the Natufian levels in Palestine. However, the new awareness among archæologists of the need to retrieve carbonised seeds and plant remains and the increasing cooperation of natural scientists in the examination of such materials is beginning to yield data about the domestication of plants and a general pattern has begun to emerge.

Among the cereal plants wheat and barley growing wild on the hilly flanks of the Fertile Crescent were harvested with composite sickles made of bone or wooden hafts mounted with stone sickle blades. The domestication of cereals was a gradual process and it took place in several stages. Initially, the cereal plants were gathered by sickles and no attempt was made to preserve the seeds and sow them in season. The second stage is marked by the increase of mutations adapted to more efficient harvesting by the selection of cereals with non-brittle rachis (Hawkes, 1969:22). The third and final stage is marked by sowing of carefully retained seeds in the more or less prepared soil of fields or gardens round the dwellings.

Here it is important to distinguish between the collection stage and the true domestication of plants. Zohary (1969:59) has rightly observed that

> where a cereal is harvested and *all* the grain yield obtained is used as food, we are dealing with a collection stage; when a cereal is harvested and later *one* part of the yield is used as food, while the second part of the grain is *intentionally planted* by man, we are dealing with *domestication*.

How was this domestication achieved? This phenomenon has been perhaps best summed up by Helbaek (1959a:184-5) in the following words:

> In wild grasses the spike axis is brittle. This is an important quality, for the individual spikelet, with the grains still in it, is released at maturity and subjected to transport by wind and animals. In some grasses, for instance the wild cereals, there is a recessive tendency to develop a tough axis, and the grains of such tough spikes loose their ability of dispersal. All the grains fall with the spike in one spot, and all but a few are choked in the competition.
>
> When man started to sow and reap the wild wheat, the recessive quality became an asset to him. He was apt to get the whole spike only when it was tough, while he would lose a certain amount of the grains of the brittle ones. Thus the tough-axis genes enjoyed priority in his harvesting, and eventually, as his technique became more summary, only the tough spikes were recovered. This was the actual act of domestication, as the tough axis cereals were no longer able to exist without the agency of man. They had become the serfs of man, but at the same time man had become the servant of the cereals, having made his new mode of life dependent upon them.

Archæological evidence demonstrates that the first domesticated cereal plants were wheat and barley and both were grown side by side. There is no instance of an early village farming community based upon only one of these cereals. Both occur in their wild state on the foothills of the highland areas which border the Fertile Crescent. These cereals were chosen for their versatility as they could adapt themselves to greatly varying soils, climate and altitude.

On the basis of the evidence obtained from western Asiatic sites during recent years for the domestication of various species of cereal plants, the position can be summarised as follows:

Emmer

By far the earliest and the commonest cereal cultivated in the Neolithic Near East was the tetraploid glume wheat called emmer (*Triticum dicoccum*). It is believed to have been domesticated from the wild emmer

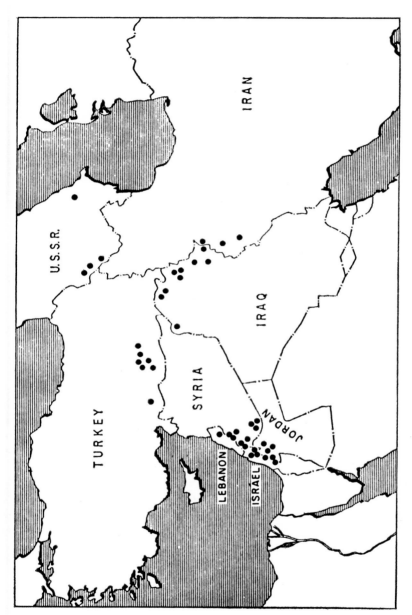

Fig. 71. Distribution of known and reasonably certain sites of wild emmer.

(*T. dicoccoides*). Wild emmer occurs in the earliest levels at Çayönü where it was harvested in the initial stages but its cultivated species has been reported from the upper levels at this site. Emmer (*T. dicoccum*) was grown at PPNA Jericho where the existence of an irrigation system has been suspected (Kenyon, 1959:40). Two grains of emmer have been found in the PPNA phase at this site. Among the sites of the eighth millennium BC and later, emmer was grown at Beidha where it is supposed to be a transitional form on the way to full domestication. Emmer has been reported from the Bus Mordeh phase in Deh Luran and from Aceramic levels at Hacilar. Among the settlements of the seventh and sixth millennia BC emmer has been reported from Late Neolithic Hacilar, Çatal Hüyük, Es-Sawwan, Choga Mami, Umm Dabaghiyah and the Ali Kosh and Mohammad Jaffar phases in Deh Luran. Helbaek (1960:103) believes that wild emmer (*T. dicoccoides*) grows from Palestine and Syria to the Zagros mountains and that it was brought to the west from northeastern Iraq. But Zohary (1969; also Harlan and Zohary 1966) believes that it is restricted to Israel, south Syria and Trans-Jordan. Harlan and Zohary (1966:1079) observe that emmer was probably domesticated in the upper Jordan watershed. This seems to be in conformity with the archæological evidences as its domesticated species has been reported from the PPNA phase at Jericho. The priority of the domestication of emmer over einkorn is shown at Jericho where einkorn occurs only from phase PPNB onward. A similar situation prevails in Deh Luran.

Einkorn

The next important variety of wheat grown in the Neolithic western Asia is a diploid glume wheat, einkorn (*T. monococcum*). Earlier, Helbaek (1959b:366, 1960:106) believed that einkorn was a descendant of the wild diploid *T. aegilopoides* Bal. but now he agrees (Helbaek, 1969, 1970) with Zohary (1969) that wild *T. boeoticum* is the ancestor of cultivated einkorn. Wild einkorn was collected at Mureybit in the ninth-eighth millennium BC. Wild einkorn has also been reported from Aceramic Hacilar, Choga Mami and from the Bus Mordeh phase in Deh Luran. The earliest evidence for the domestication of this species comes from Jericho where it occurs in the PPNB phase. Domestic einkorn, together with emmer, occurs at Ramad, Late Neolithic Hacilar, Çayönü, Jarmo Çatal Hüyük, Es-Sawwan and Choga Mami.

Zohary observes that wild einkorn (*T. boeoticum*) has a relatively wide distribution as it occurs in the Fertile Crescent belt of southern Turkey, northern Iraq and adjacent territories in northern Syria and again in west Anatolia. Helbaek postulates that einkorn may have been at first grown

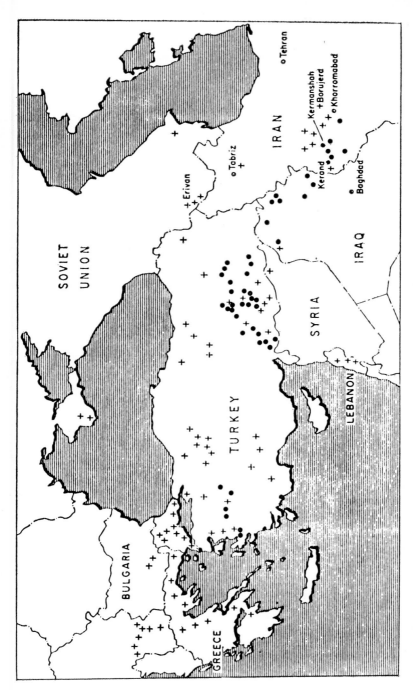

FIG. 72. Distribution of known and reasonably certain sites of wild einkorn wheat (solid circles); Fairly primary habitats (crosses).

unintentionally together with emmer and only later selected in itself as a crop. He also believes that this selection may have taken place in Cilicia where it seems to have thrived unusually well in antiquity. But Harlan and Zohary (1966:1079; also *cf*. Zohary, 1969:59) believe that einkorn was first domesticated in southeast Turkey.

Barley

The second cereal which played an important role in the diet of Neolithic man is barley. It is classified into two main groups, the two-row and the six-row types. The earliest cultivated barley is the two-row type (*Hordeum distichum*) which is believed to be derived from the wild two-row barley (*H. spontaneum*). Wild barley was collected at Mureybit but its domesticated variety was the chief crop at Aceramic Neolithic Beidha. The same species (*H. distichum*) is present in the PPNA level at Jericho and two-row hulled barley has been reported from Aceramic Hacilar. Two-row hulled barley closely resembling the wild *H. spontaneum* but obviously with tough axes was grown at Jarmo (Helbaek, 1960:117). Again, it is present in the Bus Mordeh phase in Deh Luran where it continues to be grown in the suceeding Ali Kosh and Mohammad Jaffar phases. It was also cultivated at Ramad (phase I), Choga Mami and at Es-Sawwan. Naked barley is present at Çatal Hüyük.

A new mutant of barley, the hulled six-row form (*Hordeum vulgare*) seems to have been grown at a comparatively late stage and it occurs for the first time in the middle of the Mohammad Jaffar phase in Deh Luran (Helbaek, 1969:395). These levels are datable to *c*. 5800 BC. This variety has also been recovered from Late Neolithic Hacilar and Can Hasan. Six-row naked barley (*H. vulgare var. nudum*) is also present at Late Neolithic Hacilar and was grown at Es-Sawwan, Umm Dabaghiyah and Choga Mami. Harlan and Zohary (1966; also Zohary, 1969) observe that the wild two-row brittle barley (*H. spontaneum*) the sole ancestor of all barley, is spread in a wide area in an arc in the Fertile Crescent starting from Israel and Trans-Jordan in the southwest, stretching north towards south Turkey and bending southeast towards Iraqi Kurdistan and southwest Iran and it could have been domesticated almost anywhere within this area.

Other Species

Among the leguminous plants the earliest domesticated species seems to be lentil which has been reported from Aceramic Hacilar. Wild lentil was harvested at Mureybit but its domesticated variety occurred at Late Neolithic Hacilar, Çatal Hüyük, Jarmo, Choga Mami and the Ali Kosh

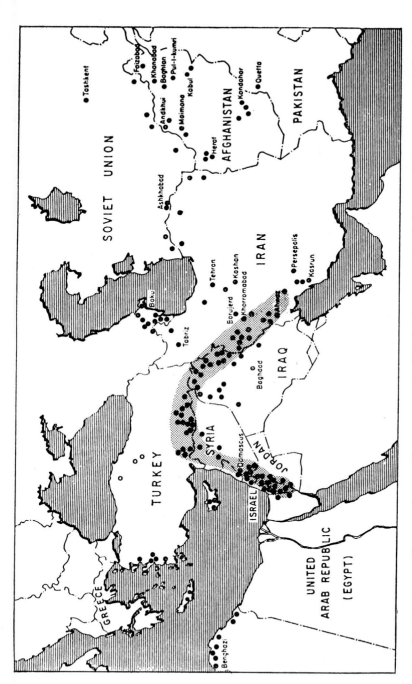

FIG. 73. Distribution of known and reasonably certain sites of wild barley. Massive stands in fairly primary habitats may occur within the shaded area. Elsewhere, wild barley may be abundant, but confined to highly disturbed habitats.

and Mohammad Jaffar phases in Deh Luran. Several leguminous plants have also been identified at Beidha. Wild vetch has been collected from Mureybit and Çayönü and bitter vetch from Late Neolithic Hacilar and Ramad. Blue vetchling occurs at Jarmo. Peas have been recovered from Late Neolithic Hacilar and field-pea occurs at Jarmo and Çatal Hüyük. Among the Neolithic Man's favourite fruits, pistachio seems to be the most important. Pistachio nuts have been recorded from Mureybit, Beidha, Çayönü, Ramad, Çatal Hüyük, Jarmo and Late Neolithic Hacilar. Pieces of shell or occasionally whole fruits of pistachio have been recorded from the Bus Mordeh phase in Deh Luran. Almond has been found from Neolithic levels at Ramad, Çayönü and Çatal and from chalcolithic levels at Hacilar. Acorn was recorded at Beidha, Jarmo and Çatal. Hackberry (*Celtis australis*) occurs at Çatal and Aşikli and hawthorn has been reported from Ramad.

Among the grasses three types, viz: goat-face, rye and oats, are very common in Neolithic settlements in western Asia. The first, goat-faced grass (*Aegilops crassa*), has been reported from Beidha, Es-Sawwan and from the earliest three phases in Deh Luran. Rye, (*Secale cereale L.*) occurs at Beidha and in the Bus Mordeh to Mohammad Jaffar phases in Deh Luran. Wild oats (*Avena fatua L.*) have been reported from Beidha and the first three phases in Deh Luran.

The practice of early agriculture is associated with the problem of the introduction of irrigation. Here it may be remarked that all the crops mentioned above were grown in the natural rainfall zone (of 200 mm per annum) during the ninth to sixth millennia. Jericho seems to provide the first evidence for the existence of an irrigation system, although the existence of one has been suspected by Kenyon in the PPNA phase but this remains to be established by positive evidence. The occurrence and the size of linseed at Es-Sawwan has led Helbaek (1964:47) to observe that some sort of irrigation was employed at this site. He believes that the seasonal flood waters of the river were checked in favourable spots by primitive damming and spill pools were exploited. More seemingly positive proof comes from Choga Mami where a series of water channels, some of which are believed to have been irrigation ditches, have been identified. Further, it has been claimed that by Çatal Hüyük VI (*c.* 6000 BC) and Hacilar VI-I, (*c.* 5600-5000 BC) irrigation agriculture had taken over from dry farming (Mellaart, 1972:282) but this claim remains to be substantiated by other studies.

Domestication of Animals

A review of the faunal material from the Neolithic sites of western

Asia reveals that the domestication of animals like that of plants, was a gradual process that took place in different regions at different times. This is best exemplified on the Neolithic sites of southwestern Turkey. Thus while several species were domesticated on sites like Çatal Hüyük and Late Neolithic Hacilar, no domestic animal, except the dog, was reported from the contemporary site of Suberde, only 80 km southwest of Çatal. Similarly, while the domestication of sheep had already taken place at Zawi Chemi in the beginning of the ninth millennium BC, no animal was domesticated at Mureybit even in the late ninth or early eighth millennium BC.

Dog

Dog, the close companion of man in the hunt and other daily pursuits, is believed to be, perhaps rightly, the first domesticated animal although no skeletal remains of this animal are forthcoming from such early sites as Zawi Chemi. However, dog was the only domesticated animal among the hunting communities of Aceramic Hacilar, Suberde and the lower levels at Çayönü. The possibility of the domestic dog being present in the Natufian levels of Mt. Carmel has now been discounted (Reed, 1960:127). According to Zeuner (1958) dog is present in the lower "plaster floor levels" (PPNB) at Jericho but in a recent study, Clutton-Brock (1969) is not clear whether the bones and teeth are definitely of dog and not of the local wolf. Terracotta figurines of dog have been reported from Jarmo but the claim that skeletal remains of this animal were found (Braidwood, 1952) has not been substantiated in the renewed excavation of this site in 1955 when all the excavated canid bones belonged to foxes and wolves (Reed, 1960:128). Among the later sites, dog bones have been reported from Choga Mami and Çatal Hüyük. Dog is also represented in a hunting scene of Level III at the latter site.

Sheep

Reed following Ellerman and Morrison-Scott (1951), believes that the first domestic sheep were derived from the wild *Ovis orientalis*. Until recently, it was believed that besides the dog, the earliest domestic animal was not sheep but goat. But the evidence from Zawi Chemi shows that domestic sheep were present at this site in the early ninth millennium BC (Perkins, 1964). Here the percentage of immature *Ovis* reached approximately 50 % and Perkins believes that domestic sheep, morphologically identical to their wild ancestors, were introduced to Zawi Chemi from some other region. Evidence for the presence of domestic sheep is not forthcoming from chronologically immediately succeeding sites; no domestic sheep are present at Jericho and the evidence from Belt cave (Coon, 1951) is not acceptable to scholars (Reed, 1960). However, domestic sheep are present in the upper levels at Çayönü and Stampfli thinks, (quoted by Reed, 1969), that sheep at Jarmo were also probably domesticated. Sheep were herded in the Bus Mordeh phase in Deh Luran along with goat but the latter animal is ten times more numerous here than sheep. A similar situation prevails in the succeeding Ali Kosh phase but the proportion of sheep gradually increases towards the end of the Mohammad Jaffar phase. Among the later sites, domestic sheep are present at Ramad (Phase III), Es Sawwan and Choga Mami but this animal remained wild at Suberde where it accounts for 85% of the sheep/goat bones.

Goat

It is now generally accepted that the domestic goat was derived from the Asiatic bezoar or pasang (*Capra hircus aegagrus*), the only wild goat found in southwestern Asia. Zeuner (1955) believes that the earliest domestic goats from this region were not screw-horned but scimitar-horned. The earliest domestic goats were supposed to be present in the Natufian III-IV levels at El Khiam in the wadi Kharaitun (Vaufrey, 1951) but are now not accepted as such (Reed, 1960:132). Three horn cores of goats have been reported from PPN Jericho and Zeuner (1955:75; also *cf*. Reed, 1959:1631) believes them to be domestic but a recent study of these remains by Clutton-Brock (1969:340) reveals that they were still wild. Reed is convinced that domestic goat were present at Jarmo and they are believed to be domesticated at Sarab and the Belt cave. Among other early sites, goats are the only domesticated animal at Beidha (Perkins, 1966:66-7). That this animal was domesticated at Ganj Dareh is suggested by the presence of hoof-prints of goat/sheep on oval bricks from Level D. This has also been confirmed by the preliminary studies of the faunal remains of this site by Perkins (quoted by Smith, 1972:167-8). Goats were also domesticated in Deh Luran. They were herded in the Bus Mordeh phase where, as noted above, they were ten times more numerous than sheep. Goats still outnumber sheep in the succeeding Ali Kosh phase in this region. This animal was domestic in the upper levels at Çayönü but it seems to have remained wild at Suberde and Çatal Hüyük. In an unpublished study Flannery (quoted by Mortensen, 1972:295) states that goat horn cores, sufficiently medially flattened to suggest the domestic form, were already present in the lower levels at Guran and the goats in those levels represented anywhere from 80% to 100% of the ungulate remains. Among the late seventh millennium and the early sixth millennium sites, domestic goat is present at Ramad III, Es-Sawwan, Choga Mami and at the Halafian site of Gird Banahilk.

Pig

Reed (1960) believes that pig was domesticated from the wild *Sus scrofa* and that its domestication occurred at different times in different places. The earlier claim of Vaufrey (1951) that pigs were perhaps domesticated at the Natufian site of El-Khiam is no longer acceptable as it is based on a solitary phalanx of *Sus*. Wild pig is present at Suberde. Perhaps the earliest domesticated pig comes from the upper levels at Çayönü and a similar situation prevails at Jarmo where wild pigs are present in the lower levels but their domesticated species occurred in the upper layers with pottery (Reed, 1969). Domestic pig is present at Ramad III, Choga Mami and Belt cave. Thus on the present showing it seems that pig was not domesticated prior to the first half of the seventh millennium BC. In an unpublished study, Stampfli (quoted by Reed, 1969) states that pig bones are found on numerous sites but nowhere are they more than 5 % of the bones of food animals. They were, however, more numerous (25 %) at Matarrah.

Cattle

Long-horned wild cattle (*Bos primigenius*) were distributed throughout southwest Asia prior to the historic times and, like the pig, were domesticated almost two thousand years later than the first domestication of sheep and goats. An earlier claim of Vaufrey that domestic cattle were probably present in the Natufian El-Khiam, is no longer tenable as it is based on insufficient data. Cattle remains were extremely rare at Jarmo and Stampfli could not find any evidence of domestic cattle there. In recent excavations, wild ox has been found at Suberde. Cattle bones were prominent (90 %) at Çatal Hüyük and domestic cattle are present here in Level VI. It is believed that these were also present in the earliest excavated levels (Levels X-XII) at this site. Cattle were domesticated a little later at the Belt cave and at Tepe Sabz in Deh Luran. Domestic ox is present in Ramad III, Choga Mami, Yarim Tepe and Amuq D. On the present evidence, it seems reasonable to believe that cattle were domesticated in southwestern Asia in the later half of the seventh millennium BC. At approximately the same time, cattle domestication was taking place elsewhere outside this nuclear zone. Domestic cattle have been reported from Argissa-Maghula (6500 BC) in Greek Thessaly and at the next oldest site of Nea Nikomedeia in Macedonia (Reed, 1969: 372-3).

Among other animals, it has been suggested that gazelle were probably tamed and kept in herds to be killed as needed but this remains to be established by positive evidence.

Pottery

Recent researches in the prehistory of western Asia have revolution-ised our earlier ideas regarding the origins and antiquity of pottery making. An attempt is made here to examine the new evidence regarding this industry.

Pottery, once considered to be the hallmark of the Neolithic, is now no longer a diagnostic trait as many preceramic settlements have been discovered. Perhaps, the best example of this type is Jericho, where an aceramic stage spanned several centuries of occupation divisible into two sub-phases. A similar situation also obtains at Ganj Dareh, Jarmo, Guran, Shimshara, Ramad, Bouqras and Munhata where the first habitation started with an aceramic culture and pottery appears at a subsequent stage. Sites like Beidha, Mureybit, Aşikli Hüyük, Suberde, Çayönü, Asiab, and Bus Mordeh in Deh Luran have no pottery at all and they all end in the preceramic stage. However, before the art of pottery making was discovered, Neolithic man made and used vessels of soft stone. That stone vessels antedate the invention of the potter's craft is demonstrated by the occurrence of stone vessels on a number of preceramic sites in western Asia. The rims of a stone bowl and limestone plates with diameter ranging from 23-35 cm have been reported from Mureybit and a similar rim fragment comes from Çayönü. Fragments of bowls, ground from a soft stone, come from the Bus Mordeh phase in Deh Luran. Bowls with carefully polished sides and made of locally available alabaster and gypsum, are present at Bouqras in Level I (preceramic) and 14 fragments of bowls of pink or cream coloured marble come from the aceramic levels at Shimshara. But the richest example of this industry comes from Jarmo where a thousand fragments of marble bowls were recorded from the preceramic levels in one season alone. This industry did not die out with the discovery of the potter's art and stone vessels were present along with pottery vessels at Late Neolithic Hacilar, Çatal Hüyük and Guran, and a large collection of alabaster vessels, associated with pottery, has been made at Es-Sawwan.

Besides stone vessels, containers of wood and other perishable materials were also made by the Neolithic folk. Evidence for such materials has been found only in cases where the objects or impressions of them have survived in exceptionally favourable conditions. A wooden palette, 40 cm in diameter, and a bitumen-coated basket with a diameter of 45 cm have been discovered in the aceramic Neolithic levels at Beidha. An oval wooden box, represented only by shadows in the soil, was also discovered at this site. "Wicker" baskets, water-proofed with asphalt, have been reported from the Ali Kosh phase in Deh Luran. This tradition continues even after the introduction of the potter's craft as is seen by the occurrence at Çatal Hüyük of wooden vessels like large dishes with handles, oval bowls, and small boxes with lids. This site has also yielded baskets made of wheat-straw.

The invention of the potter's craft had far-reaching effects and

> once the basic ceramic techniques were mastered clay proved so much more workable than stone that it quickly became not only the most abundant source of objects in man's material repertory, but also the readiest medium for reflecting every change in his artistic taste and expression (Hallo and Simpson, 1971: 16).

Chronologically, the earliest pottery does not appear either at Jericho or Jarmo. Until recently, Çatal Hüyük had the privilege of being the earliest Neolithic settlement with pottery present in a context datable to 6500 BC. Here it may be pointed out that virgin soil was not reached at this site and further excavation may push the antiquity of the ceramic art still earlier. Pottery is present in the earliest excavated level in the form of a heavy-built, burnished ware known as the Cream Burnished ware. It is hand-made and ill-fired. As may be expected at this early stage, only simple shapes such as bowls, shallow basins and one or two oval vessels have been recorded. These are devoid of any incised or painted decoration.

The antiquity of pottery has been pushed back by almost half a millennium by the recent work at Ganj Dareh in the Gamās Āb valley where pottery has been reported from a site datable to 7000 BC or even earlier. Such unmistakable shapes as fragments of large jars have been found from the upper levels at this site. The lower levels remain inadequately explored and more work, currently under progress, is likely to bring forth interesting data.

Among other early sites in Iraq and Iran, pottery is present in the upper one-third deposit at Jarmo, in the Mohammad Jaffar phase in Deh Luran, at Sarab in the Kermanshah plain and in the middle layers at Guran and Shimshara. At all these sites, the pottery is hand made, ill-fired and has a burnished surface, but in contrast to Çatal Hüyük in Anatolia once the potter's art was discovered, it gained momentum at a comparatively fast pace and painted wares occur almost immediately alongside the plain wares. The shapes remain simple, and mainly various forms of bowl; but great innovations were made in the technique of manufacture and

H

surface decoration. Several fabrics (e.g. five fabrics at Guran and three in the Mohammad Jaffar phase) have been recorded. As has been rightly remarked, the making of painted pottery requires a technical accomplishment of a relatively high order.

> It necessitates baking in a kiln which prevents access of free flames to the pots, and firing to a high temperature; moreover, it demands a knowledge of the empirical chemistry involved in choosing and controlling the composition of slips and paints which will fire to the desired combination of colours or tones (Clark and Piggott, 1970: 177).

Painted pottery is present at Jarmo, Sarab, in the Mohammad Jaffar phase, as also at Guran and Shimshara.

Ceramic art in the Levant underwent an intermediary stage of development and at sites like Ramad and Bouqras, true pottery is preceded by the manufacture of a kind of white vessel in moulded plaster (called *vaisselle blanche* by the excavators). This ware is present at Ramad II and Bouqras II. True pottery appears in the succeeding phases at both these sites and is datable to the beginning of the sixth millennium BC. It is designated "Dark-Faced Burnished ware". This pottery is handmade and is generally devoid of any surface decoration except for some incised designs on the exterior. A similar situation obtains at Munhata where *vaisselle blanche* is absent and the pottery shows more shapes and surface decorations, both incised and painted. Thus, by about the close of the seventh millennium BC pottery becomes an integral part of the Neolithic cultures throughout the whole of the Near East and shortly afterwards, regional ceramic industries begin to manifest themselves in different parts of western Asia.

The Obsidian Trade

That the Neolithic village-farming communities of western Asia had trade contact with each other is demonstrated by the occurrence of obsidian, a kind of volcanic glass, used in prehistoric times for the manufacture of chipped tools. Obsidian in its natural state is plentiful in Anatolia and two major geographical foci of obsidian sources have been identified. Of these, one is in central Anatolia (Cappadocia) and the other is centred in the Lake Van region of eastern Turkey. For this reason obsidian is the principal material of stone tools in the early cultures of Anatolia. The chipped stone tools of Çatal Hüyük are almost exclusively (about 95 %) made of obsidian and this material accounts for 99·9 % of the chipped stone industry at Aşikli Hüyük. It accounts for 90 % of the tools at Suberde and 42 % at Late Neolithic Hacilar. All the chipped stone tools of Mersin are made of black obsidian and there is an abundant obsidian industry at Çayönü although its percentage there is not known.

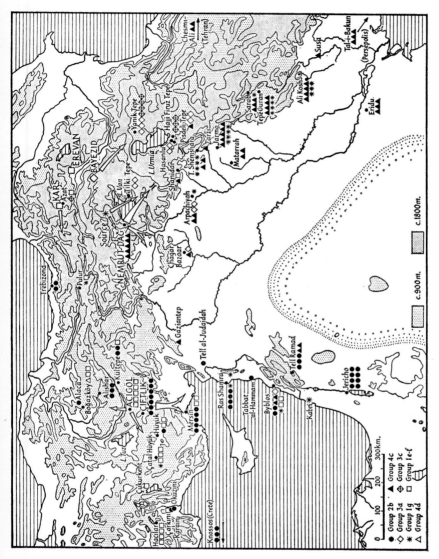

Fig. 74. Map showing the obsidian trade in the prehistoric Near East. Sources are shown in capital letters.

This abundance of obsidian was responsible for such exotic uses as the manufacture of mirrors, beads and pendants at Çatal Hüyük Level VI (5700-5600 BC) and inlays and figurines in Level I at Hacilar.

Outside the Anatolian centres this material is not plentiful and its presence is the result of trade contacts with them. There is no known source of obsidian in western Turkey, Iran, Iraq and the Levant, and the proportion of obsidian in the total chipped stone industry on sites in these countries tends to vary inversely with the distance from the nearest source. Wright (1969:25) remarks that no obsidian is reported from the Natufian sites in the Levant and it first appears during the PPNA phase at Jericho and Nahal Oren. At the former site it accounts for less than 1 % of the raw material of the lithic industries and its supply further diminishes in the succeeding PPNB phase. Renfrew, Dixon and Cann (1966) remark that all the obsidian fragments from the pre-pottery levels at Jericho derive from Çiftlik, about 40 km northwest of Niğde, on the road to Nevşehir, Central Anatolia. Obsidian is extremely rare at Mureybit, where, in a collection of 70,000 pieces of stone tools, only five pieces of this material were identified. It accounts for very few pieces at Beidha and a similar situation prevails at Ramad where only a few pieces were reported from Level I. It becomes more plentiful there in Level II but its percentage declines in Level III. A similar situation obtains at the contemporary site of Bouqras where it is present in limited quantity in Level I but becomes plentiful in Level III, which is partly contemporaneous with Ramad II. However, obsidian is rare at Munhata.

Turning our attention to the foothills of the Zagros and the Kermanshah plains, we find that obsidian, though known on early sites, was extremely rare. So far, it is totally absent at such early sites as Ganj Dareh and only a dozen pieces have been recorded from Shanidar cave, Level B. A single piece comes from the contemporary site of Zawi Chemi. Six pieces of obsidian have been reported from Karim Shahir and two bladelets come for M'Lefaat (Renfrew, 1969:430). Gird Chai has a total of eight pieces only. However, by about 7500 BC, obsidian trade starts on a limited scale and its supply gradually increases in later times. At Sarab it accounts for 1·7 % of the total chipped stone. It accounts for 1 % of the tools in the Bus Mordeh phase in Deh Luran and the volume of trade increases to 2·5 % in the succeeding Ali Kosh phase but drops again to 1·5 % in the Mohammad Jaffar phase (Wright, 1969). By about the middle of the seventh millennium BC the obsidian trade flourishes on a considerably larger scale. At Jarmo it accounts for 28 % in the pre-ceramic stage and it rises to 45 % of the tools during the ceramic phase. Its percentage fluctuates at Guran where it accounts for 46 % in Level T and only 6 % in Levels S and O (Wright, 1969). However, at Shimshara in the grassy valley south of Rania, most of the chipped stone material (87 %) was obsidian (Renfrew, 1970:140). The volume of trade seems to have been maintained in northern Mesopotamia in the sixth and fifth millennia BC. At Arpachiyah obsidian is as common as flint and 94 pieces of this material have been collected at Matarrah. It is present in all the five phases at Es-Sawwan and is found in large quantities on all the Halafian sites even after the introduction of the metal tools.

The spatial and chronological distribution of obsidian presented above, leads us to conclude that the nuclear zone of this material was Anatolia. It began to be exported in trade to the Levant around 7500 BC and at about the same time eastwards to the Zagros and Deh Luran region. While this trade did not flourish to any appreciable extent in the Levant, its volume increased greatly in the eastern region during the following millennia. Thus beginning with the Karim Shahir phase, it is present in all the sites in the early stages of settled life in the Zagros range.

A trace element analysis by optical spectrography of obsidian artefacts from different sites in the Near East by Renfrew et al. (1966, 1968) has brought forth interesting results regarding the ancient trade patterns. They conclude that the obsidian of Çatal Hüyük was brought from the Acigöl region, about 200 km northeast of this site and that of Aşikli came from the Çiftlik source in central Anatolia. The obsidian of the Levant was imported from long distances. The obsidian of Beidha came mainly from the Çiftlik source as also from the Lake Van district, about 900 km north-east of Beidha. Wright (1969:61) remarks that obsidian from the Lake Van region entered southern Levant by the PPNB phase and it reached Deh Luran in the Bus Mordeh phase. As has been noted above, the Çiftlik source was responsible for all the obsidian fragments present in the PPN Jericho. About 90 % of the obsidian found at Ramad I came from Cappadocia and the remaining 10 % from Nemrut Dağ, and east of Bingöl in eastern Turkey. The obsidian of Bouqras came from sources in eastern Anatolia and Renfrew et al. argue that this material reached the Levantine sites like Ramad and Beidha via Bouqras. However, the recent radio-carbon dates of Bouqras do not substantiate this hypothesis. While this hypothesis may be true for Ramad, Beidha had been practically abandoned when the settlement at Bouqras came into existence. All the obsidian of Shimshara came from East Anatolia and the high percentage of this material there indicates that the site was on the periphery of the eastern Anatolian supply zone. Renfrew (1970:141) remarks that Shimshara was in

fairly close cultural contact rather than simply in trading contact with the inhabitants of the supply zone and the area occupied by the obsidian sources of eastern Anatolia.

Renfrew *et al.* (1966) argue that the obsidian sources were probably visited by specialists at regular intervals and that this material was carried on foot. They also argue that trade along the Levantine coast, from Mersin as far south as Jericho was probably by sea but in the Zagros area and in Anatolia, trade must have been on foot. In the absence of beasts of burden—unless the sheep was used as a pack animal at that time, as sometimes in Tibet today—traders presumably carried their own merchandise (Renfrew, 1969:433). The pattern of prehistoric Near Eastern trade will be much clearer when we have scientific studies of such materials as turquoise, dentalium and cowrie shells. Turquoise matrix in lumps found at PPN Jericho is believed to have come from Sinai and the cowrie shells at this site from the Mediterranean. Turquoise occurring in the Ali Kosh phase in Deh Luran is supposed to have been brought from the mines near Meshed (Wright, 1969:57).

References

BRAIDWOOD, ROBERT J. (1952). *The Near East and the Foundations of Civilization.* Oregon: Eugene.

CLARK, GRAHAM AND PIGGOTT, STUART (1970). *Prehistoric Societies.* Harmondsworth: Penguin Books.

CLUTTON-BROCK, JULIET (1969). Carnivore Remains from the Excavations of the Jericho Tell. *The Domestication and Exploitation of Plants and Animals* (P. J. Ucko and G. W. Dimbleby, eds). London: Duckworth, pp. 337-45.

COON, CARLETON S. (1951). *Cave Explorations in Iran in 1949.* Philadelphia: The University Museum.

ELLERMAN, J. R. AND MORRISON-SCOTT, T. C. S. (1951). *Checklist of Palæarctic and Indian Mammals, 1758 to 1940.* London: British Museum, Natural History.

FLANNERY, KENT V. (1972). The Origins of the Village as a Settlement Type in Mesoamerica and the Near East: A comparative Study. *Man, Settlement and Urbanism* (P. J. Ucko, Ruth Tringham and G. W. Dimbleby, eds). London: Duckworth, pp. 23-53.

HARLAN, JACK R. AND ZOHARY, DANIEL (1966). Distribution of Wild Wheats and Barley. *Science, N.Y.,* **153,** 1074-80.

HAWKES, J. G. (1969). The Ecological Background of Plant Domestication. *The Domestication and Exploitation of Plant and Animals* (P. J. Ucko and G. W. Dimbleby, eds). London: Duckworth, pp. 17-30.

HELBAEK, HANS (1959a). How Farming Began in the Old World. *Archæology,* **12,** 183-9.

HELBAEK, HANS (1959b). Domestication of Food Plants in the Old World. *Science, N.Y.,* **130,** 365-72.

HELBAEK, HANS (1960). The Paleoethnobotany of the Near East and Europe. *Prehistoric Investigations in Iraqi Kurdistan* (SAOC 31) (R. J. Braidwood and Bruce Howe, eds). Chicago: Chicago University Press, pp. 99-118.

HELBAEK, HANS (1964). Early Hassunan Vegetable Food at Es-Sawwan Near Samarra. *Sumer*, **20** (1-2), 45-8.

HELBAEK, HANS (1969). Plant Collecting, Dry Farming and Irrigation Agriculture in Prehistoric Deh Luran. *Prehistory and Human Ecology in the Deh Luran Plain* (F. Hole, K. V. Flannery and J. A. Neely, eds). Ann Arbor: University of Michigan, pp. 383-426.

HELBAEK, HANS (1970). Plant Husbandry of Hacilar: A Study of Cultivation and Domestication. *Excavations at Hacilar*. (James Mellaart, ed.). Edinburgh: Edinburgh University Press. Vol. I, pp. 189-244.

HALLO, WILLIAM W. AND SIMPSON, WILLIAM KELLY (1971). *The Ancient Near East: A History*. New York: Harcourt Brace Jovanovich.

KENYON, KATHLEEN M. (1959). Some Observations on the Beginnings of Settlement in the Near East. *J. R. Anthrop. Inst.*, **89**, (1), 35-43.

MELLAART, JAMES (1972). Anatolian Neolithic Settlement Patterns. *Man, Settlement and Urbanism* (P. J. Ucko, Ruth Tringham and G. W. Dimbleby, eds). London: Duckworth, pp. 279-84.

PERKINS, DEXTER, JR. (1964). Prehistoric Fauna from Shanidar, Iraq. *Science, N.Y.*, **144**, 1565-6.

PERKINS, DEXTER, JR. (1966). The Fauna from Madamagh and Beidha. *Palestine Explor. Q.*, 66-67.

PERKINS, DEXTER, JR. (1969). Fauna of Çatal Hüyük: Evidence of Early Cattle Domestication in Anatolia. *Science, N.Y.*, **164**, 177-79.

REED, CHARLES A. (1959). Animal Domestication in the Prehistoric Near East. *Science, N.Y.*, **130**, 1929-39.

REED, CHARLES A. (1960). A Review of the Archæological Evidence on Animal Domestication in the Prehistoric Near East. *Prehistoric Investigations in Iraqi Kurdistan* (R. J. Braidwood and Bruce Howe, eds). Chicago: Chicago University Press, pp. 119-45.

REED, CHARLES A. (1969). The Pattern of Animal Domestication in the Prehistoric Near East. *The Domestication and Exploitation of Plants and Animals* (P. J. Ucko and G. W. Dimbleby, eds). London: Duckworth, pp. 361-80.

RENFREW, COLIN. (1969). The Sources and Supply of the Deh Luran Obsidian. *Prehistory and Human Ecology of the Deh Luran Plain* (F. Hole, K.V. Flannery and J. A. Neely, eds). Ann Arbor: University of Michigan, pp. 429-433.

RENFREW, COLIN. (1970). Tell Shimshara and the Traffic in Obsidian. *Tell Shimshara: The Hassuna Period* (Peder Mortensen, ed.). København: Kommissionaer, Munksgaard, pp. 139-148.

RENFREW, COLIN, DIXON, J. F. AND CANN, J. R. (1966). Obsidian and Early Cultural Contact in the Near East. *Proc. Prehist. Soc.*, **32**, 30-72.

RENFREW, COLIN, DIXON, J. F. AND CANN, J. R. (1966). Further Analysis of Near Eastern Obsidians. *Proc. Prehist. Soc.*, **34**, 319-31.

SMITH, PHILIP E. L. (1972). Ganj Dareh Tepe. *Iran*, **10**, 165-168.

VAUFREY, RAYMOND. (1951) Étude Paléontologique. I. Mammifères. *Archives de L'Institut paléontologie humaine. Mémoire*, **24**, 198-217.

WRIGHT, GARY A. (1969). *Obsidian Analyses and Prehistoric Near Eastern Trade: 7500 to 3500 B.C.* Anthropological Papers, Museum of Anthropology University of Michigan No. 37. Ann Arbor: The University of Michigan.

ZEUNER, F. E. (1955). The Goats of Early Jericho. *Palestine Explor. Q.*, 70-86.

ZEUNER, F. E. (1958). Dog and Cat in the Neolithic of Jericho. *Palestine Explor. Q.*, 52-55.

ZOHARY, DANIEL. (1969). The Progenitors of Wheat and Barley in Relation to Domestication and Agricultural Dispersal in the Old World. *The Domestication and Exploitation of Plants and Animals* (P. J. Ucko and G. W. Dimbleby, eds). London: Duckworth, pp. 47-66.

Appendix I: Radiocarbon Dates from Neolithic Sites in Western Asia

All dates in BC and based on the Libby half-life

Laboratories

BM, British Museum
C, Chicago
F, Freiberg
Gak, Gakushuin University
GL, Geochronological, London
Gro, Groningen
GX, Geochron Laboratories Inc.
W, U.S. Geological Laboratory

H, Heidelberg
I, Teledyne Isotopes
K, Copenhagen
P, Pennsylvania
SI, Smithsonian Institute
UCLA, University of California, Los
   Angeles

The Levant

Beidha

6600 ± 160	K 1085	Level II
6942 ± 115	P 1382	Level II
6815 ± 102	P 1381	
6780 ± 160	K 1084	
6840 ± 200	BM 111	Level IV
7178 ± 103	P 1380	
6690 ± 160	K 1083	Level V
6596 ± 100	P 1379	
6765 ± 100	P 1378	
6760 ± 130	K 1082	
6990 ± 160	K 1086	Level VI
6900 ± 150	K 1410	
6820 ± 150	K 1411	
6770 ± 150	K 1412	

Jericho

Mesolithic

9216 ± 107	P 376
7950 ± 70	Gro 942
7900 ± 240	F 69
7850 ± 240	F 72

PPNA

8230 ± 200	BM 110
8350 ± 200	BM 106
8300 ± 200	BM 105
8350 ± 500	BM 250
7440 ± 150	BM 251
7370 ± 150	BM 252
7705 ± 84	P 379
7632 ± 89	P 377
7825 ± 110	P 378
6770 ± 210	GL 40
6870 ± 210	GL 40
6775 ± 210	F 40
6850 ± 160	F 39

PPNB

7220 ± 200	BM 115
7220 ± 200	BM 111
6760 ± 150	BM 253
6660 ± 75	P 380
6708 ± 101	P 381
7006 ± 103	P 382
6250 ± 200	GL 28
5850 ± 200	GL 38
5850 ± 160	F 38
6720 ± 200	F 40
6950 ± 70	Gr 942
6835 ± 100	Gr 963

Mureybit

8142 ± 118	P 1216	} Stratum I
8056 ± 96	P 1215	
8265 ± 117	P 1217	Stratum II
8018 ± 115	P 1220	Stratum X-XI
7542 ± 122	P 1224	Stratum XVI
7954 ± 114	P 1222	Stratum XVI-XVII

Ramad

6250 ± 80	Gr N 4428
6140 ± 50	Gr N 4821

5970 ± 50	Gr N 4427
5950 ± 50	Gr N 4822
6260 ± 50	Gr N 4426
5930 ± 55	Gr N 4823

Bouqras

6190 ± 60	Gr N 4818	Level I
6290 ± 100	Gr N 4852	}Level II
6010 ± 55	Gr N 4819	
5990 ± 60	Gr N 4820	Level III

Turkey

Suberde

5957 ± 88	P 1385
6045 ± 76	P 1386
6326 ± 289	P 1387
6226 ± 79	P 1388
6299 ± 91	P 1391
6570 ± 140	I 1867
5634 ± 85	P 1389

Çayönü

6840 ± 250	M 1609
6620 ± 250	M 1610
7570 ± 100	Gr N 4458
7250 ± 60	Gr N 4459

Aşikli Hüyük

6857 ± 128	P 1238
6661 ± 108	P 1239
7008 ± 130	P 1240
6843 ± 127	P 1241
6828 ± 128	P 1242

Hacilar

6750 ± 180	BM 127	Aceramic Level V
5393 ± 92	P 314A	Late Neolithic IX
5820 ± 180	BM 125	Late Neolithic VII
5590 ± 180	BM 48	Late Neolithic VI
5399 ± 79	P 313A	Late Neolithic VI
5219 ± 131	P 326A	Chalcolithic IIA
5037 ± 119	P 315	Chalcolithic 1A

Çatal Hüyük

6142 ± 98	P 782	Level X
6240 ± 99	P 779	Level IX
5588 ± 89	P 778	Level VII
5754 ± 91	P 777	Level VIB
5679 ± 90	P 797	Level VIB
5574 ± 90	P 781	Level VIB
5962 ± 94	P 770	Level VIB
5629 ± 86	P 827	Level VIAB
5555 ± 93	P 769	Level VIA
5622 ± 91	P 772	Level VIA
5690 ± 91	P 776	Level V
6087 ± 96	P 775	Level IV
5571 ± 77	P 796	Level II

Iraq

Zawi Chemi Shanidar

8920 ± 300	W 681	Layer B

Shanidar Cave

8650 ± 300	W 667	Layer B1

Jarmo

9250 ± 200	W 665	
9300 ± 300	W 657	
7090 ± 250	W 607	
6880 ± 200	W 651	
6000 ± 200	H 551—491	
4757 ± 320	C 113	
4656 ± 330	C 742	
4745 ± 360	C 743	
4700 ± 170	F 44	
4620 ± 165	F 45	
6575 ± 175	H 551—491	
5800 ± 250	W 608	
6000 ± 200	W 652	

Shimshara

8080 ±	K 981	Level 10
5990 ±	K 951	Level 13
5870 ±	K 972	Level 11
5350 ±	K 960	Level 9

Hassuna

5090 ± 200	W 660	Level V

Matarrah

5620 ± 250	W 623

Tell Es Sawwan

5506 ± 73	P 855	Earliest Level
5359 ± 86	P 856	
4858 ± 82	P 857	

Choga Mami

4896 ± 182	BM 483

Iran

Ganj Dareh

8450 ± 150	Gak 807	Ganj Dareh 1
6960 ± 170	Gak 994	Ganj Dareh 2
6938 ± 98	P 1486	Level B
7289 ± 196	P 1485	Level C
7018 ± 100	P 1484	Level D

Tepe Guran

6460 ± 200	K 1006	Level U
5810 ± 150	K 879	Level H
1220 ± 120	K 856	

Tepe Sarab

6006 ± 98	P 466	Level 5
5655 ± 96	P 465	Level 4
5698 ± 89	P 467	Level 1

Tepe Siabid

3865 ± 83	P 442

Hajji Firuz

5319 ± 86	P 455	Stratum D-15
4945 ± 83	P 502	

Pisdeli Tepe

3688 ± 84	P 505	Stratum 10
3568 ± 81	P 504	Stratum 5
3510 ± 160	P 157	

Dalma Tepe

4036 ± 87 P 503

Tepe Yahya

4302 ± 180 GX 1509 Level VIIID
3280 ± 170 GX 1734
3245 ± 465 W 876   Level IVB

Belt Cave

6135 ± 1500 Neolithic
8160 ± 610 Mesolithic (upper levels)
6595 ± 50 Mesolithic (upper levels)
6054 ± 1010 Mesolithic (Base of the
                                   Lower Mesolithic)

Ali Kosh and Tepe Sabz—Deh Luran Plain

4100 ± 140 I 1499
4220 ± 200 SI 203
4110 ± 200 SI 204
3750 ± 250 SI 205
3910 ± 230 I 1503   Bayat Phase
3820 ± 120 SI 156
4110 ± 140 I 1502
4120 ± 100 UCLA 750A
3460 ± 160 I 1500
4520 ± 160 I 1493   Mehmeh Phase
5510 ± 160 I 1501
4975 ± 200 UCLA 750B Khazineh Phase
5250 ± 1000 SI 206
4790 ± 190 I 1497
7100 ± 160 UCLA 750c Sabz Phase
A.D. 490 ± 400 SI 255
5270 ± 160 I 1495
6970 ± 100 SI 160
6940 ± 200 SI 160R   Mohammad Jaffar Phase
5870 ± 190 I 1494
5790 ± 600 SI 207
6150 ± 170 I 1491
8000 ± 190 I 1490   Alikosh Phase
6300 ± 175 Humble
                      01-1845

5820 ± 330	Humble 0-1848	
6475 ± 180	Humble 0-1833	
6475 ± 180	Humble 0-1816	Alikosh Phase
6460 ± 200	Shell 1246	
6900 ± 210	Shell 1174	
5430 ± 180	I 1496	
5720 ± 170	I 1489	Bus Mordeh Phase
7950 ± 200	UCLA 750D	

Author Index

Numbers in italics refer to pages on which a reference is listed at the end of a chapter

General Index

Sites and Localities Index